Developing Your Conflict Competence

On the Web: Take the Conflict Dynamics Profile® With a 1/2 Hour Review Session at a Substantial Discount

The Conflict Dynamics Profile® assessment instrument helps you better understand how you currently respond to workplace conflict. It enables you to leverage areas of strength and modify behaviors that don't work well. The instrument provides specific measures on fifteen different constructive and destructive behaviors. It also looks at conflict "hot buttons"—situations and behaviors in others that can irritate you and trigger conflict.

In addition to an eight-page report and forty-page development guide, you will also receive a half-hour telephone session with an experienced consultant who will review your results with you.

Link: www.conflictdynamics.org/special

Code word for discount: CCD3

Price: $150.00, a greater than 25% discount

FREE
Premium Content
▼

JOSSEY-BASS™
An Imprint of
Ⓦ **WILEY**

This book includes premium content that can be accessed from our Web site when you register at
www.josseybass.com/go/Runde
using the password *professional*.

Developing Your Conflict Competence

A HANDS-ON GUIDE FOR LEADERS, MANAGERS, FACILITATORS, AND TEAMS

Craig E. Runde
Tim A. Flanagan

JOSSEY-BASS
A Wiley Imprint
www.josseybass.com

Center for
Creative
Leadership
NORTH AMERICA EUROPE ASIA
www.ccl.org

Published by Jossey-Bass
A Wiley Imprint
One Montgomery, Ste. 1200, San Francisco, CA 94104—www.josseybass.com

Library of Congress Cataloging-in-Publication Data

Runde, Craig E.
    Developing your conflict competence : a hands-on guide for leaders, managers, facilitators, and teams /Craig E. Runde, Tim A. Flanagan.
        p.   cm.
    "A joint publication of the Jossey-Bass business & management series and the Center for Creative Leadership."
    Includes bibliographical references and index.
    ISBN 978-0-470-50546-5 (cloth)
        1. Conflict management.   2. Interpersonal conflict.   I. Flanagan, Tim A.
II. Center for Creative Leadership.   III. Title.
HD42.R864 2010
658.3'145—dc22

                                                                                    2009044800

Printed in the United States of America
THIRD EDITION
HB Printing   10 9 8 7 6 5 4 3 2

A Joint Publication of
The Jossey-Bass
Business & Management Series
and
The Center for Creative Leadership

For all those challenged by conflict (pretty much everyone in the world).
May you find new ways to make the best out of differences!

CONTENTS

WHAT'S A HANDS-ON GUIDE AND WHY SHOULD I BE INTERESTED?

Our first two books, *Becoming a Conflict Competent Leader* and *Building Conflict Competent Teams,* generated a good deal of interest (Runde and Flanagan, 2007, 2008). We were pleased with the reviews and the number of invitations we received to speak and present. We were also intrigued by the volume of inquiries from readers regarding how they could put the principles of conflict competence into action.

We had designed *Building Conflict Competent Teams* to be user friendly. Our intent was that teams could use portions of it as a handbook as they developed norms for interaction and encountered the challenges of conflict. We discovered that team leaders, coaches, consultants, and trainers loved this notion. We also found that they wanted even more. Thus, the concept for this book, *Developing Your Conflict Competence,* is unquestioningly one of practicality and usability for individuals, teams, trainers, facilitators, and coaches.

We didn't enter into this third book in the series lightly. For us, tackling a hands-on guide means covering the concepts we presented in the first two books without pure (boring) replication. At the same time, our intent isn't to break much new ground. Rather, we are committed to providing examples, suggestions, and tools for embracing the opportunities and meeting the challenges of conflict. Our goal is to provide a resource that makes it easier to address conflict when it occurs. After all, conflict is not only inevitable, it also contains elements of diversity, innovation, and creativity that can result in more satisfying interactions and better solutions.

What this guide is *not* is an exhaustive review of every step you could take for every aspect of conflict possible. We believe it is critical to help you make the most of your time. Therefore, we decided to err on the side of "less is more." Our focus, as always, is on actions, behaviors, and steps.

We are indebted to our many friends and colleagues who have contributed to this book. They are cited specifically in the text for their stories and suggestions. Without them, this guide could not exist. We also want to thank our editors and marketers at Jossey-Bass, without whom this book would never have been published. Kathe Sweeney, Brian Grimm, Mary Garrett, and Dani Scoville are a wonderful team who make our job much easier and more pleasant. We'd also like to thank Kathy Runde and "Mac" Flanagan for their help in proofing the manuscript.

In short, our hope is that you will find *Developing Your Conflict Competence* both engaging and useful. The stories and examples come from our own experiences and from practitioners in the field. The tips, suggestions, and tools have been developed over time and used in a variety of settings. We welcome your feedback and wish you the very best.

St. Petersburg, Florida   Craig E. Runde
December 2009   Tim A. Flanagan

Introduction

When we talk with leaders, team members, and individual contributors, we find universal agreement that conflict is an inevitable part of organizational life. Survey after survey supports the notion that conflict is all around us. In fact, a recent study by the Center for Creative Leadership found that 85 percent of leaders experience conflict on a regular or continual basis (Center for Creative Leadership, 2009). So the question isn't one of whether or not you'll experience conflict or how to reduce or avoid it. Instead, the question is what will you get out of conflict when it does occur. Depending on how you respond, that something can be good or bad, constructive or destructive, invigorating or debilitating.

During nearly all of our presentations, we ask participants what words come to mind when they think of conflict. In just a few moments, we collect dozens of words. Next, we ask the audience how they would characterize most of the words they shared. The response is always the same: most of the words are negative. A few of the words, though, such as *opportunity* or *interesting,* are positive. This tells us a couple of things. First, the vast majority of people experience conflict as negative. Second, there is also a natural, albeit infrequent, response to conflict that is favorable. Next, we ask the audience how they learned to deal with conflict. Many say they followed the lead of models (most of them poor models). Others say that they just tried to avoid or minimize conflict when it happened.

Finally, when we ask how their "conflict education" has worked out, we usually hear a smattering of nervous laughter.

We can virtually guarantee that using traditional approaches to dealing with conflict (avoidance, minimizing, "eye for an eye," and so on) will result in the same poor outcomes that generate the negative words most associate with conflict. It simply doesn't have to be this way. Rather, it is possible to prepare for and respond to conflict in ways that reduce the negative or harmful aspects and promote positive, mutually satisfying outcomes. This field guide provides simple, focused tools and suggestions for doing just that.

DEFINING CONFLICT COMPETENCE

Conflict competence is the ability to develop and use cognitive, emotional, and behavioral skills that enhance productive outcomes of conflict while reducing the likelihood of escalation or harm. The results of conflict competence include improved quality of relationships, creative solutions, and lasting agreements for addressing challenges and opportunities in the future. As with all competencies, people can learn ways to improve, change, and develop.

We believe that those individuals who possess a keen sense of self-awareness are well positioned to develop conflict competence. This requires honesty and objectivity. It requires seeking feedback from others. We recommend using assessment instruments for a thorough analysis.

It is also helpful to understand how conflict begins and unfolds. Cognitive understanding of the "mechanics" of conflict helps to demystify the impact of conflict. In addition, preparation for conflict is critical. In nearly all cases, we find that those who are best prepared for conflict have the best outcomes, the fewest issues, and the most satisfying relationships with their conflict partners.

Most important, we believe that developing skills, learning mental models, and applying basic principles are the keys to developing conflict competence. Our model is simple and involves three key steps: cooling down, slowing down, and engaging constructively. We address the components of the model fully in the pages to follow. In short, though, the model suggests that those who deal well with emotions, are mindful of the ramifications of conflict, and use effective skills during conflict have the best chance of productive outcomes.

Ten Principles of Conflict Competence for Individuals, Teams, and Organizations

Conflict competence applies to individuals, teams, and organizations. It is relevant at work, home, and in community settings. The following principles capture the key elements of conflict competence and can be used to frame effective training efforts.

1. *Conflict is inevitable and can lead to positive or negative results depending on how it is handled.*

When we talk with people, they readily admit that conflict is inevitable. Their life experience has confirmed that when people interact with one another their different perspectives and needs lead to conflicts. They are keenly aware of the negative aspects of conflict but less so about its potential benefits.

2. *While people generally see conflict as negative and prefer to avoid it, better results can emerge from engaging it constructively.*

Research in organizational conflict has identified various types of conflict that lead to different outcomes. Two important types include *task* conflict, which focuses on resolving the issues that stem from differences, and *relationship* conflict, which emerges when people are more interested in placing blame than they are solving problems. Task conflict can lead to creative solutions and improved decisions, whereas relationship conflict nearly always leads to interpersonal tension and poorer performance. People have more experience with relationship conflict and as a consequence see conflict as a negative to be avoided. This often leads them to respond ineffectively and guarantees that they experience the dysfunctions that come with that type of conflict. When they are able to engage conflict effectively, though, they are more likely to attain the benefits that can come from task conflict.

3. *In order to overcome reluctance to address conflict, people need to believe it is important to do so—thus recognizing the tremendous value of managing conflict effectively.*

Motivation is as important as knowledge in developing conflict competence. Changing established beliefs and patterns of behavior is difficult, and unless people see value in doing so, it won't happen. Helping them understand the benefits that emerge from managing conflict effectively is critical in providing the rationale and impetus to undertake this work.

4. *Individual conflict competence involves developing cognitive, emotional, and behavioral skills that enable one to cool down, slow down, and engage conflict constructively.*

When faced with conflict, people respond in a variety of ways. They think about what is happening. They experience emotional reactions that are influenced by the ways they view and interpret the conflict. They also take action to address the concerns that the conflict raises. In order for people to be able to deal effectively with conflict, they need to be able to improve their cognitive, emotional, and behavioral skills so they can cool down, slow down, and engage the matter constructively.

5. *Cognitive skills include developing self-awareness about one's current attitudes and responses to conflict and an understanding of conflict's basic dynamics.*

As with most leadership skills, self-awareness plays an important role in dealing with conflict more effectively. This includes an understanding of how people currently view conflict, because their attitudes can affect their responses to it. Self-awareness also involves understanding what triggers a person in the first place as well as how he responds when conflict emerges. This awareness allows him to leverage effective responses and at the same time work on improving areas where he is using ineffective behaviors. This development work plays out better when people recognize some of the fundamental dynamics of the conflict process.

6. *Emotional skills include understanding one's emotional responses to conflict, regulating those responses to attain and maintain emotional balance, understanding and responding to the emotions of one's conflict partners, and when necessary slowing down to allow extra time to cool down.*

In order to use constructive behavioral responses to conflict, a person first needs to be able to manage his emotional responses. This allows him to become curious, and curiosity is a key factor in engaging one's conflict partner constructively. Conflict is all about emotion. Being able to manage one's emotions provides a foundation from which to choose and use constructive behavioral responses.

7. *Behavioral skills include engaging constructively by understanding others' perspectives, emotions, and needs; sharing one's own thoughts, feelings, and interests; collaborating to develop creative solutions to issues; and reaching out to get communications restarted when they have stalled.*

Considerable research and publishing have been done in the field of conflict, and there is considerable agreement about the kinds of behaviors that work well to resolve conflicts. These include *listening to understand* how other people see an issue, *sharing* one's own perspectives, *working together* to develop effective solutions to problems, and *keeping communications going*. When these behaviors are used, conflict can move in more productive directions. Of course, it can be a challenge to use these behaviors. If it were simple, people would already handle conflicts better.

8. *Engaging constructively also involves reducing or eliminating the use of destructive behaviors characterized by fight-or-flight responses to conflict.*

One of the reasons that responding constructively can be a challenge is that people are more likely to default to destructive fight-or-flight behaviors, either because these are the kinds of responses they have learned to use or because they are upset and turn to reactive behaviors in order to protect themselves. Reducing the use of these kinds of responses depends in large part on developing and practicing new, more constructive approaches and on regulating emotional reactions to conflict.

9. *In team settings, conflict competence includes creating the right climate to support the use of the "cool down, slow down, and engage constructively" model among teammates so they can have open and honest discussions of issues. Creating the right climate includes developing trust and safety, promoting collaboration, and enhancing team emotional intelligence.*

In order to manage conflict effectively, team members need to be able to discuss issues openly and honestly. When they can robustly debate issues without turning a task-focused conflict into one involving relationship conflict, they can develop better, more creative solutions. This is not easy to do and requires developing norms that produce the right climate for managing conflict constructively. This includes changing attitudes about conflict so that it is not just something to avoid. It also means creating a safe environment in which team members trust that what they say won't be used against them. Working together with team spirit produces collaborative effort that can enable people to give others the benefit of the doubt when conflict emerges. Managing emotions is important in team settings as well as in individual contexts, because emotions are contagious and if not addressed can spread tension throughout the team. Team members also need to use constructive behaviors when addressing conflicts in order to keep a solution-oriented focus to their discussions.

10. *In organizational contexts, conflict competence involves creating a culture that supports the "cool down, slow down, and engage constructively" model. This includes aligning mission, policies, training programs, performance standards, and reward structures to reinforce the conflict competence model. It also includes creating integrated conflict management systems to support these cultural changes.*

In order to be conflict competent, an organization needs its leaders, managers, supervisors, and employees to be individually conflict competent. At the same time, it needs to align its conflict management processes with its mission, values, policies, performance standards, and reward structures in order to reinforce the kind of conflict behaviors it wants its personnel to use with each other and with its vendors and customers. This involves creating systems to reinforce its conflict model and to provide multiple avenues for employees to address conflicts, preferably at the lowest possible level at the earliest possible time.

Individual Conflict Competence Model

Our model of individual conflict competence looks at cognitive, emotional, and behavioral aspects of how people respond to conflict. Key elements of the model are shown in Figure 1.1.

Cool down relates to strategies to help regulate emotions so that a person can maintain or regain emotional balance before proceeding further. If you are upset, your cognitive faculties are impaired and it is easy to slip into use of destructive behaviors. So a key first step is to make sure that your emotions are managed effectively. Since emotions can come and go rather quickly, it may be necessary to cool down several times during a conflict.

Slow down involves developing a strategy for what to do when cooling down is not working. Strong emotions can be challenging, and despite our best intents, there will be times when our efforts to calm down will not be entirely effective. In these cases, it is important to have ways to slow things down. Taking a time-out to enable your emotions to calm down is much better than going too far and saying something you will later regret. These foot-in-your-mouth comments usually escalate the conflict and prove very hard to undo.

Once you have used cool down and slow down to allow you time to gain a more balanced state, you can then move on to engage the other person using constructive behaviors.

Figure 1.1
Individual Conflict Competence Model

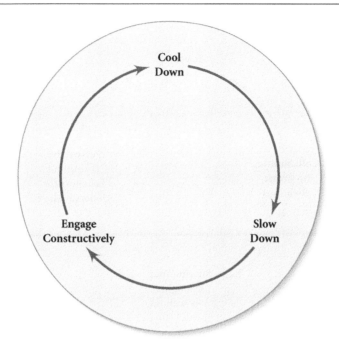

Engage Constructively   The key behaviors associated with the *engage constructively* part of the Individual Conflict Competence Model are reaching out, perspective taking and listening for understanding, sharing thoughts and feelings, and collaborating to create solutions. Figure 1.2 provides a graphic view of these behaviors.

Reaching out is a behavior that involves working with the other person either at the very start of conflict to get communications moving or later on to get things back on track.

Perspective taking and listening for understanding involve listening for how the other person sees the situation, using empathy to understand how the other person is feeling, and asking about what he or she wants. Through this process you can develop new insights about the conflict and help lower tensions.

Sharing your thoughts and feelings involves telling the other person how you see the situation, how you feel about it, and what you want for yourself and the other person.

Figure 1.2
Engage Constructively Model

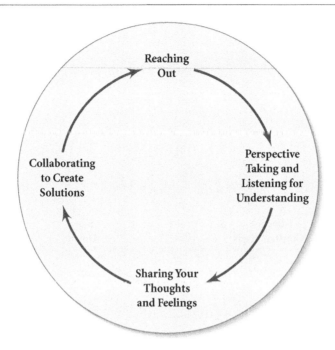

Collaborating to create solutions involves trying to find answers to the issues raised by the conflict that will work for both parties. It includes reflecting on the merits of alternative solutions, brainstorming with the other person to develop new approaches, and remaining flexible so you can make the best out of whatever solution is devised.

Team Conflict Competence Model

Team conflict competence includes creating the right climate to enable open, honest discussion as well as using constructive communications techniques to discuss issues. Team members know that conflict is an integral part of team life. Yet, most teams don't take the time to figure out how they want to deal with it when it emerges. The team model in Figure 1.3 shows some of the important elements that teams must address to manage conflict effectively.

Figure 1.3
Team Conflict Competence Model

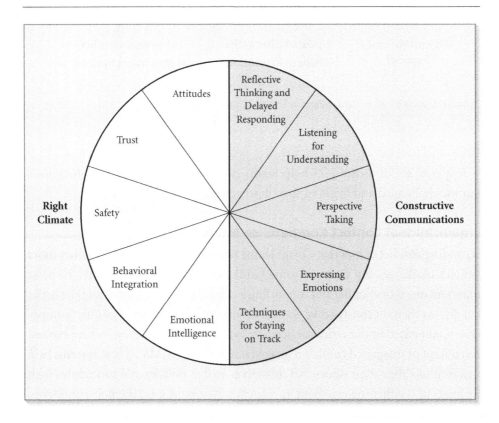

The *right climate* includes five elements that teams can use to help support open discussion. The first involves changing attitudes toward conflict so it isn't looked upon only as negative. The second and third deal with creating and preserving a sense of *trust* and *safety* among members of the team. The fourth component involves creating a collaborative spirit in the team. The final element concerns improving the team's emotional intelligence.

Once the right climate is set, then team members can use *constructive communications* techniques to keep discussions focused on solutions and away from finger pointing. These constructive techniques include reflective thinking and delayed responding, listening for understanding and perspective taking, and expressing emotions as well as thoughts.

Figure 1.4
Organizational Conflict Competence

Source: Adapted from a model developed by Jennifer Lynch, QC (Lynch, 2005).

A special set of techniques help teams *stay on track* when communications become challenged and begin to turn destructive.

Organizational Conflict Competence Model

Expanding conflict competence from teams to entire organizations presents more complex challenges, but there are some fundamental similarities. Perhaps the most important one is developing and supporting a culture in which people can raise issues and discuss them in constructive ways. Our view of organizational conflict competence is influenced by our colleague, Jennifer Lynch, QC, and others who have evolved the concept of integrated conflict management systems (ICMS). These systems help organizations align their values and mission as well as policies and procedures with the kinds of conflict management approaches they want used by their employees. Figure 1.4 is an adaptation of Jennifer's model for an ICMS (Lynch, 2005).

In this model, *organizational support* refers to the skill development that enables individuals to develop individual conflict competence together with the leadership, coordination, communication, and evaluation required to create an ICMS.

An *updated alternative dispute resolution* system involves elements such as mediation, fact finding, arbitration, and other processes that can be used to deal with conflict that has reached a point where the individuals themselves are unlikely to resolve it without the involvement of third parties.

Together, the organizational support and the updated alternative dispute resolution components create and sustain the ICMS that in turn helps transform an organization's culture into one that supports conflict competence.

Cognitive Aspects of Conflict

The first element of individual conflict competence deals with the cognitive aspects of conflict, including improving current attitudes about conflict, appreciating the value of managing conflict effectively, and understanding how you currently respond to conflict. This chapter explores ways of improving cognitive skills in these areas.

CONFLICT ATTITUDES

In our programs and presentations, we often ask questions of participants to get them thinking about their current attitudes toward conflict. People clearly have thoughts and feelings about conflict, but these often go unexamined. Yet, these attitudes affect the ways that people act when conflict arises even if individuals have not thought about them. We find it helpful to get people thinking about their relationship with conflict, and one way is by having them explore their attitudes.

Exploring Current Conflict Attitudes

It would be helpful to consider your own attitudes about conflict. Do you think it is something bad, to be avoided? Are there positive aspects of conflict? What has affected your understanding and approach to conflict? When we run programs, we ask people a number of questions about conflict to help them reflect on their attitudes. We share them next as if you were conducting a program with others. If you are doing this exercise by yourself, answer the questions based on your own thoughts and feelings toward conflict. In either case, we believe you will discover some interesting answers!

1. We suggest you begin by having people first think about conflict and then share words that come to mind to describe it. You will probably hear lots of words like *stress, frustration, anger,* and *fear.* Less frequently you may hear words like *opportunity* and *resolution.* Once you have solicited a number of terms, ask your participants how they would characterize most of the words they've just heard. If your group is like the hundreds that we have asked, they will describe the words as *negative.*

2. At this point, shift your inquiry to how people deal with conflict. You could ask a question such as, "How do you or most of your colleagues respond to conflict at work?" While a few people may say they react to it aggressively or move to resolve it, most of the answers will be something like, "We avoid it."

3. You may ask at this point, "How well does the combination of viewing conflict as negative and avoiding it work out?" People usually chuckle at this point, as they begin to see how ineffective this approach is.

4. We also suggest asking people, "Why do you think conflict seems to be so difficult to manage?" You will likely hear a variety of responses. "It is emotionally distressing." "I'm afraid I might hurt the other person" (or its converse "I'm afraid they might hurt me"). Eventually, someone will probably suggest, "I've never learned how to deal with conflict." You'll see a lot of others nod in agreement with this statement. It is easy to follow up with, "How many of you learned how to deal with conflict in school?" Rarely will you see more than 1 percent of hands raised. Some people may joke that they learned how to deal with conflict on the playground. School conflict management programs have improved in recent years, so eventually we will see more people who did learn effective ways of dealing with conflict in school. We also ask our participants, "How many of you learned to deal with conflict at work?" A few more hands will go up but rarely more than 10 percent.

5. We suggest one more preliminary question: "How many of you believe that conflict is something that inevitably arises in the workplace?" Nearly everyone usually agrees with this, largely because of their personal experiences. This point can be further emphasized by referring to the Center for Creative Leadership study we mentioned earlier that found that 85 percent of leaders encounter conflict on a regular or continual basis (Center for Creative Leadership, 2009).

6. At this point it may be helpful to recap: Conflict is inevitable. We generally use negative words to describe it (but there are a few positive words as well).

We generally use avoidance techniques when it arises. It can be emotionally distressing, and we've never learned how to address it effectively. With all of that, participants readily agree that there is little doubt why conflict is such a vexing problem.

Connecting Attitudes to Conflict Results

People find it interesting to look at their conflict attitudes and see that theirs are similar to those of most people. They also begin to see that their attitudes probably make it harder to deal with conflict effectively. We like to strengthen this connection by relating attitudes with research on organizational conflict. In both *Becoming a Conflict Competent Leader* and *Building Conflict Competent Teams,* we explored research on organizational conflict. Since the mid-1990s, researchers have looked at two very different types of conflict. One type, called *relationship* or *affective* conflict, describes situations in which people have apparently incompatible differences and focus more on who is at fault or to blame than on how to solve the problem caused by the differences. We then talk about the researchers' conclusions about the outcomes of this type of conflict: increased stress, people avoiding or pulling back from one another, decreased creativity, lowered morale, and poorer decision making (DeDreu and Weingart, 2003). When we describe this type of conflict to participants, they usually are very familiar with it. When we ask about their own experience with relationship conflict, they quickly realize that the negative words they used earlier to describe conflict essentially describe *this* form of conflict. So most of their experience is with relationship conflict, and most of what they get out of conflict is something bad. No wonder they would prefer to avoid it!

We then talk about the second type of conflict, called *task* or *cognitive* conflict, with which people have less experience. Task conflict emerges when people appear to have irreconcilable differences but they stay focused on ways of solving the problems caused by those differences in mutually beneficial ways. When people are able to stay focused on solutions, which we understand is not easy, they often come up with more creative solutions and effective decisions and implementations (Roberto, 2005). Participants are typically less familiar with this type of conflict, but they recognize that the positive words they shared earlier, like *resolution* and *opportunity,* describe task conflict and its more favorable outcomes.

So, conflict is inevitable and you are likely to either experience it as relationship conflict, with its bad outcomes, or task conflict, with its more favorable outcomes. Our point to participants is that the way you think about conflict can have an effect on whether you get more good or more bad results from it. Our next step is to look at how to improve attitudes.

Changing Conflict Attitudes

Since most people have negative attitudes about conflict that can flavor and affect the ways they respond to it, we enable people to begin looking at conflict in new ways—ones that help them see it as something to embrace rather than just avoid. Again, we have framed this as a group exercise, and it can be helpful to do this with others. If you are alone, though, you can still profitably reflect on these questions and your answers to them.

1. We typically divide participants into groups of three or four. We then ask them to start by thinking about any conflict they have experienced that had some kind of a positive outcome. This itself can take some doing. We tell them to first write down a description of the conflict and the positive outcomes that came from it.

2. Once they have completed the first step, we ask participants to think about what caused the conflict to have a good result. We ask them to think about the types of behaviors and approaches people used that seemed to help the conflict move in a more positive direction.

3. After everyone has had a chance to describe a conflict that turned out well and list some contributing factors for the success, we ask the participants to share their stories and comments with others in their small groups. We ask them to look for common factors that seemed to lead conflict in a positive direction and for some common types of successful outcomes. After sharing in the small groups, a representative from each group reports their key findings. As this is being done, we encourage participants in other groups to ask questions and provide comments about what they are hearing. When participants are from the same organization, these questions and comments are often more specifically related to the substance of the conflicts, but even in groups of people from different organizations this interaction usually leads to additional insights.

APPRECIATING THE VALUE OF DEALING WITH CONFLICT

As we noted, people generally prefer to avoid dealing with conflict. Leaders are just as or even more conflict averse than everyone else. As a consequence, we feel it is important to have people reflect on why they should overcome their reluctance to engage conflict.

What is the cost of conflict for you? How much time do you spend either dealing with conflict or thinking about it? Does it affect your relationship with others? If you are the leader of an organization or team, how is conflict costing your organization? Are your employees empowered to debate issues so that you get more creative results, or is your organization one in which people keep quiet, avoid rigorous discussion, and settle for mediocre compromises?

If you are training others, you can put program participants in groups and have them come up with reasons why dealing with conflict effectively is of value to them personally, as well as to their organization. You may want to prime the pump by providing the groups with an example. One good one is to ask them whether managers in their organization waste much of their time dealing with conflict. You'll probably get an affirmative reaction to this example, as numerous surveys have confirmed that a typical manager can spend 20 percent or more of his or her time on conflict (Thomas and Schmidt, 1976; Watson and Hoffman, 1996; Center for Creative Leadership, 2003). After 10–15 minutes, you can ask groups to share their results with the larger group. As each point is raised, we recommend spending time discussing the costs associated with it and how handling conflict better could result in either savings or improved results for an organization. During this time we also encourage participants to share personal experiences, which increases the interest and relevance of the exercise.

Another more formal way to help people evaluate the cost side of conflict is the use of the Dana Measure of Financial Cost of Organizational Conflict (*Dana Cost of Conflict Survey,* 2009). This online calculator helps people explore the cost of conflict to their organization. We find that the calculator is the best tool for focusing people on the multiple costs of conflict, such as wasted management time, retention problems, absenteeism, health costs, grievances, complaints, sabotage, and violence. Dan Dana notes that these costs are often unexamined or at least not thought of as conflict issues. When we have participants in our programs fill out his online calculator, we recommend that they be very conservative in their estimates of various costs. Yet, when they get back the results of their estimates, they are usually astounded by how much conflict can cost. The costs of managers' time can be particularly profound. At even 20 percent of managers' time, conflict can be a tremendous financial burden to an organization.

The out-of-pocket costs of conflict are easier to calculate, and make for easier return on investment arguments. When we are working with organizational leaders, we like to explore other value propositions associated with conflict, such as enhanced creativity and improved decision making. Again, we put participants in small groups and ask them to talk about the kind of interactions they have around conflict. In particular, we prompt them to explore the degree to which their top management teams engage in robust discussions about different approaches to issues. We recommend having a facilitator placed with each group. The facilitator's purpose is to prompt participants to make connections between their ability to engage conflicting approaches and the quality of the ideas they are able to produce and the decisions they make. This discourse generally leads to recognition that robust discussion brings more creative options, because as people bounce ideas off one another they come up with new concepts that had not been considered before. This interaction also allows for more complete vetting of alternatives and leads to better decisions. Implementation is better as well, because members of a team have felt part of the process even if their proposal was not chosen. Dan Dana has found that clients appreciate this part of the value proposition.

"The out-of-pocket costs of workplace conflict certainly catch people's attention. Yet, it is the effects of conflict on decision quality that seem to make the greatest impression. When I discuss this with clients, they initially say that they never really thought about the connection. Upon reflection, they readily agree that this happens on a regular basis and leads to some poorly considered, costly decisions" (Craig's discussion with Dan Dana on July 8, 2009). If, however, conflict is addressed effectively, better decisions can be obtained.

UNDERSTANDING HOW YOU CURRENTLY RESPOND TO CONFLICT

Self-awareness is a key component of most leadership development programs. The gap between a person's intention and his or her impact on others can be of particular importance in conflict contexts.

Take a minute and ask yourself a few questions:

- How often do I face conflict in the workplace?
- When conflict occurs, do I prefer to avoid dealing with it or give in to others?
- Do I come off too aggressively at times?
- Do I take time to listen to other people's thoughts on an issue?
- When conflicts emerge, am I aware of my feelings and those of others?
- Do I rush to solve problems before I'm sure of what the issues are?
- Do I collaborate with others to come up with solutions, or do I make most of the decisions on my own?

When people reflect on these and similar questions, they begin to get a better sense of how they approach conflicts. We don't often take the time to consider such things. As a consequence we are often unaware of how we truly think and feel about conflicts and are sometimes surprised by our reactions to conflict.

Using Instruments

While various forms of self-reflection can be helpful, we find that people seem to pay more attention when we use assessment instruments as part of their development work. The instruments contribute an additional sense of objectivity and credibility to the process. The powerful impression they can have on people also underscores the importance of making sure you use assessments that have been properly tested and validated and that they are administered by competent professionals. In this section we talk about one instrument that focuses on conflict behaviors and a group of others that deal with conflict styles.

The Conflict Dynamics Profile   We often use the Conflict Dynamics Profile® (CDP) in our programs. Yes, it was developed at Eckerd College, where we work, but there is more to it than just that. The course of conflict is heavily influenced by the behaviors people use when dealing with it. The CDP looks at behaviors that tend to move conflict in both positive and negative directions. It measures behaviors in others that can trigger people's negative emotions that lead to tension and exacerbate conflict. It also reveals the responses or reactions we use once conflict is initiated.

The CDP was developed by Drs. Sal Capobianco, Mark Davis, and Linda Kraus in the late 1990s and was influenced by research on organizational conflict that focused on two different types of conflict: cognitive or task conflict and relationship or affective conflict (Amason, 1996). The former type of conflict is characterized by discussion, creative thinking, and good decision making, and the latter by blaming, emotional tension, and dysfunction.

The CDP authors suggested that the kind of conflict that is experienced is largely determined by the kinds of behaviors that people use when they are faced with conflict. They identified a set of constructive behaviors that when used would lead to the more productive task conflict and another set of destructive behaviors that usually generated relationship conflict. The CDP measures the frequencies with which people use the various constructive and destructive behaviors.

In addition to behaviors, the CDP also measures conflict triggers. These behaviors in others that cause irritation in an individual and can lead to destructive reactions are called *hot buttons*. The hot buttons as well as the behavioral scales are normed against a large adult population so that recipients can see how their patterns compare against other people. Hot buttons are described in greater depth in the chapter on emotions.

Administering the CDP   To administer the CDP, one must be certified in the instrument, which comes in both multirater and self-assessment versions. While it is available in both online and paper-and-pencil formats, most people use the online version.

When we use the 360-degree version of the instrument with a group, we ask participants and their respondents to complete the instruments using the instructions that come with it. If we use the self-assessment version of the instrument, only the individuals respond to questions.

During the program, we review the model underlying the instrument using a PowerPoint slideshow that comes with the certification materials. We make sure that people understand the specific scales that are presented on the CDP report so that people are clear about the data they will be reviewing. These are described in some depth in chapters Three, Four, and Five of *Becoming a Conflict Competent Leader.*

The main scales include a set of nine hot buttons, seven constructive behaviors, and eight destructive behaviors. The *hot buttons* measure behaviors in other people that tend to irritate us. In particular, they measure the degree to which a person gets upset when he or she encounters someone who behaves in specific ways. We describe these in more depth in Chapter Three. They include the following types of behaviors:

1. *Abrasive*: Arrogant, sarcastic, and demeaning
2. *Aloof*: Isolating, not seeking input, hard to approach
3. *Hostile*: Angry, yelling, losing temper
4. *Micro-managing*: Constantly monitoring and checking on others
5. *Overly analytical*: Focus on minor issues, perfectionistic
6. *Self-centered*: Care only about self, believe they are always correct
7. *Unappreciative*: Fail to give credit, seldom praise good performance
8. *Unreliable*: Miss deadlines, cannot be counted on
9. *Untrustworthy*: Exploit others, take undeserved credit

The *constructive* scales deal with behavioral response patterns that when used tend to move conflict toward more positive outcomes. We address these in more detail in Chapter Four. They include:

1. *Perspective taking*: Trying to understand the way the other person thinks and feels about the conflict
2. *Creating solutions*: Brainstorming with the other person to develop solutions to the problem
3. *Expressing emotions*: Telling the other person openly and honestly how you feel about the conflict
4. *Reaching out*: Working with the other person to start or keep communications going to resolve a conflict
5. *Reflective thinking*: Considering the pros and cons of different approaches for solving the issue

6. *Delayed responding*: Taking a time-out to let emotions cool down before returning to discuss the problem

7. *Adapting*: Remaining open and flexible so as to make the best out of the situation

The *destructive* scales address eight response patterns that tend to prolong conflict and result in the negative outcomes found in relationship conflict. As with the constructive scales, we address these in greater detail in Chapter Four. They include:

1. *Winning at all costs*: Trying as hard as you can to get your way in the conflict

2. *Displaying anger*: Acting out and showing anger towards others

3. *Demeaning others*: Belittling or putting down a person with whom you are experiencing conflict

4. *Retaliating*: Getting even with the other person

5. *Avoiding*: Staying away from another person to prevent having to deal with the problem

6. *Yielding*: Giving in to the other person in order to not have to address the conflict

7. *Hiding emotions*: Covering up the way you feel about the conflict

8. *Self-criticizing*: Ruminating about the ways you mismanaged the conflict

As we discuss the different behaviors, we show people some of the questions that are asked for each scale and have them discuss how they characterize each scale. We review a sample report with the participants so they can understand how data will be presented before receiving their own report. At that point we share participants' reports with them individually and give them a chance to review their results. We encourage you to consider taking the CDP; we provide you with information about it in the beginning of this book.

Debriefing the CDP　After people get their results on the Conflict Dynamics Profile, we set a time to meet with them to debrief their results. It can be unsettling to get feedback on how one responds to conflict, so it's helpful for someone knowledgeable in the instrument to work with the recipient of a report to make sense of it. We go through the data in the report with individuals and ask them what they make of the responses—either their own responses or those of other people. In particular, we ask why they think others may see them the way they do. People are often surprised that others see them differently than they see themselves, but often after reflecting on the matter, they begin to appreciate why that may be the case. Even in instances when they do not understand reasons for differences, they're able to think about how they may talk to the individuals who gave them their responses in order to find out more why those people see them differently.

In addition to helping them understand the data in the report, we also help them to think about ways in which they are already effective and behaviors that they're already using appropriately. We also help them consider what behaviors they may want to improve or what hot buttons they may want to cool down. This process of prioritizing areas for development is aided in the 360 version of the CDP by a section dealing with the organization's perspective on conflict. This part of the report looks at how particular behaviors could enhance or be detrimental to one's career development. People are then able to compare their own use of behaviors to see which ones could be problematic if not done well. This helps prioritize areas for development.

We also help people explore connections between their hot buttons and the ways they respond to conflict when those buttons are pushed. For instance, it may be the case that the participant gets upset when she encounters a hostile individual. We ask her how she responds if that is indeed a hot button for her. If she says that she, herself, gets angry and pushes back against the other person, it may not be a surprise if, in her behavioral data, she finds that her Displaying Anger score is higher than she might otherwise expect.

When we're debriefing the CDP in groups, we often use a consolidated report to look at the overall patterns of the group. We see which constructive or destructive behaviors may be unusually high or low within the group. We can also look in the 360 version at a larger sample of people's perspectives on what behaviors are acceptable and unacceptable in the organization. These group reports enable people to compare their behaviors against the norms of the group to see when they are generally in sync with others or display behavioral patterns different from their teammates.

Talking About Conflict

One of the benefits of using an assessment instrument like the CDP is that people who use it are able to talk about conflicts using a common model and vocabulary. This is illustrated in a story from Sue Strong, a consultant and colleague of ours. She calls the story, "It's All About the Business."

IT'S ALL ABOUT THE BUSINESS

The Business Situation

A well-known consumer products company conducted an internal survey to assess the effectiveness of one of its most critical business processes. The success of this process is directly linked to competitive advantage in the marketplace, which, as we know, equates to product sales. While there were a variety of elements that constituted how effectively the process worked, a critical component was the ability for multiple, cross-functional teams to partner in achieving outcomes that would be in the best interests of the company.

There was only one problem. The members of the team each reported into different functional areas within the organization, and there was no hierarchy within the team that would suggest a final decision maker. In other words, they needed to figure out a way to work together and reach mutual decisions . . .

A perfect storm for conflict! *And,* a perfect opportunity for innovation! Which way would it go?

The Process

Up until the time I was brought in, the feelings on these multiple teams ranged from high energy in some cases to lethargy and frustration in most. The same people tended to dominate discussions and the same people tended to say nothing at all. It wasn't uncommon to feel that a key approach to success was, "I Win, You Lose." Not that anyone was saying that, however.

I viewed this as a perfect place to use the CDP not only to deal directly with the success of these teams but also to begin shaping a culture in which people would begin to think in different ways. Because time was tight and I was dealing with busy people who were not about to spend a lot of time on development without kicking and screaming, I chose to use the Individual version of the CDP. It was administered to more than fifty people online.

As the data came in, I realized that these individuals were all over the place in terms of how they dealt with different opinions. This was, of course, part of the problem. Not only did they look at issues from different business angles, they also addressed their differences in a wide variety of ways. Of course, everyone thought his or her approach was the right approach. At times, approaches were polar opposites. For example, on the Destructive scale of the CDP, as many people scored *Yielding* as a behavior they used to deal with conflict as those who scored it as something they very rarely did. On the Hot Buttons scale we saw a similar phenomenon. As many people saw *Overly Analytical* as a hot button as those for whom it wasn't an issue at all.

The Outcome

The CDP allowed us to do several things:

1. It opened a conversation that permitted us to define conflict as something that was not "bad."

2. It illuminated the reality that there are different ways people handle conflict and that some of those strategies worked and others didn't.

3. The CDP offered participants the opportunity to self-reflect and think about what they needed to do differently for the good of the whole.

4. We were able to dialogue about how different behaviors could, unknowingly, feed off of each other and cause a downhill spiral— for example, *Yielding* and *Winning* as potentially the flip sides of the same coin.

5. It also pointed out strategies for taking something Constructive and using it to minimize a behavior that was Destructive: for example, *Expressing Emotions* versus feeling the need to *Display Anger.*

The critical outcomes were that people left the meeting with a new interpretation of conflict and its potential value to them as a competitive strategy, a better appreciation of the pluses and the minuses of their approaches to conflict, and the ability to talk to each other about something that often is "undiscussable."

Removing the taboo of conflict has opened up a dialogue that will be continued in the organization as the strategies offered in the CDP are put to use and even carried to this group's counterparts overseas. Culturally, it offers the organization an opportunity to use the synergy of its people in ways they had never previously considered.

Style Instruments   There are a number of instruments that measure people's conflict styles, such as the Thomas Kilmann Conflict Mode Instrument (TKI) and the Hiam Dealing with Conflict Instrument. Style instruments typically look at two domains. The TKI domains are concern for self (getting what you want out of the conflict) and concern for other (wanting the other person to get what they want out of it). The Hiam instrument looks at the importance of relationship in relation to importance of outcome of the conflict. In both cases, depending on the relative importance of the two domains for an individual, he or she is characterized as having one of five different styles:

1. *Competing.* This style on the TKI indicates more concern for self than for other; on the Hiam it shows more importance for outcome than for relationship.

2. *Avoiding.* On the TKI, this style indicates low interest in self and other concerns and a desire not to have to deal with the conflict; on the Hiam it shows low perceived importance in the relationship and the outcome.

3. *Accommodating.* Low concern for self and higher concern for the other mark this style on the TKI, as does higher importance for the relationship and lower importance for the outcome on the Hiam.

4. *Compromising.* This styles splits the difference and shows partial interest in both domains on both the TKI and Hiam.

5. *Collaborating.* This style shows high concern or importance for both domains on both instruments.

When people understand their own styles of approaching conflict, they can reflect on situations where their style generally works well, as well as instances where it usually doesn't. They can then begin to adjust their approach based on their style and the circumstances. They can also appreciate styles of others and learn how to reach out to those with different styles. Our colleague, Beverly Fletcher, who is a faculty member at the Federal Executive Institute, does an excellent job using exercises that help people understand their conflict styles and the relevance these styles have for conflict settings.

We appreciate her sharing her approach.

DISCOVERING YOUR CONFLICT STYLES

The primary focus of this best practice is on participants' understanding of conflict styles. It uses adult learning techniques and is heavily *experiential* and thus avoids long lectures and demonstrations.

The process described here provides an example for trainers to use in helping participants understand the grounding theory underlying five conflict styles described by several different theorists. This best practice was designed to provide an opportunity for participants to examine and develop, firsthand, the underlying theory and constructs involved in the five "styles" utilizing the theoretical constructs developed by Kenneth W. Thomas and Ralph H. Kilmann (Thomas-Kilmann Conflict Mode Instrument); the five styles presented by Alexander Hiam (Dealing with Conflict Instrument); and five conflict strategies presented by David W. Johnson in *Reaching Out; Interpersonal Effectiveness and Self-Actualization* (Thomas and Kilmann, 1974, 1976; Hiam, 1999; Johnson, 2008).

This example sets up experientially basic information about how people differ in their approaches to conflict; it provides an opportunity for participants to develop a language to use in discussing these differences and the interaction between people with various differences. It also enables trainers to conduct an initial process upon which to build additional and more complex experience-based training in the area of conflict management.

The success of this process depends upon several things:

- The trainer's belief in the perspective that adult learners are naturally curious, creative, resourceful, and fully able to understand and articulate the nature of conflict styles
- The trainer's understanding of the five conflict styles
- The trainer's experience with adult learning technologies, and
- The trainer's ability to actively listen, to use provocative inquiry techniques, and to give constructive feedback.

The trainer must do her homework to understand the styles, must be able to ask good open-ended questions in the moment, and must have the skills to take participants as fully as possible through the adult learning cycle. The trainer must listen and build upon what is said in order to assist participants in developing the concepts underlying each style. Trainers must also be able to support participants by providing concise constructive feedback.

BEVERLY'S APPROACH

- Explain objectives of the process. Understand your primary style, explore advantages and disadvantages of different styles, determine how to diagnose the conflict situation, and determine the most appropriate style in that situation to guide your behavior.
- Introduce the style instrument being used in your session.
- Have the participants complete the instrument and put it away for later. They do not yet score their instruments.
- Emphasize that the five styles are "situational" and have the quality of being neither "right" nor "wrong" nor "good" or "bad." *Briefly* describe each style using visual metaphors that represent the styles (visual metaphors affect us at a deeper level than word labels). Have participants take notes and each select his "primary" style based on his perceptions of his own behavior. (*Note*: This should take less than 5 minutes. Do the descriptions *after* the

participants complete the instrument to prevent unduly skewing the instrument results.)

- Set up separate flip charts for each style. Have all participants stand by the flip chart with the style they select. Give participants at each flip chart 15 to 20 minutes to discuss and record the advantages and disadvantages of their style. Also have them record an example of an inappropriate and an appropriate use of the style. Figure 2.1 shows an example of a flip chart using a turtle symbol adapted from Johnson to indicate a group that tends to avoid conflict.

- Each group reports out. Explain that we are all capable of and probably have at one time or another used each of the five styles. Have the person "reporting" stand by with a marker to add additional insights into advantages and disadvantages from other

Figure 2.1
Turtle Style: Avoiding Conflict

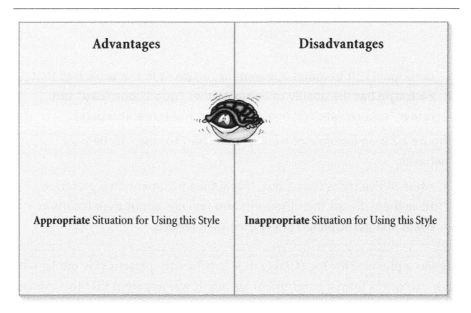

Advantages	Disadvantages
Appropriate Situation for Using this Style	**Inappropriate** Situation for Using this Style

Source: Adaptation from Johnson (2008) by Beverly Fletcher.

Figure 2.2
Problem-Solving Wheel

Advantages	Disadvantages
• Stay in comfort zone • Less risk • Buy time to think • Able to pick place and time • Preserve energy • Give time to calm down	• Make it worse • Prolong conflict • No solution • Doesn't address root causes • You look weak, indecisive • Holding hostage, passive aggressive, controlling
• When need time to cool down and think • When it's time to let things go • When goal is not important	• Long-term, festering problem, especially one that impacts a number of people and requires everybody's input.

participants. (It becomes apparent at this point in the workshop that each style has the quality of being neither "good" nor "bad" but rather "appropriate" or "inappropriate" given the situation.)

Figure 2.2 is an example of a completed chart for the "Turtle" behavior.

- After all five styles report out, reveal the instrument interpretation. Have them discuss their thoughts and feelings about their results in dyads and participants review their own reports.

It was a pleasure for me (Craig) to watch Beverly present this model with senior executives from a government agency. It was apparent that this exercise goes over well in a group setting and allows people to explore their own style and recognize that others may have very different styles. This sheds light on why it can be difficult to engage others in conflicts.

DECONSTRUCTING CONFLICT: A METHOD FOR UNDERSTANDING THE DYNAMICS OF CONFLICT

People are often confused by how conflict unfolds and changes. So we use an exercise that helps them better understand how the dynamics of conflict form their personal perspectives. We ask participants to think of and write down a description of a conflict that they've experienced recently. We then engage in a series of steps to help clarify how the conflict played out. Try answering them yourself:

1. How did you first become aware that there was a conflict? Can you determine the first time that you felt either some tension or thought that there was some kind of a difference that mattered with another person? It is not easy, sometimes, for people to remember these early stages. They get covered up by the subsequent interactions with the other person, and they no longer remember the conflict's origin. In many feuds, people no longer remember why the feud occurred; they just remember that they're supposed to dislike some other person or group.

2. When the participants can remember the earliest time they became aware of a conflict, we ask them what their thoughts were about the actions of the other person involved. In effect, what we want to do is to have them consider how they saw the other party. Our hope is that they remember what the other person said or did. The next step is to have them focus on how they understood the meaning of what the other person said or did. As they begin to flesh out their sense of what the other person's intentions may have been and what their actions probably meant, we ask them how it was that they came to that conclusion based on what they saw or heard. We also ask them to consider whether there are any other possible interpretations of those same facts or circumstances. If they indicate that there were alternatives (and usually this takes some effort to draw them out), we ask them why they think they chose the particular interpretation that they did at the time. Sometimes, this is influenced by a person's history with the other person. If he or she has had negative encounters in the past, it's very easy

for an individual to draw a negative interpretation about a new situation based on history.

3. After we've had the individual consider his or her interpretations of the situation, we then ask that person to talk abut how he or she felt about the matter. We want her to link the way she felt with the thoughts she was having and the interpretations she was giving to the situation. It's oftentimes difficult for people to clearly express their feelings, and we spend some time helping them get to what they felt at the time.

4. Next we ask them to think about what actions they took once they had experienced their initial thoughts, interpretations, and feelings about the situation. In other words, what did they say or do with respect to the other person in the conflict? We ask participants to be as specific as possible in sharing what they said or did.

5. Finally we ask how he or she thinks the other person would have interpreted or likely interpreted the actions that he or she took. If they were in the other person's shoes, how might they have reacted to what they had said or done toward that other person? We ask them how might they have interpreted their actions if they were in the other person's shoes. How might they have thought about those actions, and what kind of feelings might they have had? Then, we ask them how the other person responded, and is his or her response understandable—even though, perhaps, not reasonable in light of how they thought and felt about the behavior. Slowing things down and beginning to analyze, step by step, how a conflict unfolds begins to give us a sense of why people do the things they do. We also ask the person to reflect on whether his actions, based on his thoughts and feelings, were likely going to get him the result he wanted. In the moment of conflict, behaviors that feel so right oftentimes are unlikely to get us what we want out of the situation. So, we ask participants to think about whether their actions would likely get them what they wanted, and if not, what different kinds of actions would have been more likely to succeed.

There are obviously other factors that come into play—questions about differences in power between people, differences of culture—all of which can affect how conflict unfolds. But in general, the fundamental factors of how individuals see things, what sense they make of them, how they feel about them, how they respond, and what they really want in the situation are key elements of any conflict. If people can begin to understand better how these facets interact with one another, it becomes easier to be aware of them as conflicts emerge. It becomes less of a complex enigma. Individuals are able make more sense of conflicts and, as a result, can begin to develop skills and strategies to enable them to address conflicts more effectively.

The Emotional Side of Conflict

There are many wonderful books and courses dealing with conflict. If people could easily follow the recommendations found in these sources, conflict would not be such a confounding problem. We work with a lot of very smart clients, and while they easily understand concepts related to constructive conflict behaviors, they usually have difficulty using them in their daily lives. While practice helps polish the behaviors, we find that an even more fundamental issue concerns emotions.

Conflict is much more than just an intellectual battle of opposing ideas. It involves emotions, and often they are the greatest obstacle to resolving differences. In order to become conflict competent, people need to develop their emotional intelligence. More specifically, they need to understand how they respond emotionally to conflict, develop approaches to achieve and maintain emotional balance, recognize emotional responses in their conflict partner, and learn ways to help their partner gain emotional balance.

UNDERSTANDING HOW EMOTIONS ARISE IN CONFLICT

We have defined *conflict* as situations in which people have apparently incompatible interests. When we feel our interests threatened, our biological and neurological systems kick in and help us prepare to meet the threat. Before devising approaches to help manage emotions, let us first start by looking in more detail at what happens when the conflict emerges.

When we take in sensory data (seeing, hearing, and other senses), our brains try to make sense out of it. During this interpretive process, we make inferences about what the data mean and eventually draw conclusions based on these inferences (Argyris, 1990). While this process and the conclusions we draw seem perfectly reasonable, they are often off the mark.

First of all, we don't see everything that is happening, so our conclusions are made on incomplete data. Next, our inferences based on data we do have can be biased, especially in situations in which we think there are threats to our interests. In such cases, we frequently analyze the other person's actions in negative terms. We attribute their actions to personality flaws or sinister motives. Once we have concluded that the other person is a threat, and an unprincipled one at that, we conclude that the other person is bad and needs to be punished (Allred, 2000). Research suggests that this retaliatory response is an evolutionary development meant to teach others to avoid bad behavior (McCullough, 2008).

As these processes of inference and attribution proceed, emotions are triggered. When we feel that someone is threatening us and that this is bad, we begin to feel afraid or angry. These emotions tend to fuel further negative thinking about the situation and the other person. This process of rumination has been shown to be associated with brain patterns related to negative emotions (Ochsner and Gross, 2005).

All of these steps unfold very quickly. The distance from hearing something, to thinking about it, to inferring negative intent, to feeling angry can be spanned in seconds. In some cases our brains are preconditioned to analyze certain patterns as threats so that we can respond without thinking. When a snake darts out on a trail in the forest, we automatically step back without consciously thinking about it. We humans have what psychologist Paul Ekman calls *auto-appraisers* that enable our brains to scan the environment for threats, including possible threats to our interests caused by other people (Ekman, 2003). In conflict contexts, these auto-appraisers could be called *hot buttons* (Capobianco, Davis, and Kraus, 2008). When you come across someone who pushes your hot buttons, you get upset right away without even consciously thinking about it.

When our negative emotions are aroused, it becomes more difficult to respond constructively rather than react destructively. Authors in the field of emotional intelligence distinguish between our "hot" and "cool" response systems and between the "high road" of thinking and "low road" of destructive emotions

(Edmondson and Smith, 2006; Goleman, 2007). If we don't find ways of cooling down our emotions, we are more likely to react to conflicts by using ineffective behaviors that tend to escalate and prolong tensions. If we fail to slow down when we are upset and instead use destructive behaviors, this will cause our conflict partner to get angry and react, thus leading to a cycle of retaliation (Dana, 2005).

The problems arise from a combination of perception, thinking, and emotional responses. Over the years people from various fields have looked at how people can regulate these processes. Cognitive behavioral therapy, dialectic behavioral therapy, and acceptance and commitment therapy view the problem from a psychological therapy perspective.

The work of James Gross at Stanford University analyzes emotion regulation from a chronological viewpoint. It examines what people can do at various stages to regulate emotional responses (Gross, 1998). Early on, a person could try to avoid certain situations or people to prevent being provoked in the first place. This, of course, it not easy in the workplace. Once a situation has arisen, you could try to distract or focus your attention on something else and try to defuse tensions. You could also reexamine what you have seen or heard to see if there is some innocuous explanation for what is happening. Once their emotions have been aroused, people try to find a way of dealing with them, often by suppressing them and occasionally by finding constructive methods of expressing the emotions.

Regardless of the techniques employed to manage emotions, it is crucial to remember how negative emotions emerge because that process provides a glimpse of what needs to happen to regulate them.

In this chapter we share a number of approaches that can be used to help people cool down, slow down, and gain emotional balance as first steps in dealing effectively with conflict. We share tips and techniques that we use as well as ideas from leading researchers and practitioners.

We look at ways of helping people understand their current emotional reactions to conflict so that they will not be caught off guard. We investigate the concept of conflict "hot buttons." We explore three approaches—centering, cognitive reappraisal, and mindfulness or awareness—to cooling down negative emotions when they arise.

We also look at an approach from Roger Fisher and Dan Shapiro called *core concerns,* which aims at forestalling negative emotional reactions. This involves promoting positive emotions and is grounded in the areas of positive psychology and resilience.

Finally, we share methods to help people slow things down, when despite their efforts to cool their emotions down, things are nonetheless slipping out of control. In all of these areas we present tips, practices, and stories that you can use to help yourself and others improve conflict competence around emotions.

PERSONAL HOT BUTTONS

Conflict can emerge quickly, and before a person knows it he can feel upset and emotionally off balance. We use the Conflict Dynamics Profile® (CDP) assessment instrument to help people analyze personal hot buttons. The CDP contains a section that measures people's responses to nine different types of behaviors that are typically at the root of workplace conflicts. These hot buttons include the following behaviors:

1. *Abrasive*: Arrogant, sarcastic, and demeaning
2. *Aloof*: Isolating, not seeking input, hard to approach
3. *Hostile*: Angry, yelling, losing temper
4. *Micro-managing*: Constantly monitoring and checking on others
5. *Overly analytical*: Focus on minor issues, perfectionistic
6. *Self-centered*: Care only about self, believe they are always correct
7. *Unappreciative*: Fail to give credit, seldom praise good performance
8. *Unreliable*: Miss deadlines, cannot be counted on
9. *Untrustworthy*: Exploit others, take undeserved credit (Capobianco, Davis, and Kraus, 2008)

In the CDP, people rank how upset they get when they encounter other people who exhibit specific behaviors that describe the nine hot buttons. Their answers are compared to those of thousands of other people who have taken the instrument. They are then provided with a graphic display of how their responses compare to the norm group.

We find that people are fascinated by their hot button profiles, particularly because scores can differ so widely. In group settings we ask for volunteers to share a hot button. We then ask how many others in the group also share this hot button. There are almost always others who have the same hot button, and people find comfort that they are not alone. At the same time, there are usually individuals in the group for whom the hot button is not a trigger.

Hot buttons discussions work very well in team settings. Our colleague, Dr. Edmond Bazerghi, a psychologist from Austin, used a hot buttons exercise with an executive team that was having conflict problems. They took the Conflict Dynamics Profile to get a better sense of how they were currently dealing with conflict. The group was reticent. Although they agreed to take the instrument, they were concerned about how to discuss the results. Edmond was able to overcome their reluctance by focusing the group on a discussion of their hot buttons. The group began to share their particular hot buttons and soon loosened up and were able to say things like, "When you do that particular thing, it drives me crazy," in a way that didn't hurt each other's feelings. They talked about how not everyone experiences the same reactions. Even the president of the company, who was an introvert, was drawn into the discussion. He normally avoided conflict and as a consequence didn't get to hear what people were thinking about issues. The hot buttons exercise enabled him to open up about his avoidance of conflict and his desire to change this so the group could have more substantive discussions. They also had a new language about hot buttons and behaviors they could use when frustrations arose.

If two people were in the room with another person who behaved in a particular way, one person might get angry and the other wouldn't. We ask people in our groups to reflect on whether the "button pusher" is the cause of their anger or rather is it a specific reaction to the other's behavior. This is an important question in conflict management; rarely will you have a better context to explore the true cause of the emotional upset you feel in conflict.

We also like to explore why people get angry in the face of certain hot button behaviors. We ask the people who have a particular hot button, such as Unreliable, to talk about what makes them angry when they encounter someone who misses deadlines or cannot be counted on to do what they say. This helps people reflect on the values or concerns that underlie their hot button. When doing this in a group, we ask other people who do not share that hot button to talk about why they do not get upset when they encounter someone who behaves in that way. When people recognize that it is their own reactions that are at the heart of their hot buttons, they can become more open to exploring ways to cool down.

Before looking at ways to cool down, we ask participants to think about why they would want to do so in the first place. When people feel righteous indignation about their hot button responses, it is difficult to think about cooling down. The natural response is to want to "fix" the button pusher. To overcome this, we first help people think about what cooling down is all about.

The idea of lessening the intensity of our hot button responses is primarily about maintaining our own emotional balance. When we get angry at someone else's behavior, we become more susceptible to engaging in destructive, reactive responses. To prevent this from happening, we want to decrease the level of our anger. We still may not approve of the other person's behavior, but in addressing it we will be able to use more constructive approaches. So by dealing with our hot buttons, we are better positioned to effectively address the button pusher.

Once people see that lessening the intensity of their hot button reactions can be helpful, the next question is how to do it. The techniques described in the rest of this chapter can help lessen the emotional tension felt when hot buttons have been pushed.

REFLECTING ON HOT BUTTONS

1. Pair up with someone.

2. Have each person identify one of their hot buttons.

3. One person shares her hot button with her partner and describes what about the hot button causes her to get upset. We recommend that the person describe a real situation where the hot button was pushed and how she felt.

4. The partner then asks the individual to describe the "button pusher." The person who is experiencing the hot button carefully describes the actions of the button pusher and talks about how she interprets the motivations behind the button pusher's actions. If there is history behind the relationship, the person should also describe it and talk about how it affects the attributions she makes about the button pusher's intentions. Finally, the person should talk about how her view of the actions, motivations, and history of the relationship affected her emotional reactions to the situation.

5. The partner then asks the individual to speculate about any other possible reasons for the button pusher's actions. If the button pusher was abrasive and condescending, it might be explained by the person feeling superior and treating others as inferiors. It might also suggest that the button pusher was insecure and used the abrasive behaviors to try to cover up a sense of inferiority. The partner can brainstorm with the individual to come up with other possible explanations. The partner then asks the person how she would feel about the situation if one of the alternate interpretations was correct. Would this change the intensity of the irritation she was feeling? If it does, this may be one approach for cooling down the hot button reaction.

6. An alternative approach is for the partner to ask the individual if there are any helpful aspects of the button pusher's behavior. It is easy to spot the problematic aspects of the behavior but more difficult to look for positive ones. For example, if the individual has a hot button of Micromanaging, it would be easy to see the downsides of someone else acting in that manner. Is there anything positive, though, about people who micromanage? Perhaps they are good at details and make sure to keep things on track, even though the way they do it can be aggravating to some. Again, the partner can brainstorm possible positive aspects of a particular hot button behavior and then ask the individual how she would feel about the behavior when looked at from this context.

7. When this process is complete for one person, then the partners switch positions and repeat the exercise.

8. When the process is completed, the participants continue to follow a similar approach for each of their hot buttons. The key is to do this *in advance* of the time they encounter the hot button, so that it is no longer a mystery. Exposing hot buttons to the light of this analysis lessens the likelihood that they will take a person by surprise and will decrease the intensity of the emotions that will be felt. If there is an opportunity, the person could work with a coach

> to role-play hot button contexts to let the individual practice dealing with exposure to the behaviors and work to put new perspectives on them into practice.

As we have said, people have very different reactions to hot buttons. This probably stems from life experiences that have taught us to regard different behavior patterns as threats to our interests. In our work as consultants, we find that most people taking the CDP have one or two hot buttons out of the nine that are measured. For those people, we explore which of the hot buttons might be pushed in their workplace settings and how much difficulty the buttons present when they are pushed. We explore how an individual typically responds when a button has been pushed. We try to help him determine which, if any, hot button might be worthwhile to cool. It is usually too difficult to work on multiple hot buttons at once, so we recommend starting with one that is particularly problematic and moving on to others after the first is adequately addressed.

Some people have many hot buttons. Lots of behaviors can upset some individuals. We find they can even be upset about having lots of hot buttons. Often we see this in people who have very high standards for themselves and for others. If they don't live up to those standards, they can get down on themselves. If others don't meet their standards, it pushes a hot button. We reassure people with this type of pattern that having high standards is not a bad thing. When these standards lead to hot buttons being triggered, it can be difficult but it can also be managed. We take the same approach of working on one hot button at a time. Once the person addresses one hot button, then she can move on to the next.

A bigger problem occurs when a person who has lots of hot buttons that are getting pushed lacks a way to deal with the emotional upset these cause. If the person holds the anger inside, the anger can build up until it is released in unhealthy ways. Similar approaches can be used to lessen the intensity of an individual's hot button responses, but any approach needs to be coupled with work on lowering negative emotions and expressing how the person is feeling in more constructive ways.

A smaller selection of people have few if any hot buttons. These folks do not seem to get upset by other people's actions, which can make their lives a little easier. This pattern is not without its problems, though. Some people without hot buttons can be insensitive to the fact that other people do have them. We run into people who have no hot buttons and who are seen by others as real "button pushers." It is as though the person's attitude is, "It doesn't bother me; why should it bother you?" In these cases, we focus on how they can keep from pushing others' buttons without knowing it. The exercise in which people pair up to talk about hot buttons can be useful here. Instead of telling about their lack of hot buttons, they can talk in more depth with a partner who does have a hot button. The key task is to acknowledge and affirm that the other person's hot button is authentic, and that even though one person doesn't get upset by that behavior, the other person genuinely does. So if he acted in that manner, he could be upsetting the other person even without intending to do so and even if the same behavior would not upset him.

Understanding hot buttons is a rich area in emotions and conflict. It can provide helpful insights into what triggers people's emotions. If you want more information on the hot button concept, you can take a mini-survey at: http://www .conflictdynamics.org/cdp/hotbuttons/index.php. This survey does not substitute for scoring the hot buttons component of the CDP, but it does provide a first glance.

ADDRESSING FEARS

While we often think of anger when we consider conflicts, perhaps fear is the key underlying emotion. We may fear losing out on substantive issues or losing face. Bob Acton, a psychologist and organizational development consultant, provides us with an interesting approach to reducing fear.

As a conflict advisor, I assist individuals and organizations using a variety of tools such as organizational assessments, individual assessments, conflict coaching, training, and organizational effectiveness interventions.

As a psychologist, I attend to many factors involved in a conflict situation, such as an individual's thinking (for example, attitudes, interpretations, expectations, thoughts), behavior (for example, aggression, avoidance, withdrawal), emotions (for example, fear, anger, disappointment), and the context of the situation (for example, past history of conflict, organizational structure and functioning, current work environment).

Conflict frequently involves negative emotions for nearly everyone involved. Anger, of course, is the most common negative emotion associated with conflict, and the outcome of anger is all too often aggressive behavior. I believe it is important to pay particular attention to the participants' emotional reactions to the conflict itself while assisting them to reduce conflict. While anger is frequently noticed, there are other emotions that need to be assessed, as they can significantly influence behavior. Moreover, some emotions seldom are overt; they are frequently hidden, suppressed, or denied by people because of the associated anxiety or embarrassment associated with a specific emotion.

Fear is an emotional reaction that individuals experience in response to aggressive behavior or angry outbursts in others. But acknowledging fear or anxiety in response to aggression or anger can be embarrassing for some and hence can be uncomfortable to talk about. However, if a conflict advisor does not attend to the underlying emotional reaction, it will continue to undermine successful resolution of the conflict and may, in fact, lead to more conflict.

An example of this relates to my work with a manager of a small group in a unionized, not-for-profit organization. There had been significant conflict between the manager and some members of the group. It was serious enough that the union had frequently been consulted, grievances had been filed, and investigations were conducted. This required time-consuming and costly involvement from upper management and human resource professionals. However, no positive change had occurred, and I was asked to conduct an assessment and provide some solutions.

The assessment determined that the manager would become insistent about his perspective, increase his emotional reactions, and become more focused on the rules (how it was *supposed* to be done) when faced with what he perceived to be irrational employee behavior that was contravening industry standards and rules. The staff members in question would frequently respond to the manager's behavior by becoming accusatory, withdraw or yell, and then file a grievance. Thus the focus was shifted to the individuals' emotional reactions and subsequent behavior rather than the issue of the job performance, which was the key issue.

The manager was accurate in his belief that the employees were not following procedures correctly and that this placed the organization at risk for substantial fines by various authorities. But despite the fact he was correct, his reactions and behavior had not resulted in changing the employees' behavior. And, in fact, his emotional reactions provoked such a storm in the employees that typically the desired change in work procedures was lost.

A series of solutions was suggested, including conflict coaching for the manager. The coaching was designed to assist him to develop a new repertoire of responses to negative or confronting behavior by the staff.

I adopted a consulting role that included information provision, questioning, teaching, and empathetic understanding. We began with setting manageable, concrete goals that were accompanied by activities, including developing an understanding of conflict, recognizing the value in using effective conflict strategies, and role-playing effective conflict management techniques. The manager, however, seemed to struggle with enacting the expected behavior even in role play situations. In fact, I could provoke the behaviors experienced by his staff in the manager quite quickly (that is, emotional responses, rule-focused reactions, and so on). It was apparent that a hidden emotional reaction may have been creating a barrier for the implementation of new conflict resolution actions.

Through more exploration, it became clear that the manager's immediate reaction to employee noncompliance or overt defiance was fear. This fear stemmed from his worry that he would be seen as inept by his boss, the union, and human resources. It was his belief—that others would identify his presumed inadequacy—and the accompanying worry or fear that triggered his self-protective anger and his insistence that the employees act appropriately. This emotional response triggered a number of maladaptive behaviors and prevented opportunities to learn more adaptive behaviors. Until we were able to negate the impact of this emotion, no amount of training or teaching would suffice.

In situations such as this, one strategy that is quite effective is to assist the person to examine the truth behind the emotional reaction. Often people will hold a belief that not only is incorrect but also provokes a strong negative emotion that, in turn, leads to unproductive behaviors. In this case, we examined the "truth" of his sense of personal inadequacy.

I often use the metaphor of trying to put the issue on the table. In this strategy, I try to get the client to focus his or her attention on a table in front of us by imagining the issue is "on the table." This externalizes the problem and allows the individual to reduce his or her emotional reactions so that he or she can be more rational and thoughtful about it. Then we examine evidence, as one might do in a court of law, about the belief, and we look for evidence that is supportive or contrary to the belief. In the case of the manager, there was an overwhelming set of evidence that he was very competent (for example, past performance evaluations, statements by his boss) and no evidence that he was inadequate. He learned that he couldn't use his worry as evidence. He acknowledged that his propensity to think that others viewed him as inadequate was an influence from early experiences growing up and that it was clearly not true in the present context. This insight allowed him to develop a new belief that had solid evidence: "I am a competent manager dealing with a difficult situation."

In order to help him to deal with his anxiety and to focus on the task at hand, I taught him a technique to breathe effectively and maintain his attention and focus in the present moment. The idea of being fully present can be a powerful tool for individuals involved in conflict. Once he was able to breathe effectively and maintain his attention in the present moment, I asked him to remind himself of his new belief. He spontaneously created a mantra or internal cue for himself of "Breathe, Present, I'm okay," which he eventually shortened to BPOK. This held specific and powerful meaning for him.

When he became comfortable with these techniques, I was able to teach effective conflict resolution techniques (listening, clarifying, paraphrasing). I helped him to understand that his fear response may continue or recur, as it was likely that this response was embedded in his reactions to events. It is important for conflict advisors to predict that the old reactions may occur again but that the client can have greater control over it with the new skills. This emphasis on competency rather than mastery is important in helping individuals cope with "slips" rather than become discouraged and give up.

Relatively quickly, the manager was able to use the process of breathing, being present, and recognizing his competence even when his fear was triggered. He was able to use newly learned conflict management techniques in both provocative role play situations and ultimately in real-life situations when having difficult conversations with the staff.

At the end of our work together, he was able to stop his negative, anger-inducing reactions and replace them with appropriate conflict management techniques that resulted in the work-related issues being addressed without a great deal of conflict. The manager's work stress reduced significantly, and conflict in the department reduced to an acceptable and manageable level. The manager felt confident and competent in his newfound awareness and skills. The manager, his staff, and the team were able to return their focus to their individual and collective strengths and the core activities of the workplace.

Fear and other distressing emotions can cause us to lose balance and react in negative ways. Our next section looks at one approach to regaining balance.

CENTERING

The process of *centering* has its roots in the martial arts. Our friend and colleague Judy Ringer is an instructor in the martial art of *aikido* and a conflict management trainer in New Hampshire. She makes wonderful use of metaphors and lessons from aikido in her conflict training. We find her work with centering to be particularly valuable and are happy that she was willing to share the following tips and stories. We hope you find her stories and tips to be valuable as well.

People *will* push our buttons. Conflict *will* happen. What choices will we make? As Craig and Tim write in *Building Conflict Competent Teams,* "Once you understand the behaviors that can push your hot buttons, begin to look at ways to keep them from getting out of control."

In aikido, the Japanese martial art that I practice and teach, we use a physical centering practice that offers this kind of control through focused awareness on the breath, the body, and the environment. On the mat and moving from center, I align with the attacker's energy and redirect it while disarming the attack. Similarly, off the mat and breathing from center, I can acknowledge my emotional energy and manage it more intentionally. Whether on the mat or off, when I center, I collect myself physically and emotionally. I'm present to my surroundings and ready for whatever may come.

You can try centering yourself right now. Your physical center of gravity is an internal balance point approximately two inches below the navel. In aikido, we call it *tanden,* or one-point. You center yourself by focusing on this balance point. Stop reading, stand up, and focus your thoughts on your center, your *tanden.* Direct your weight toward that spot. Breathe in and out from center. Do you feel calm? Confident? More present? Ask a partner to gently push on you. You'll notice that you're stable and can redirect the push through your center into the ground.

You can increase your understanding of center by moving in and out of the centered state and identifying the differences in the quality of your being. Once you become familiar with the feeling of centeredness, you will access it quickly and easily. It only takes a thought to bring you back.

To choose center under pressure takes awareness of our uncentered state. When rising emotion and tension take hold of my body, if I can notice the tension coming over me, I can make a choice to center myself and create the next moment with awareness and purpose. I move from reaction to response, and I regain flexibility, balance, and power. Acquiring this life skill takes time, practice, and commitment to making the change in ourselves.

My own experience with the practice of centering, as well as the stories of students and colleagues, reinforces my conviction that as we become more centered, the social intelligence of our environment changes. Our centeredness is contagious. As we change, we influence the energy in the room, on the phone, and yes, even in that e-mail!

Examples of centering and its effects in the workplace are numerous. One participant, Sam, wrote me that after attending a conference workshop I presented on centering and purposeful communication, he was immediately offered an opportunity to put centering into practice. Upon returning to his office that day, he was surprised by an unanticipated meeting concerning a policy conflict that had been keeping him up nights—a meeting that could easily have turned confrontational but did not.

Sam is the director of a multifamily housing program in northern New England. Among his responsibilities is interpreting complex and controversial Housing and Urban Development (HUD) policy changes. One recent change affected how homes are appraised, and many area appraisers were unaware of the new policy. As a consequence, their appraisals of properties were coming in high.

One particular transaction was questioned by HUD and ended up in limbo for five months. When Sam explained that the appraiser's methodology put the transaction at risk and quite possibly thirty elderly residents out of a home, the developer and his consultant accused Sam of interfering.

The afternoon Sam retuned from the conference, the developer and consultant arrived unexpectedly to talk about the conflict with Sam's boss. Sam was caught off guard and unprepared.

In Sam's words:

Upon learning that the developer and consultant were in the building I made sure to begin some centered deep breathing. I reminded myself that this wasn't about me and thought about how this could be an opportunity to hear their side of the story and find some common ground. I asked that they be shown into a neutral meeting room rather than meet in my office and spent a few minutes gathering my thoughts and staying positive. Instead of focusing on whether I was right or wrong and defending my position, I projected confidence in the process that was about to unfold.

We sat around the oval table in the meeting room, and I tried to find a relaxed position. I continued to breathe and remind myself that this could be a good opportunity to find a new path that would allow us to acknowledge differences and reach a better outcome.

After some introductory conversation while waiting for my boss, the developer and consultant began to rather emotionally present their position. I forced myself not to defend myself and instead focused on really listening to what they had to say. . . . This was very hard to do. Reminding myself to stay calm and centered, once they finished, I acknowledged some things that they had said that I did agree with and talked about the need to be accurate, consistent, and fair in how we approach the appraisal issue. Some good information was shared, and I felt a shift in the flow of the conversation.

As I continued to relax, I sensed that they, too, were transitioning from a position of challenge and confrontation to one of cooperation and purpose. We all wanted to see the sale happen for the same reasons, and there were valid issues on both sides. Rather than getting caught in the trap of digging in on our respective differences, we were able to move to a place where new ideas and approaches could be used to solve the problem and both end up in a better place.

The upshot is I slept better over the weekend and communicated with others involved about what we might do as a result of the difficult conversation. I could finally let go, and instead of fear and defensiveness, I could look forward to problem solving in a more enlightened and forward-thinking way.

This kind of story is common. When one person decides to cool down, slow down, and engage constructively, all are affected. Everything changes.

Susan is the manager of a quality control team in an international biomedical corporation. Things had not been going well at work. She'd lost her top performer, and the rest of the team was making frequent and unacceptable mistakes. The stress of having to pick up the missing teammate's work was affecting Susan mentally and emotionally. She, too, was waking up nights thinking about what to say to her team about their poor performance.

The morning of their staff meeting, Susan woke in a bad mood, after one more restless night. She felt like screaming at her team to get their act together. On the way to work, however, she realized if she went into the meeting with these negative feelings it would only make matters worse.

She decided to center. As she focused on her breathing, her center of gravity, and on her positive intention, she began to reframe the conflict and see her team differently. They were not working against her or trying to undermine her. She saw them as one team, all there to do a job and facing the challenges together. As she took a few more minutes in the car to breathe and find her center, she focused on welcoming the energy from the group and redirecting it toward solutions.

At the meeting Susan remained relaxed and centered; the team began to brainstorm ideas on how to manage the workload without their star teammate; and together they made plans to meet their challenges.

Sam and Susan were able to create their environments on purpose. For them, centering is a mind-body practice they think about and engage in regularly, not only in difficult moments. If we want to get better at something, we have to practice, and there is no limit to the ways we can practice centering.

When you center yourself, you access a state of being that helps you notice, appreciate, and manage your hot buttons, transform your relationships, and enjoy being alive.

COGNITIVE REAPPRAISAL

New biological research has shown that a process called *cognitive reappraisal* can be a potent method for regulating emotions (Ochsner, Bunge, Gross, and Gabrieli, 2004). Reappraisal (also known as *reframing*) involves a cognitive process through which the facts underlying a conflict are reexamined for nonthreatening, alternative explanations.

Professor James Gross from Stanford University is a leading expert on emotion regulation. He shared with us some insights about how to use this approach and why it is effective (Craig's conversation with James Gross, April 20, 2009). Key suggestions and observations include:

- Cognitive reappraisal involves using alternative interpretations of the meanings about situations.

- Emotions have control precedence in crises (so if you want to manage conflict, you need to manage emotions).

- It is helpful to understand how emotions unfold and to recognize that you have options other than just acting them out or suppressing them.

- Emotions emerge over time, regenerating in waves that ebb and flow.

- Reappraisal can be used at any point during an emotional sequence.

- Being aware of your current emotional state is important so that you can know when you are off balance and need to use reappraisal.

- Recognizing that being upset isn't in your best interest can provide impetus to reappraise the situation.

One approach is changing the meaning of what you see. Dr. Gross gives the example of seeing someone crying on the steps of a church. At first, you might see this as an unhappy situation, such as a funeral. Alternatively, the person might be crying for joy, after a wedding. Our first impressions and interpretations are often affected by our own life experiences. So, two people viewing the same scene may construe it very differently.

In workplace contexts, many conflicts arise from just such misinterpretations. One person may say, "I'll be glad to take on that task," with the intention of helping others out. The recipient of the message may interpret it as an attempt to invade his turf. On the one hand, this describes the gap between the intention and impact of the speaker. It also describes how a particular reading of the situation on the part of the recipient can result in negative impressions and upset feelings.

To use cognitive reappraisal, you have to challenge your original construal. Is it the only way of seeing the situation? Are there rational, nonthreatening ways of understanding the matter?

When you are able to develop and consider such alternatives, interesting changes occur in the brain. Brain imaging shows that patterns associated with negative emotions begin to lessen, and those associated with more positive emotional states emerge (Ochsner and others, 2004). People begin to calm down and are more able to access and use constructive behaviors.

A second approach involves reconsidering the personal importance of the situation. This is equivalent to the notion, "Don't sweat the small stuff." While it may be true that the other person's actions if construed in a particular way might be irritating, is it worth bothering yourself about it? Looking at the broader perspective can help temper our emotional reactions.

Professor Gross admits that most people have little practice using the technique of cognitive reappraisal. Fortunately, walking through sample conflicts can be an effective practice technique.

There are several approaches we suggest for doing this. One involves remembering a conflict in which you got upset. Carefully note how you initially saw or interpreted what was happening and what the motives of the other person were. At this point, we suggest thinking about other possible explanations. You may initially want to reject these other alternatives as unrealistic, particularly given your "knowledge" of the other person. We encourage you to withhold judgment and participate in the brainstorming effort, assuming for the moment that the other person wasn't acting out of a malevolent intent. Remember, the point of this exercise is not to discern the objective truth about what happened, but rather to come up with possible alternative ways of appraising the situation. The more you can remain open to the *possibility* of alternate scenarios, the more effective the exercise becomes. By seeing alternatives, tensions begin to recede because the conflict threat is no longer so certain. Again, it is important to stress that you are using this technique to regulate your emotions so that you can more effectively use constructive engagement techniques. You may ultimately find out that your initial understanding was correct and that you will want to take action to address that situation, but at least you will be able to do so from a more balanced emotional state.

Another approach that can help people practice reappraisal and reinforce its validity involves thinking of a conflict in which they misinterpreted or misunderstood someone else and became angry or afraid. As an individual recalls a story, she describes the situation and her initial interpretation of it—the one that turned out to be wrong. As she describes her original appraisal, she describes why it was an understandable one given the circumstances or her history with the other person.

At that point, she shares what really was going on and what the other person's real motivations were. It is useful to also have her explain why the original construal was a reasonable, understandable one for someone in her shoes. This helps reinforce the notion that our original interpretations and attributions often seem eminently reasonable even though they turn out to be wrong. We sometimes get people to talk about other times when they felt *certain* their initial impression was correct only to have it turn out wrong.

If you can get people to admit that first impressions can be and perhaps often are wrong, it helps them open up to alternative explanations. In effect, it makes it easier for them to use cognitive reappraisal.

We have participants in our programs talk about how things turned out when the misunderstanding was clarified. We ask if they were surprised by the final explanation of the situation. Could they see how this version, which escaped their initial awareness, was probably a believable alternative from the start?

Finally, we ask them to talk about how they felt about the other person and the situation once things were cleared up. While the individual may initially talk about how he felt guilty, silly, or sorry for the misunderstanding, he reconsiders how he *felt* toward the other. Did his anger, fear, or resentment lessen? Did he feel better about the other person, perhaps less threatened by or suspicious of them? Did he feel more positive about moving forward?

When people are able to recognize that they are upset, and slow things down, they can consider how they are looking at the situation and then begin to look for other nonthreatening alternatives. When successful, this helps bring down tensions and enables people to achieve emotional balance. At that point, they can begin to use more constructive communication techniques to effectively resolve conflicts.

The process of reappraisal may be helped by the next emotion regulation technique we address, known as mindfulness (Garland, Gaylord, and Park, 2009).

MINDFULNESS

The approach called *mindfulness* or *awareness* has its origins in contemplative or meditative traditions. It is based on the belief that our thinking affects our emotions and vice versa. When we are in conflict, distressing thoughts about the issue or the other person can lead to fear and anger, which in turn provide fuel for further negative thinking. Mindfulness is an approach to breaking this cycle and helping us regain emotional balance. One definition is, "Mindfulness is the awareness that emerges through paying attention on purpose, in the present moment, and non-judgmentally to things as they are" (Williams, Teasdale, Segal, and Kabat-Zinn, 2007).

People use different terms to describe this process, such as *awareness, presence, observing, disengagement,* and *going to the balcony.* In conflict contexts, the process involves slowing down, stepping back, and observing what you are feeling and thinking rather than being caught up in the thoughts and feelings.

Although the practice derives from meditative traditions, it can be used without reference to its spiritual or religious roots. In more recent times, mindfulness has been used to help people deal with anxiety and depression in clinical settings. A process called Mindfulness Based Stress Reduction (MBSR) was developed at the University of Massachusetts Medical School to help patients deal with pain and anxiety. More recently, mindfulness has been used to address depression in a practice called Mindfulness Based Cognitive Therapy.

Mindfulness allows people to see thoughts and feelings as passing phenomena. Just as cloud shapes come and go, so too do thoughts and feelings. What feels so overwhelming in the moment can change and dissolve after a short time—unless we continue to ruminate about the matter. When we are able to step back and disengage from being obsessed about what the other person did to cause the conflict and how mad we feel about it, the intensity begins to diminish and we are held less captive by our emotions. The cycle of negative thoughts begetting negative emotions begetting more negative thoughts is broken. We no longer identify our sense of self with the negative thoughts and feelings, and as a consequence they lose their hold over us (Tolle, 2008). We also become more open and curious to what is happening and less likely to use avoidance behaviors.

Mindfulness changes brain functioning. Researchers have found that when people use mindfulness techniques, their brain patterns change from ones associated with negative emotions to ones associated with more positive affect (Siegel, 2007; Davidson and others, 2003; Begley, 2007). So if people can effectively use this approach, they change not only their thinking but their brains as well.

Mindfulness Techniques

A variety of approaches can be used to help develop awareness skills. Let's go back to the definition just presented. Mindfulness involves purposely paying attention, being in the present moment, and suspending judgment.

In conflict, this means paying attention to your thoughts and feelings—observing them rather than being swept away by them. It means doing this in the present moment. When we are upset, we often think more about what has happened to cause the conflict (in the past) and about what we intend to do about it (in the future). We have difficulty staying in the present—being in touch with the sensations we are feeling in our body (tightness, unsteadiness), what thought patterns are occurring, and what emotions we are feeling. We are experiencing all of these sensations, thoughts, and feelings, but we are relatively unaware of them. It is as though we are on autopilot and not very conscious of what is happening to us.

Being mindful involves suspending judgment for the moment. If we observe our thoughts and feelings and then berate ourselves for having them, we launch a new set of negative things to dwell on. Being observant while withholding judgment allows things to settle down and for balance to return.

So what are some of the techniques that can be used to practice mindfulness? You can try being mindful about all kinds of things in your life. A number of books provide exercises that you can follow. We particularly like *The Mindful Way Through Depression* because it provides a wide range of exercises; an accompanying CD by Jon Kabat-Zinn, who was a key developer of the MBSR program; and a framework that can be used to connect the various practices (Williams and others, 2007).

I (Craig) had the pleasure recently of attending a mindfulness retreat hosted by the Florida Community of Mindfulness. Participants were provided with opportunities to experience mindfulness in different circumstances—including a number described in *The Mindful Way Through Depression* book. After an introduction to the concept of mindfulness, participants tried being very aware of their breathing. As we became aware of the feelings associated with both inhalation and exhalation, a certain calm emerged. Our minds slowed down. Thoughts would come and go, but we were encouraged to gently bring our attention back to our breath when we were aware that it had strayed. We were reminded that distractions happen naturally and frequently. We needn't berate ourselves when it happened (in other words, we could be nonjudgmental).

Later in the retreat, we participated in two walking exercises. The first occurred inside and involved walking in a circle with other participants. The key was paying attention to each step, noticing how our body was balanced and where each foot was placed for each new step. It took awhile to get used to the practice, but over time we found our minds less full of thoughts and more relaxed.

The second walking exercise was outside, through a local wildlife park. We walked in silence and were encouraged to just observe things. Rather than trying to name all the plants or calculate how many birds we saw, we were encouraged to stay in the moment and just observe what we saw, heard, or felt. This included observing the sensation of the sun on your skin or how a breeze felt when it passed.

Once again, as we became more observant of what was happening here and now, there was a slowing of thinking. Occasionally one's mind would turn to an errand you wanted to do later or some work-related problem, but when you became aware of it, you would gently return to the present moment and begin observing what was here and now anew. Again, an easing of tensions and a general positive mood emerged.

We practiced mindfully doing some stretching and yoga exercises. We were encouraged to move slowly through these exercises and be very aware of feelings in our bodies. When we stretched, we looked for areas of tightness and the sensations that occurred. It was fascinating to feel the tingling, almost burning sensation when a tight muscle began to be stretched. We didn't push hard, so as to avoid injury, but enough so we could feel the body's response. It was possible to focus on sensations, even those that were a little uncomfortable, in a new way. We learned not to immediately pull back just because something was unpleasant. We could observe it dispassionately and with a sense of curiosity, and we noticed our relationship to the sensation begin to change. It no longer caused us to immediately react. It was possible to stay aware, open, and curious about the feeling. These, of course, are key elements of being able to manage conflict effectively.

The retreat included a lunchtime exercise in eating mindfully. In a society that is always on the go, eating often means grabbing something quickly and not having time to savor the meal. Our retreat lunch was completely the opposite. We were given guidance in how to make the meal into a mindfulness exercise. In particular, we ate slowly and carefully observed how the food felt in our mouths (texture; tastes—salty, sour, bitter, sweet; hot or cold), the flavor as we chewed it, and how it felt as we swallowed. The experience was rich and dramatic compared to an ordinary eating experience.

Similar kinds of practice can be done with thoughts and feelings. As described in *The Mindful Way Through Depression,* you can invite a difficult situation (like a conflict) into your mind and then focus on how it makes you feel. You can notice any physical sensations (increased heart rate, tightness, sweating, and so on).

You can be aware of what thoughts arise in your mind around the conflict and what emotions are evoked by it. By being aware and open to these elements, you accept them rather than try to push them away. We particularly like the approach described in the book to enhance acceptance by saying to yourself, "It's okay. Whatever it is, it's already here. Let me be open to it" (Williams and others, 2007, p. 152).

I (Craig) have practiced this technique with interesting results. I think of a conflict that I've had or am having and begin to stew about it for a moment. I remember some of the thoughts and feelings I originally had. At some point I started observing my thoughts and feelings. As I observe them rather than being wrapped up in them, I feel my agitation recede and an openness and curiosity emerge. At that point I try to change pace and get immersed in the thoughts and feelings again. I could feel the tension rise again. At that point I would try the mindfulness processes again and regularly found that the anxiety would decrease.

Our colleague, Michael Hoppe, a former instructor at the Center for Creative Leadership, also used an adaptation of mindfulness in exercises. He and his coinstructors would create a space in the room where participants could go when they began to feel upset about something. More than just a time-out space, this *witnessing perch* or *balcony,* as it was called, was a place where people could go to observe and reflect on what was happening to themselves and with others in a group. The person could objectively look at himself or herself and disengage from the thoughts and emotions that were causing turmoil. The program facilitator could intervene when someone appeared upset and encourage them to go to the witnessing perch. The rules and norms of the program gave legitimacy to people going there on their own volition or for the facilitator to suggest that participants do so. This made it much easier to take advantage of this approach to cool down when one's emotions were getting the best of him (Craig's conversation with Michael Hoppe, May 5, 2009).

Practice Builds Skill

Since conflict is so prevalent, there will be plenty of chances to practice these techniques should you choose to do so. At the same time, it takes practice to build new skills, particularly when the need for them arises in stressful contexts.

Fortunately, mindfulness skills can be developed in nonstressful contexts. When the phone rings, don't answer it on the first ring. Take that short moment to slow down and become aware of how you are feeling. When you're eating your breakfast, try eating at least a part of it very consciously. Rather than reading the paper or talking, spend a few moments being very aware of the eating experience. As you enhance your skills, your ability to focus and become aware in stressful situations will improve. In the beginning it may only be after an argument that you become aware that you were not being mindful during the conflict. As you practice, the more likely you will be able to catch yourself in the midst of distress and begin to use these techniques to help gain emotional equilibrium (Tolle, 2004).

The Mindful Way Through Depression presents a helpful exercise for dealing with stressful contexts. The authors call it "the three-minute breathing exercise." When you become aware of distress, they recommend stopping and observing what you are thinking and feeling and the body sensations you are having. After this, they suggest focusing your attention on your breathing and give specific suggestions for doing this. Finally, they suggest expanding your field of awareness to include a sense of your body, posture, and facial expressions (Williams and others, 2007, pp. 182–183). This process is meant to change your stance toward what is happening. It helps stop our entanglement with negative thoughts and feelings and allows slowing down, cooling down, and regaining balance.

Dr. Daniel Siegel, author of *The Mindful Brain* and *Mindsight,* says that such exercises help activate parts of the brain that support receptivity as opposed to reactivity (Siegel, 2007, 2010). The exercises enable people to distinguish *their thoughts* from *themselves*: "You can see mental activity as something different than you are" (Craig's conversation with Daniel Siegel, June 26, 2009). By being aware of sensations, images, feelings, and thoughts, you are able to reshape your internal world and respond to conflicts in a more balanced manner.

CORE CONCERNS APPROACH

Another approach focusing on cultivation of positive emotions is the core concerns model developed by Dan Shapiro and Roger Fisher of Harvard University in their book, *Beyond Reason* (Fisher and Shapiro, 2005). They identify five core relational concerns, common to all people, which when addressed can create positive emotions that help in dealing with conflict and negotiation contexts.

The five core concerns include:

1. *Appreciation:* Acknowledging the merit of the thoughts, feelings, and actions of others and yourself. This includes understanding the other person, genuinely finding merit in what he says or does or how he feels about an issue,

and letting him know what it is that you appreciate. It also involves helping the other person appreciate you.

2. *Affiliation:* Building connections with others. This concerns finding things in common with the other person, building trust, and treating each other as colleagues.

3. *Autonomy:* Respecting the rights of others to make their own decisions as well as for you to make your own. Refraining from impinging on others' autonomy to make their own decisions while retaining the right to make your own builds respect and prevents people from being imposed upon by others.

4. *Status:* Acknowledging others' and your own areas of status. Everyone has special talents and characteristics. Treating others with the respect they deserve can enhance esteem and make people feel good.

5. *Role:* Define and support fulfilling roles for yourself and others. If you feel your role is unfulfilling, it can be disheartening. Our colleague, Bill Rusak, a longtime business executive, always made a point to emphasize the importance of all his employees' roles in promoting important organizational or societal outcomes. A sanitation worker might not have a high-profile job, but if he of she doesn't do it well, public health can be seriously jeopardized.

Shapiro and Fisher suggest that it is easier to address these core concerns than to worry about managing the myriad emotions we may experience. Their approach aims at building positive emotions while at the same time lessening the chances that negative emotions will emerge. We recommend their book and a course that Dan Shapiro teaches at the Harvard Program on Negotiation.

Showing Respect

We want to focus on one aspect of the core concerns model. This involves showing respect to others. While respect is a part of all of the core concerns, we particularly like its use in the first concern, which involves expressing appreciation for the other person's thoughts, feelings, or actions.

It costs very little to show some respect for the other person in a conflict. Our colleague, Jennifer Lynch, QC, who was appointed the chief commissioner of the

Canadian Human Rights Commission in 2007, developed a conflict model called VALUED. The elements include:

V   Validate

A   Ask (open-ended questions)

L   Listen (to test assumptions)

U   Uncover interests

E   Explore options

D   Decide (on solutions)

The first step involves validating the other person. If someone has angered us, we often respond by attacking their view of things. Jennifer says that this is the time to stop and offer some form of validation to the other person, perhaps by acknowledging that he or she feels strongly about an issue, and it is important that it be addressed. Showing respect to another person does not mean that you agree with him, just that you respect him enough to treat his ideas, feelings, and actions seriously.

We find a good way to help people develop this skill is to have them practice with past conflicts. When we are working with a group, we divide people into small groups and have them describe their conflict and the person with whom they had it with the other participants. At this point we ask if she genuinely finds merit with how the other person thought about the conflict. We also ask the person to reflect on how the other person felt about the conflict and how he acted during the conflict. This is not as easy as it seems, because many times people do not have a very good understanding of how the other person thought or felt about the conflict. In these cases, we have them reflect on how the other person probably thought or felt about the conflict. We encourage the other participants to share alternative thoughts or feelings that the other person might have had. Once this is complete, the participant is again asked to consider the potential merit in these thoughts and feelings. We do not ask them to judge whether the other person's thoughts or feelings are objectively correct. Rather, we ask them to look at them to see if they have merit. We do not want the participant to make something up. It is important for the participant to find something he genuinely believes has merit (even though it might not turn out to be correct).

After he has discovered a thought or feeling that has merit, then we have him practice how he could express appreciation to the other person about how that person thought, felt, or acted. As we mentioned before, it might be something as simple as recognizing that the person has a strong emotion about something and validating that you respect that emotion as genuine and worthy of being addressed. He might also comment on a thought that the other person had and recognize that this is a reasonable or understandable way to view the situation, even if he sees it another way.

When people feel respected it boosts their self-esteem. This can cause them to feel more positive and lessen tensions. As this occurs, people can begin to listen to one another more carefully and consider new approaches to solving their problems. Fred Eppsteiner, a psychotherapist and teacher with the Florida Community of Mindfulness, shared with us an approach for dealing with ongoing conflict called the *beginning anew ceremony*. It incorporates a process called "watering seeds" in which people in a group acknowledge positive aspects of one another. They also admit any ways they have contributed to a problem, and then talk about the emotional pain that has been caused. Fred said that this helps clear the air and enable people to move on (Craig's and Tim's conversation with Fred Eppsteiner, May 19, 2009).

We also recommend celebrating successes—small ones and large ones. The positive feelings that can come from a job well done can help lift people's spirits. Sometimes people think that doing one's job shouldn't require additional kudos. While that may be true in one sense, in terms of helping improve resilience and the ability to deal with conflicts, we say, "Celebrate!"

CHANGING FOCUS

When emotions arise in conflict settings, they are triggered by the way we think about the situation, giving rise to the conflict. One way to manage emotions is to think differently about the circumstances. It is a cognitive approach that can be very effective.

Another technique is embodied by common adages like "Take your mind off the problem" or "Think of something more positive." This approach involves changing one's focus or attention. Thomas Jefferson advised, "When angry count to ten before you speak. If very angry, count to one hundred." The reason this process helps is that it breaks the mind's absorption in the negative thoughts related to the conflict. This, in turn, disrupts the emotional reactions stemming from these thoughts.

Sometimes people suggest taking a break when things get tense and going outside for a walk to change the context. If, while on the walk, the person is able to enjoy the sights and stop thinking about the conflict, this can be helpful. If, however, the walk turns into a time when the person continues to stew about the problem, then little relief will be found.

We find it is helpful for people to think about or imagine something that is relaxing or inspiring to them. I (Craig) was once in a coaching session with a client who became quite upset in conflict settings, so much so that it prevented her from dealing with issues in a suitable manner. She wanted to find some way to calm down so she could relate to people in the way she wanted. It was obviously a problem for her, and she became tense even discussing it. I asked her about what she found to be calming. Almost at once, a smile came on her face. She began to talk about taking her boat out onto the lake and just floating quietly. As she spoke, I could see her body relax, and her mood continued to brighten. By the end of the coaching session, she determined that one technique she would use to cool down during conflicts would be to take a short break, go somewhere she could be alone, and visualize herself out on the lake, in her boat.

The benefit of imagining something positive is that a person's mood can brighten, and this not only helps emotions calm, but also supports adaptive thinking—looking for how to make the best out of a situation.

A number of people find that reflecting on religious or spiritual themes helps them deal with upsetting emotions by providing an uplifting alternative to negative thoughts. This sometimes takes the form of quotes like "This, too, shall pass" or prayers such as the serenity prayer (Niebuhr, 1987). Various meditative or contemplative practices have also been shown to lessen tension and help regulate emotions, as we saw in the section on mindfulness.

POSITIVE EMOTIONS

We have seen that negative thoughts can trigger negative emotions that can fuel more negative thoughts and so on. This in turn leads people to default into destructive types of behavioral responses. Researchers in the field of emotions suggest that negative emotions trigger *specific action tendencies* that tend to be fight-or-flight responses. It is as though we feel we have fewer alternatives for action while we are experiencing negative emotions. We have talked about ways of cooling down these enflamed emotions. What if instead we could increase our positive emotions? Would this help us deal with conflict better?

In recent years, research into the field of positive psychology and positive emotions has revealed some helpful clues to these questions. Dr. Barbara Frederickson has developed a broaden-and-build theory of positive emotions that suggests that positive emotions broaden the array of thoughts and actions that come to our mind. They increase our curiosity and ability to absorb new information. This happens not only while you are experiencing the emotion but afterward as well, as our thinking patterns are broadened in ways that help us deal with subsequent threats (Frederickson, 2001).

This suggests that cultivating positive emotions may be an effective way of addressing conflicts in which negative emotions can emerge. Frederickson suggests that positive emotions serve as antidotes to negative emotions and can help undo the narrowing tendencies they engender. They help people find more positive meaning and make more positive appraisals of stressful situations and even enable people to reflect on information in more complete and complex ways (Tugade and Frederickson, 2004; Tugade, Frederickson, and Barrett, 2004). It appears that positive emotions also help increase people's resilience, which in turn helps them deal with the stress and setbacks that can come with conflicts (Cohn and others, 2009).

Cultivating Positive Emotions

How can one go about cultivating positive emotions? A number of approaches have been suggested, such as using humor and laughter and fostering a sense of gratitude. Different types of meditative practices have been shown to increase brain function associated with positive affect (Davidson and others, 2003; Frederickson, 2008).

We suggest that you think about things that inspire you and make you happy. What brings you a deep sense of peace, contentment, and happiness? Since positive emotions seem to have a cumulative effect, we suggest you think about these things on a regular basis. This can be difficult during the hustle-bustle of the day, but it is still important. We recommend that you find and set aside a few brief times during the day when you can reflect on these uplifting thoughts. It could be at the very start of the day, right before or after lunch, and just before going home.

The key is to do it regularly so that you constantly replenish the positive emotions that can bring so much into your life.

Another interesting approach is presented by work done at the Institute of Heartmath. They have developed several techniques that involve focusing on the heart area while self-generating a positive emotion like appreciation. Research suggests these techniques can elevate people's positive emotional states. (McCraty, Atkinson, and Tomasino, 2003).

RESILIENCE

When you have experienced strong negative emotions, it takes a while to recover. In the short-term refractory period, you have to weather the storm. Sometimes, though, these feelings last for a long time and interrupt a person's capacity to respond effectively. Then it becomes important to work on improving our resilience. Conflict coaching is a mechanism of choice for Cinnie Noble, founder of CINERGY® Coaching, a Toronto-based company that provides conflict coaching and training worldwide. We appreciate that Cinnie has shared her approach, which can help people with this work.

This one-on-one process is a hybrid of executive coaching and conflict management principles, and it is both a proactive and a reactive technique. Conflict coaching began to gain popularity as a distinct mechanism in the field of alternative dispute resolution in the 1990s and has grown exponentially in both the coaching and conflict management arenas since that time.

Goals of conflict coaching in workplaces include:

- To help people increase their competency to more effectively engage in conflict
- To help individuals approach conflict proactively and prevent matters from escalating unnecessarily
- To assist individuals to effectively manage an ongoing dispute
- To help people resolve a dispute that ended in an unsatisfactory way
- To prepare for mediation or other dispute resolution forum
- To help leaders better manage their staff members' conflicts they have with their coworkers and with themselves

- To help leaders prepare for challenging conversations, such as performance reviews and appraisals
- To help participants apply and sustain their learning from conflict management training workshops

Most of my practice involves coaching individuals to improve their conflict competence, to be able to manage their disputes and engage in conflict more effectively. Similarly, as a mediator, I increasingly provide premediation using the CINERGY® model to prepare people for this process.

However, one component of conflict management that I find is often overlooked in workplaces has to do with postconflict resilience. Specifically, many people experience an adverse reaction after an altercation or after their participation in a dispute resolution process such as mediation. This fact has the potential for continuing to challenge the individuals initially involved in the conflict and other workplace relationships as well. It also has implications for the nonresilient person's ongoing and future ability to engage in conflict. Following are two examples of situations in which one of the people in a dispute identifies the impact of conflict after its occurrence.

David and John

David and John are midlevel managers who have worked in the same company for three years. Mostly they see each other at monthly meetings, at which time their competitive styles and apparent need to win at all costs are evident. At a recent meeting, David and John began to argue over the plan being proposed for restructuring several departments. After the meeting, their manager called them in and said she wanted them to participate in mediation "to get the issues between them sorted out once and for all" and to "learn how to collaborate."

At the mediation, David and John discussed what they considered the reasons for their clashes. The two men seemed to come to a truce by the end of several highly charged sessions, and they ultimately discussed a plan for how they will work collaboratively. However, a few months after the mediation, John decided to see a coach. He told him that he had been blaming himself ever since the mediation for things he said or wished he had said to David and also for "getting into such squabbles" in the first place. John added that he is now reticent to disagree with David in meetings and that he is not really sure he can be collaborative with David when he still "resents" him.

Jennifer and Victor

Jennifer and Victor work in close proximity and their desks are separated by a divider. Victor came on staff two months ago and from the beginning he found Jennifer's voice to be "loud and strident." He has sent her several emails expressing his complaints. A few times Victor also peered over the office divider and asked Jennifer to "please keep your voice down." These messages started in a friendly manner and over time have become angrier and more sarcastic in tone and content.

Jennifer initially apologized to Victor and tried to be conscious of her voice. Then, she too became angry at Victor and started to blame him for being "a bully." Last week, Jennifer screamed at Victor to "stop his nonsense and get over himself," after he sent her an email that said "PLEASE SHHHH." The two of them began to argue and blame each other for various behaviors until one of their coworkers intervened and told them they were being childish and inconsiderate of everyone else. Both Jennifer and Victor went back to their work, and they haven't spoken since. Jennifer asked for a transfer and was off on sick leave for two days. Yesterday, she went to see a coach and told her that she has been agonizing over a situation with her coworker Victor and that it's typical of her that she "never seems to bounce back after arguments with anyone."

These two examples of dissension demonstrate how conflict can have a lingering impact on ongoing interactions and how negative feelings prevail. People who repeatedly experience postconflict repercussions have typically developed conflict-coping habits that tend to repeat themselves from altercation to altercation. I have found that helping people closely examine their conflict habits through coaching, including the consequences of lack of resilience, strengthens their individual conflict competence in general. Similarly, coaching for other aspects of conflict management strengthens clients' postconflict resilience. Relevant to this discussion is also my experience that when people speak of even one factor that reflects lack of resilience, there are usually clusters of other responses to conflict that are apparent and related to the one(s) identified.

The following exercise includes a number of behaviors that are often indicative of lack of resilience and may be used to check one's Conflict Resilience Quotient (CRQ). This tool, shown in Exhibit 3.1, helps people identify a range of variables that reflect lack of resilience, so that they are able to focus on and develop those that require strengthening.

To put this exercise into a conflict coaching context, it helps to look back on the two scenarios presented earlier. John continues to focus on things he said or wished he had said to David. John criticizes himself about how he acted in the meeting and is now reticent to disagree with David.

Exhibit 3.1
Conflict Resilience Quotient

After most interpersonal conflicts, I usually tend to:	Less True			More True	
Recover quickly and do not worry, agonize, or stay preoccupied about what the other person said or did that offended me.	1	2	3	4	5
Forgive and do not bear a grudge about the other person and what s/he said or did.	1	2	3	4	5
Reflect on what I learned from the conflict that will help me manage future disagreements.	1	2	3	4	5
Reach out to make amends with the other person.	1	2	3	4	5
Take responsibility for my part of the conflict and consider what I may have done differently.	1	2	3	4	5

Not share my side of the situation with others in self-serving and distorted ways.	1	2	3	4	5
Feel hopeful that things will be better and consider how I will try to contribute positively to this happening.	1	2	3	4	5
Move on and not see myself as a victim or feel sorry for myself.	1	2	3	4	5
Not continue to perceive the other person in negative ways.	1	2	3	4	5
Not bad-mouth the other person to others.	1	2	3	4	5
Identify what may have been important to the other person that I did not realize before.	1	2	3	4	5
Apologize for my part of the conflict.	1	2	3	4	5
Have a better appreciation for and understanding of the other person's perspective on the issues, even if I don't agree with it.	1	2	3	4	5
Not criticize, blame myself, or engage in other self-deprecating behaviors about what I did or said (or didn't say or do).	1	2	3	4	5
Let go of blaming the other person for what s/he did or said (or didn't say or do).	1	2	3	4	5

Total:

SCORING KEY

15–39   Hmmm . . . I guess you already know you are not conflict resilient and coaching is highly recommended.

40–54   Your conflict resilience quotient is low and conflict coaching is recommended.

55–69   You are conflict resilient with a few areas that could use some work to strengthen your skills even more.

70–75   You are definitely conflict resilient!

Source: From CINERGY® COACHING www.cinergycoaching.com.

In his conflict coaching, John identified factors on the CRQ related to these tendencies. He was surprised how much it resonated that he "is not able to move on" and that he "bears a grudge" against David. All of these points were significant to John's coaching, which ultimately helped prepare him to have a one-on-one conversation with David aimed at finding a way for them to disagree productively and to collaborate more effectively. John acknowledged that he wanted to work on his competitive style of communicating, which has caused him trouble in previous jobs.

In the scenario with Victor, Jennifer was able to identify a number of factors on the CRQ to work on. She acknowledged that when she is in conflict, she does not readily recover and worries "endlessly," choosing to continuously avoid rather than to learn more effective ways of managing or resolving the conflict. Jennifer's coaching focused on helping her gain increased awareness about her way of responding to conflict. She explored alternate ways she could manage conflictual situations not only with Victor but also with others who might provoke her in the future. In this case, Jennifer decided not to transfer out of the work unit after all, and she said she wanted to make amends with Victor. She was coached on her goal to meet with Victor to discuss things, including how open he was to meeting together with their manager about what sort of physical setup may be more workable for them.

Some interpersonal conflicts are more upsetting than others. Depending on the person and the nature of the situation, resolution does not always occur. Even when it does, it may not be as mutual or satisfactory as one might have hoped. Conflict competent organizations contemplate the full gamut of how conflict affects the workplace and its workforce and provide ways to address staff members' postconflict resilience in their overall efforts to normalize conflict. Whether it follows an interpersonal dispute that has occurred, after mediation or other interaction or process in which staff engage, the importance of offering ways to assist people with respect to postconflict repercussions cannot be overstated. I have found that coaching staff to learn more about themselves and how they manage issues before, during, *and* after conflict is critical to increasing their conflict competence and their Conflict Resilience Quotient.

SLOWING DOWN

When conflict arises, our emotions can get enflamed. Adrenaline courses through our bloodstream to prepare us for fight-or-flight responses to perceived threats. Things speed up, and we become susceptible to reacting to situations without thinking about the consequences. We have talked about how we can work at cooling down in these situations. When these efforts are successful, we become calmer and more balanced emotionally. Yet, sometimes despite our best efforts at cooling down, our tensions continue to escalate, and before we know it, we say or do something we later regret.

An effective strategy for gaining and maintaining emotional balance also has a backup plan for when cooling down isn't working. We call this process "slowing down." It involves taking a time-out to allow yourself extra time to apply cooling down techniques.

When our negative emotions are aroused in conflicts, we enter a stage Ekman (2003) calls a *refractory period,* in which emotions hold sway over our rational mind. During this period, logical persuasion doesn't work. The stronger the emotions, the longer the refractory period can last (Goleman, 2003). During this time, it is best to slow things down to give you more time to work on cooling down.

In the heat of conflict, it can be difficult to remember to slow down or to find a good way to ask for a time-out. So we recommend developing plans in advance for what to do when things are racing in the wrong direction.

We have people develop ways of being able to know when to take a time-out in the first place. Since it is easy to get caught up in the moment and say something that is accompanied by your foot in your mouth, it is crucial to know when it is time to *stop*! One method is practicing becoming more aware of your feelings. The section on mindfulness provided some tips for practicing this through the day. As you become more conscious of your emotions, you will be able to tell when negative emotions are becoming stronger, and you can slow down. You could also ask trusted colleagues to let you know when it looks like you are getting upset. If they help you out with this, you would do well to just thank them rather than telling them in loud terms that "*I am not angry!*"

Once you are aware that your emotions are aroused, you'll need to signal your desire for a time-out. This time is meant to give you a break so you can use the techniques we described in the cooling down sections of this chapter. Depending on the circumstances, you may only need a few moments, or in some instances you may need more time to allow the cooling strategies to work. So it is good to develop a few approaches to ask for some time.

If you only need a few minutes, you might ask for a coffee break or a restroom break. In this case you are not commenting on your emotions but rather taking a little time to breathe and clear your head. In more difficult situations, you may have to ask for more time. We recommend having people write up ways in which they could ask other people for such a break. This might look like, "This is an important issue and deserves our full attention. I need a little while to reflect on this so that I can do it justice." Another approach might be, "I'm upset right now and need some time to cool down so I can listen to you with the attention you deserve." When people have in mind words that they can use when they are upset, it takes the pressure off to come up with something at the exact time when their brain is least able to concentrate to do it.

Slowing down also helps when you return to the discussion of the issue. The factors that upset you in the first place are still present and could reignite emotional reactions. We particularly like the communication processes developed by Dr. Sherod Miller for use by couples and by people in organizational settings (Miller, 2009). These processes help people become more clear about what they have perceived, thought, felt about a situation, how they have acted, and what they want out of it. The particular techniques he employs with people help them discuss these elements in a deliberate manner that helps slow things down and keep emotions in balance. We talk more about how to slow things down as part of constructive engagement of conflict later in the book.

Engaging Conflict Constructively

So far, we've focused on improving the "internal" aspects of personal conflict competence. Understanding our attitudes about conflict, recognizing the value of conflict, and investigating our natural responses to conflict help us address it intellectually. Then, learning how to cool down and slow down by managing our feelings and/or pausing before reacting helps regulate our emotional responses to conflict. Next, we prepare to actively engage with our conflict partners. In this chapter, we look at ways to improve the way we interact by utilizing constructive approaches and lessening or avoiding the temptation to engage destructively.

CONSTRUCTIVE ENGAGEMENT

During our years of experience working with individuals, we've identified four specific behavioral categories for constructively engaging in conflict. There are no completely foolproof tactics, methods, or behaviors for dealing with conflict. But the consistent use of these four approaches will dramatically increase the chances that you'll not only resolve conflicts more effectively, you will discover a wealth of unforeseen ideas and possibilities in the very differences that caused the conflict to arise.

We've identified a general sequence for engaging in these four behaviors in the model presented in Figure 1.2. Most productive conflict conversations begin (1) with one party initiating or reaching out to the other. Next, there is meaningful sharing comprised of (2) perspective taking and listening for understanding, and (3) open, honest expression of emotions, thoughts, and interests. This continues, when conducted successfully, with (4) problem solving and searching for collaborative outcomes. In between, of course, every conflict is different. Even though we suggest this general sequence, conflicts certainly don't follow a script. It's important that you use the most appropriate behavior at the right time during your interactions.

These concepts and behaviors are very easy to understand. Tim's wife, Virginia, leads a team of prevention specialists in the Pinellas County, Florida, middle schools. They teach students how to use these skills to settle disputes and manage anger without resorting to violence. Duane Collette works with a student mediation program called "Peace Makers" at an elementary school in Washington state. He reports that fourth and fifth graders are able to identify and use these same constructive behaviors when they serve as peer mediators at school. With programs such as these in progress, we have high hopes for a conflict competent world!

FOUR CONSTRUCTIVE BEHAVIORAL ELEMENTS

In the following section of the chapter, we review four behavioral elements of conflict competence. We know that these behaviors and techniques work. The emphasis here is on how to use them and when to apply them. We suggest options for practicing these behaviors and exercises to prepare for using them. In essence, we address what a person says and does when using each.

Reaching Out and Initiating Contact

Someone has to initiate the discussion. *Reaching out* involves an overt attempt to resume communications with one's conflict partner once a conflict has arisen. It includes the intent to repair emotional damage caused during the conflict. It may include an apology or making amends.

Obviously each situation is unique. There are no detailed "cookie cutter" formulas for phrasing the perfect reach out. However, there are components or characteristics common to many effective instances of reaching out. When coaching or encouraging someone to reach out, it may be useful to focus on certain characteristics. Let's look at four of the most common components of reaching out: overt invitation, intent to address emotional damage, offer to take responsibility and apologizing, and expressed interest in resolving the issue.

Overt Invitation   Sometimes, keeping the effort simple and concise is the best approach. In the case of an overt invitation, one conflict partner directly asks the other to reengage in the discussion. The most critical aspect is to phrase the question so that it invites rather than insists. Some sample invitations include:

- "Would you like to talk?"
- "I would very much appreciate an opportunity to discuss this with you again."
- "Would you please join me in reviewing our recent conversation?"

Intent to Address Emotional Damage   The key aspect of this characteristic is clear communication of one's intent. As we've discussed, most harmful conflict is connected to feelings and emotions. When one conflict partner expresses a desire to address and/or repair emotional damage, chances improve dramatically that the conflict can be resolved. Some sample phrases that communicate this intent include:

- "I'd like to talk about the damage to our relationship."
- "I'm sure your feelings were hurt. Would you like to discuss that?"
- "Can we focus on the emotional harm before we start talking about our disagreement?"

Offer to Take Responsibility and Apologizing   When it's clear that one party has said or done something that hurt the other, an offer to accept responsibility goes a long way toward reengaging in a meaningful discussion. We don't advocate making an apology when it's not warranted. However, there are very few statements more powerful than an apology for restarting a conflict discussion that's gone bad. When an apology is offered, it must include an offer to take responsibility. An apology offered with an excuse is not an apology at all. For practice, which of the following do you think are good apologies and which are excuses?

1. "I'm sorry. I didn't realize that I hurt you. Please forgive me."

2. "My mouth just engages before I think sometimes. I'm very sorry."

3. "I apologize. I was having a really bad day."

4. "I've been under a lot of stress at work lately. I didn't mean to come across that way."

5. "I am sorry. What I said was mean. I know that I hurt you. I hope you can forgive me."

6. "When you yelled at me, I should have kept my cool. I apologize."

7. "Everything happened so fast. In the heat of the moment I probably said some things I shouldn't have."

8. "Did I really sound angry? I was just trying to be very clear."

9. "Sorry. It was just one of those things."

10. "I'm sorry. Let's focus on the future rather than the past, okay?"

The correct answer may surprise some of you. In our estimation, only one of the statements constitutes a "good" apology. We hate to admit it, but we've used a number of these ourselves and wondered why they didn't work! Here's a quick review with brief restatements and/or explanations:

1. "I'm sorry. I didn't realize that I hurt you. Please forgive me." (Not realizing or remembering may be true, but ultimately is an excuse.)

2. "My mouth just engages before I think sometimes. I'm very sorry." (It's my mouth's fault, not my fault.)

3. "I apologize. I was having a really bad day." (Bad days don't excuse poor behavior.)

4. "I've been under a lot of stress at work lately. I didn't mean to come across that way." (It's my job's fault, not mine.)

5. "I am sorry. What I said was mean. I know that I hurt you. I hope you can forgive me." (This is the only good one. It acknowledges the damage, accepts responsibility, and seeks forgiveness.)

6. "When you yelled at me, I should have kept my cool. I apologize." (But you were wrong, too.)

7. "Everything happened so fast. In the heat of the moment I probably said some things I shouldn't have." (Probably?)

8. "Did I really sound angry? I was just trying to be very clear." (Let me rationalize my misbehavior.)

9. "Sorry. It was just one of those things." (It's no big deal that I hurt you.)

10. "I'm sorry. Let's focus on the future rather than the past, okay?" (Get over it already.)

While apologies should never be forced or phony, it may be helpful to think about how to deliver them effectively. Small group work can be effective for practicing apologies. The key becomes, how does the person who receives the apology understand it? The apology should make it clear to the other person that you understand what you have done that has harmed them, that you are sorry for it, and that you will not do it again (Weeks, 2003).

We sometimes use a short exercise in our workshops that enables participants to practice creating and delivering apologies.

1. Each person recalls a conflict in which they felt sorry about something they said or did to the other person, whether or not they tried apologizing about it. They write down a short apology they could have made.

2. The members of the group take turns sharing their story and the apology they wrote. The other members of the group put themselves in the position of the individual's conflict partner. They then tell the person how they would have reacted to the apology as written and delivered. The key focus is the impact that the apology has on the recipients, in this case the other members of the group.

3. After telling the person about their reactions to the apology, the group members make suggestions about how it could have been better. The person issuing the apology also participates and shares his or her reactions to the suggestions.

4. At the end of the session, the large group reconvenes and participants pair up with another person in the large group who was not in their small group. The members of these dyads then take turns describing the conflict situation and sharing their revised apology. Their new partner provides them with feedback on the impact of the revised apology. This gives another viewpoint on whether the apology is having its intended effect and whether or not it comes across as genuine.

Another important part of reaching out involves taking responsibility for your own part in the conflict and making amends where appropriate. In almost every conflict, both sides bear some fault. If you genuinely want to work through the conflict and reach a resolution, being willing to admit and apologize for your own shortcomings can begin to break the ice. As Lynn Johnston, one of our favorite cartoonists says, "An apology is the superglue of life. It can repair just about anything." Apologies, of course, only work when they are genuine and largely, if not completely, unconditional. As Kimberly Johnson says, "Never ruin an apology with an excuse."

Expressed Interest in Resolving the Issue   The final common characteristic of reaching out is demonstrating a sincere interest in finding a resolution. Genuine desire to reach agreement and resolve differences can be a catalyst for beginning the earnest discussion necessary to repair hurt feelings and focus on collaborative solutions. Demonstrating a willingness to reengage and explore the differences may generate a similar spark in one's conflict partner. Again, we acknowledge that every conflict is different and there are no absolutes when it comes to the right words to use.

EXPRESSING INTEREST

Here are several simple ways to express interest in resolving the issue:

- "I'm sure we can find common ground."
- "Although we see it differently now, I can't help but believe we can find a way to make it work."
- "We both have strong reasons for our views. Let's see if we can find some connections in our perspectives."
- "I'd like to explore this further. Will you join me?"
- "Imagine if we found a way for our ideas to work together. How great would that be?"

Reaching out and initiating contact alone do not guarantee that the conflict will be resolved. Reaching out ensures very little. What it does is give the conflict a chance to be addressed. If none of the parties involved in the conflict reach out, there is zero chance that the conflict will be resolved.

We appreciate our colleagues, Dennis Dennis and Debera Libkind, sharing a great story about how reaching out can prevent tensions from escalating as well as result in some pleasant surprises.

THE CONTAGIOUS NATURE OF REACHING OUT

Delivering consulting and training services in health care sometimes means working in less than ideal situations. The difficulties may come in the form of limited time availability of the staff and managers due to the 24/7/365 schedules they keep; sometimes their staffing needs require us to work with very small groups. But on occasion, the problem is something as simple as access to space that is conducive to creating a positive learning environment.

Not having quiet, private space was the problem when we were working with the food service staff in a medium-sized medical center. This group planned, produced, and delivered 300 meals three times a day and ensured they were as nutritionally sound and tasty as possible. One discussion group consisted of vocal and engaged staff members who were at the lowest level of the organizational hierarchy. Most of these folks had little formal education, but they were bright and personally committed to the patients and the medical center. Unfortunately, the only space available for this meeting of about fifteen employees with two consultants was at one end of an employee cafeteria.

About halfway through the meeting we had nearly finished describing the CDP concepts of hot buttons, and the constructive and destructive conflict behaviors. At that point other employees began arriving for their lunch breaks. Their tables were about 20 feet away from the back of our "classroom" and there was no physical demarcation between them. As the normal volume of lunch table conversations began to increase, we attempted to adapt (our preferred CDP behavior in these situations) by speaking a little louder and leaning in toward our audience gathered closely around the lunch room table that was serving as our "classroom."

In spite of our considerable conflict competence, as visitors we were hesitant to impose our needs on others who had no knowledge of us or what we were doing in *their* space. Apparently, it was more of a concern for at least one of our participants. He quietly got up and approached the employees at the lunch tables nearby. He politely explained that we were in a class and requested that they keep their volume down. He returned to our group, and the employees on their lunch breaks began speaking in hushed tones.

Not wanting to miss an opportunity to identify the skills already existing in the group, we highlighted the effectiveness of this man's actions by noting that he:

- Was aware of his own increased tension. In other words, his hot button was pushed. It might have been "Unappreciative"; in this case the "offenders" were completely unaware of any impact they were having on us.

- Initiated action by reaching out, a particularly powerful constructive behavior.

- Expressed emotion when he explained the situation and the impact of the noise on our class.

We also discussed the very different impact that using a destructive behavior, like displaying anger or demeaning others, could have had.

Our participants were pleased when we recognized that they did in fact already have skills that they demonstrated confidently and naturally. Too often folks believe we are working with their unit because of some deficit that needs correction. Acknowledging these skills, particularly in a group that frequently is seen as less skilled and competent than others, was a powerful tool in both building their trust in us and increasing their willingness to consider the wisdom of using constructive behaviors more frequently.

But the payoff was yet to come. Several minutes later, as another group of employees entered the cafeteria, the volume again began to rise. Before anyone in our group reacted, someone from the first table leaned over to the newcomers and explained the situation to them. Hushed tones were again the only thing we heard. This is the real power of using constructive conflict behaviors—they are contagious, even in a medical center.

What makes it even more difficult is our natural resistance to reaching out. The one inexorable truth in conflict is that if no one initiates a conversation about the conflict, the conflict has no chance of being resolved. Reaching out is the only way to give resolution a chance.

By the way, did we mention that it sometimes takes several attempts at reaching out before your conflict partner accepts? Have patience, be resolute, and keep reaching out until either your partner acknowledges the effort or you determine that the work situation or relationship no longer requires effective interaction between you and this conflict partner. Please use extreme caution when deciding the situation or relationship no longer warrants your efforts. In today's world, it's not uncommon to reconnect years later with people you thought you'd never see again. We encourage giving every conflict your best shot.

REACHING OUT ACTIVITY

1. Imagine a recent conflict. This conflict should be one where your feelings were hurt or your conflict partner made you frustrated or angry.

2. As you think of this conflict situation, be sure that this is a case in which your conflict partner has behaved worse than you.

3. In fact, this situation is one where you're sure that your conflict partner owes you an apology and there's no chance that the conversation can continue until that happens.

4. Do you have this image pictured clearly in your mind?

5. This is the exact moment for you to reach out to your conflict partner!

For most people, this demonstration seems extreme. The thought process goes something like this: "If I'm owed an apology, there's no way I'm going to reach out!" This kind of mental story-telling is exactly what prevents many of us from reaching out.

Perspective Taking and Listening for Understanding

We have long declared that perspective taking is the single most powerful behavior associated with conflict competence. Nothing in recent years has changed our position about this. The ability to see the situation from your conflict partner's point of view is unsurpassed as a way toward resolution of differences.

We like to break the entire concept of perspective taking into three distinct parts. First comes listening for understanding. This serves as a prerequisite for the act of perspective taking. If one is unable or unwilling to listen with the intent to understand, true perspective taking simply isn't possible.

Second is perspective taking with a focus only on the substance or tangible issues related to the conflict. This requires the ability to effectively summarize the other party's points of view, positions, and/or ideas. In other words, one must demonstrate understanding to the satisfaction of the conflict partner.

Finally, there is perspective taking with a focus on the other party's emotions. We refer to this as demonstrating empathy or acknowledging the feelings of one's conflict partner. Again, this must be accomplished to the satisfaction of one's conflict partner.

Next we offer ideas and exercises on how to polish one's skills and abilities for perspective taking by reviewing each of these three components.

Listening for Understanding   The essence of listening for understanding is placing one's full intent and focus on hearing and comprehending what is being said. The entire purpose of the act is to grasp the words, context, and emotion of the speaker. We often contrast listening for understanding with listening to respond. Both are valuable communication skills. *Listening to respond* is listening with a focus to communicate back to the speaker. The skill of *listening for understanding* isolates the act of listening for the sole intent to comprehend what is being said.

You are not effectively listening for understanding when:

- Your mind wanders while your conflict partner speaks.
- You say, "Yeah, but . . ." (or any of scores of similar responses).
- You contemplate points or counterpoints you wish to make while "listening."

Signs that you are effectively listening for understanding include:

- You are genuinely curious about what the speaker is saying.
- You approach the speaker's communication with a sense of wonder.
- You can accurately summarize the speaker's statement.
- You ask follow-up questions for clarification.
- Your attention is fully upon the speaker's words, mannerisms, and delivery.
- You're not thinking of your position.

The purest form of listening for understanding happens with a sense of wonder and curiosity. Think of the last time you saw something truly remarkable or engaging. Perhaps you witnessed a magic trick that left you wondering, "How did they do that?" Maybe you saw a powerful play or a performance that left you moved. You wanted to know how it was possible. That same sense when applied to listening for understanding during conflict can be the key to freeing you from a position and enabling you to grasp another's perspective. Of course, during conflict a sense of wonder and curiosity may not occur naturally. You may have to work at it. Our colleague Rita Callahan offers an exercise for improving the ability to listen for understanding.

When I use this exercise for participants to practice listening and summarizing and paraphrasing, I continue to be amazed at how difficult it is for many people to allow others to communicate a different view. Many people are challenged just to listen without interrupting and offering their own point of view. Often, even when they think they have summarized another's view, they just can't resist also offering their alternate viewpoint before understanding what has been said.

The purpose of this exercise can be twofold:

1. Participants understand that there are different views, all perceptions are accepted, and no one perception or interpretation is "right."
2. Participants practice listening and summarizing and paraphrasing when others express a different point of view.

While training people to develop conflict management or communication skills, I value this exercise because it engages everyone, includes movement, builds skills, and the instructions are simple. By varying the statements, I can direct the degree of intensity, interaction, and practice to match the skills of the participants.

Agree/Disagree Only

Learning Objective:	Participants experience that there are at least two points of view for any topic, and all views are accepted.
Time:	Flexible. Recommend a minimum of 10 minutes.
Number of people:	Flexible. Ideal is a minimum of ten people. The more people the better to illustrate the point.
Space:	Almost any room where people can move into two groups.
Preparation:	A number of statements and two signs ("Agree" and "Disagree") are posted in different parts of the room. The number of statements varies with the time allotted.
	The statements can be on any topic and can be on a PowerPoint slide or written one at a time on chart paper. Only one statement is displayed at a time. If groups are in conflict, begin with more neutral statements and work up to more relevant or more controversial statements.
Instructions:	Begin by saying, "In a minute, a statement will be displayed. Read the statement and then move to the side of the room that represents your view. You must

agree or disagree. Choose a side. There's no middle of the road." After people are grouped, choose one side (the one with fewer people) to offer their views about the topic. If there are many people, limit each person to just one point that supports their view. Keep this moving fast so everyone is engaged. After hearing from one side, repeat the same process for the other side. After hearing from everyone, ask who is right. Repeat for the number of statements.

Sample statements: Cell phones and other technology contribute positively to my life.

Schools are getting better.

This community is a good place to raise children.

TV is a good baby-sitter.

Employees at [this organization] are fortunate to have a job.

Managers care about employees.

Employees want to be productive at work.

People can change.

To work together, everyone must agree.

Agree/Disagree with Summarizing or Paraphrasing

Learning Objective: Participants practice listening to understand, summarizing, and paraphrasing.

Instructions: After hearing all the points from one side of the room, ask participants from the other side of the room (before offering their point of view on the topic) to summarize (or paraphrase) the points they have heard. Usually, especially when the participants feel strongly about the topic, the participants will rush in with their points and ignore the request to summarize. As the facilitator, interrupt them and remind them of the request to summarize. Continue to make the request to summarize.

Most people will enjoy the challenge and some will recognize the difficulty in summarizing or paraphrasing before offering their own point of view. Continue to ask for different points to be summarized by the listeners before hearing their points of view. After hearing all points, ask the original speakers if they feel understood or if there are additional points not yet mentioned. (The listeners have still not yet offered their points of view.) Only after making sure the speakers have been understood, allow the participants to offer their alternate points of view.

After several statements, the group improves by listening and summarizing (or paraphrasing), before offering their points of view.

Debrief: Facilitate a discussion about the value of these skills when dealing with people in conflict. Participants will conclude that there are many points of view that are accepted, and they recognize the value of listening and summarizing (or paraphrasing) to understand before adding their points of view.

An additional opportunity is to identify the importance of tone of voice when expressing one point of view to deescalate a disagreement or conflict.

Perspective Taking: Focus on Content   Perspective taking on content focuses on the other party's points of view, positions, and/or ideas. It is for most people the easiest kind of perspective taking. One primary tool for demonstrating this is the art of summarizing. Others include checking for understanding and asking related questions. Suggestions for how to effectively demonstrate content-focused perspective taking include:

1. *Summarize frequently.* You can summarize mentally, by jotting notes, or verbally. The key is to do it with enough frequency to remember what is being said. Do your best to summarize the speaker's thoughts, feelings, positions, and ideas throughout the conversation.

2. *Check for understanding.* When you genuinely don't understand something the speaker says, ask for clarification. Be clear about what you don't understand by saying, "When you said *X*, I'm not sure I followed you. Can you explain?"

3. *Ask questions related to the content.* Questions can demonstrate your interest in the speaker's thoughts. Be cautious about making challenges through your questions. The idea is demonstrate interest, not to put the speaker on the spot. A safe way to ask is by seeking comparisons or analogies.

4. *Demonstrate your understanding.* Once the speaker has said his piece, ask if you can take a stab at reviewing what he's said. Offer a summary of the points and a grasp of the rationale. The idea is to show him that you truly understand the essence of his perspective.

We use ColourBlind, a challenging exercise originally designed for use with air traffic controllers, in some of our workshops. Participants are seated around a table, blindfolded, and are asked to solve a problem. The problem involves identifying the shapes and colors of small plastic playing pieces. Participants must describe their shapes to each other without touching or trading pieces. The facilitator will tell participants the color of a shape when asked, but nothing more.

This exercise very clearly enables participants to experience the art of perspective taking. As each participant describes the shape of a piece, the others examine their pieces trying to determine whether they are holding the same piece. Questions abound regarding the length of sides, contours of curves, degrees of angles, and other identifying characteristics. All the while, participants are "seeing" mental images of the shapes and attempting to discern if they have matches.

When individuals involved in conflict use perspective taking, they make the same kinds of attempts. They listen carefully to their partner's descriptions. They ask questions to clarify. They summarize what's been described. They display curiosity about their partner's perspectives. And they try to find ways to be clear about each other's viewpoints.

Obviously, when the viewpoints are shared accurately, both parties are clear about the similarities and differences. Even when the viewpoints are not fully clear, genuine attempts at perspective taking can help a conflict reach more satisfying conclusions. Without perspective taking, most conflicts cannot be resolved.

Perspective Taking: Focus on Emotions Perspective taking with a focus on feelings and emotions is often more powerful and more complex than content-focused perspective taking. As we've emphasized throughout our work, most destructive conflict is connected to ineffective communication regarding emotion. The ability to show empathy during conflict is the most effective way to demonstrate emotion-focused perspective taking.

When people in conflict show regard for one another's feelings, the results are validation and a sense of safety. When validated and safe, conflict partners are more likely to share and explore differing views. As the sharing and exploration expands, so does opportunity for finding common ground. Even better, such expansion invites the discovery of new ground, additional perspectives, and novel solutions.

Teaching people to demonstrate empathy requires knowledge, experience, mechanics, and genuine concern for others. Of these, no one can "teach" concern for others. We believe all of us have that capacity. It's up to each of us to tap into it and choose to display it. We do have some suggested activities for gaining knowledge and experience, as well as practicing the mechanics of empathy. Here are two recommendations.

EXERCISE 1: IDENTIFYING EMOTIONS

1. Create a deck of "emotion cards" by listing common feelings and emotions on 15 to 20 index cards. (Examples include sad, proud, joyful, frustrated, angry, exhilarated, upset, surprised, alarmed, and scared.)

2. Assemble a group of participants and distribute one card to each person.

3. Ask each to tell a story illustrating a time when they felt the emotion listed on their card *without* revealing the emotion.

4. When the story is complete, other participants try to identify the emotion.

5. Repeat this process until everyone has had a turn.

6. Debrief the exercise by asking questions such as:

   • Which emotions were most difficult to identify? Why?

   • Which emotions were most similar?

- What clues did you hear or see that helped you identify emotions?
- Which were more meaningful in identifying feelings, words, tone, nonverbals, and so on?

EXERCISE 2: I UNDERSTAND

1. Ask for a volunteer to share a story about a time when he or she was extremely happy or proud. The story will need to be several minutes long.

2. Ask for a second volunteer to listen to the story with the instruction that all he or she can say to the storyteller is, "I understand how you feel." Tell the listener to say this at least three times during the story.

3. Ask all others (if it's a group) to observe and comment afterward.

4. Debrief the exercise by asking questions such as:
   - (To the storyteller) How did you feel about the listener's level of empathy?
   - (To the listener) How did you affect the storyteller?
   - (To observers) Did you observe empathy?

5. Discuss alternatives to "I understand how you feel" that would effectively demonstrate empathy.

Activities such as these help build awareness and skills for demonstrating empathy. The surest way to successfully demonstrate empathy is by labeling the feeling you've observed. When you observe or discern an emotion, label it! For instance, "You must be very frustrated at the way I've responded." Even if the label is slightly off, there's still credit given for recognizing that a feeling is present. The response might be, "I'm not frustrated, but I was surprised."

Unfortunately, most people attempt to demonstrate empathy by saying something like, "I really understand how you feel." The result of this statement, regardless of the intent, is often the opposite of understanding or acknowledgment. "What do you mean you really know how I feel? You're not in my shoes!"

In practice we attempt to bring these three concepts (listening for understanding, content-focused perspective taking, and emotion-focused perspective taking) together by using a tool dubbed "the perspective-taking worksheet." The worksheet asks a person in conflict to review the conflict situation. First, the person is asked to briefly summarize the issue and the people in it. Next, she responds to series of questions (including content and emotions) from her conflict partner's perspective. Finally, she must reconsider her approach and steps for addressing the conflict anew.

Debra Dupree, a conflict management consultant in San Diego, offers advice and activities she uses in her practice.

READING BETWEEN THE LINES

Whether it's in dialogue or full-blown conflict, people often listen for content—what's being said, rather than what's being conveyed. Listening for content frequently fuels the fire further as we react to what we hear rather than what the speaker intended. Oftentimes, we are busy processing in our minds what we're going to say before the other person has even finished speaking. This approach seldom helps us resolve differences and instead may escalate the situation, leading to the "retaliatory cycle" as coined by Dr. Dan Dana in *Managing Differences* (2005, p. 134). Instead, successful conflict conversations are marked by very different sets of dynamics.

In mediation and related conflict engagement processes, listening for meaning is much deeper and requires that we listen without doing anything else. And, when appropriate, we probe for underlying interests—what's important to people about certain issues, challenges, or obstacles. When we key into what's important to people, the visible signs of making a connection are incredible. Passion and clarity emerge and true understanding evolves. The *aha!* magical moments of mediation appear and work their transformation . . . in any conversation!

But how do you teach that to clients who are in the midst of a personal or professional conflict? And, in a relatively short but meaningful period of time, so that they can truly benefit from a change in strategies and techniques?

In my teaching of mediation, I have used a number of techniques from noted scholars that have proven most effective. Drawing upon the works of Dr. Dan Dana, should be Michelle LeBaron, James Champion, and Dr. Nancy Love, my practice today incorporates a series of simple strategies that serve to bring out what's truly important to people. As the commander of a major naval station in Southern California recently voiced, "Why didn't they teach us this in elementary school? Years of professional development and leadership experience would have been much better served!"

So here are a few tips and strategies, building upon the work of many notables, that serve to sharpen one's listening and speaking skills in just a few short activities.

Activity 1: Getting to Know You: An Exercise in Deep Listening

Introductions of participants in any group process are critically important. Going beyond the usual name, position, years of service, here's an opportunity to engage participants in the first step of deep listening. To focus participants on underlying interests, engage them in "listening for the sounds of the BEACH": Beliefs, Expectations, Assumptions/Attitude, Concerns, and Hope (Dr. Nancy Love, www.pulseinstitute.com).

Ask participants to tell where they're from, one unique thing about him- or herself, and one memorable life experience. While each person is speaking, the other participants simply listen. When each person is finished speaking, the participants take 1–2 minutes to jot down brief highlights of what they heard. The facilitator asks for three or four participants to share with the speaker what they heard. The facilitator is the last to share what he or she heard, modeling listening for underlying interests. As the sharing process continues, the other participants continue to get sharper and more articulate in their listening by going beyond the facts presented and highlighting the meaning conveyed. Participants inevitably feel much more connected and learn much more about their fellow participants.

Activity 2: Hot Buttons

Another quick and effective way to help people become aware of the different approaches to conflict is to engage them in the Conflict Dynamics Profile Hot Buttons exercise found at: http://www .conflictdynamics.org/cdp/hotbuttons/index.php. Having participants engage in this before a group activity allows for interesting discussion and awareness of the things that trigger people into conflict while building commonality and shared purpose. Strategies for cooling down and slowing down help people connect and develop communication strategies jointly. Engaging in a facilitated dialogue helps transform understanding from intent to impact.

Activity 3: The Animal Exercise: The Power of Open-Ended Questions

This is a quick little exercise that opens the eyes and minds of people to the power of asking open-ended questions. As the facilitator, you select an animal in your mind. The task presented to the participants is that they must guess the name of the animal by asking only closed (Yes or No) questions. The facilitator keeps track of how many questions are asked before someone guesses the animal (if they reach twenty-five questions, call a stop to this part of the exercise). Announce to the participants how many questions it took to guess (or not) the right answer. Now repeat the process of identifying an animal; however, this time, participants may ask *only* open-ended questions, generally starting with *What* or *How.* If they ask a "closed-ended question," simply refuse to answer the question. Frequently, participants will start with "What does the animal look like?" While this is great, and as a facilitator one should reinforce this response positively, there is a more basic open-ended question that captures it all: "What is the animal?" Participants marvel at how quickly they can get where they want to go by simply framing the questions more appropriately. This is a great opportunity to demonstrate how open-ended questions are used effectively by starting broadly and then probing further based on the response to the first question and subsequent questions.

Activity 4: Three Minutes of Passion
(Adapted from Michelle LeBaron's *Cultural Issues in Conflict Management,* 2003)

This exercise draws upon *emotional intelligence*, which is central to successful relationships. It allows one to refocus, recharge, and reinvigorate. It enhances listening while also building connections. Pair up participants and select one to be A and one to be B. Starting with A, the first speaker begins by filling in the sentence "I am passionate about . . ." Speaker A continues to repeat that phrase and fill in the blank for 3 minutes (facilitator calls time). Listener B listens . . . for changes in intensity, themes, and patterns. If Speaker A gets stuck, Listener B asks, "What else are you passionate about?" When the facilitator calls time, the Speaker and Listener sit in silent reflection for 1–2 minutes to process what was said and what was heard. A and B then reverse roles and repeat the exercise.

When debriefing, first ask the speakers for what they noticed about what they experienced and what they said. Then ask the listeners for what themes emerged, what shifts in content developed, and what they observed about the speaker's verbal and nonverbal behavior. This is an excellent exercise to help people listen beyond the content to the meaning conveyed both verbally and nonverbally.

Each of these activities takes just minutes, yet the learning experienced is powerful and contributes to enhanced understanding of how people listen and how they engage in communication and conflict!

Perspective taking and listening for understanding are simply the most critical behaviors for handling conflict competently. When those in conflict practice these behaviors, outcomes are better than ever imagined.

Expressing Emotions, Thoughts, and Interests

This is consistently where we get the greatest degree of resistance when coaching, facilitating, or presenting on conflict competence. Participants' initial reaction to this set of behaviors is that they appear soft. Many people tell us they were brought up to meet force with force, trade an eye for an eye, and certainly never let the other side see you sweat. To do so would be a sign of weakness. On the contrary, we assert that the effective expression of emotions, thoughts, and interests is a sign of strength, forthrightness, and honesty. To do otherwise is tantamount to concealing the truth and fosters mistrust. And fostering mistrust is exactly the opposite of what is necessary for resolving conflict. When participants in conflict are skilled at expressing their emotions, thoughts, and interests effectively, the ensuing discussion of conflicting ideas, issues, and positions can flow productively.

The problem is, paradoxically, many of us conceal our true feelings or thoughts from our conflict partners at the exact moment when revealing them would be most meaningful. In fact, not only do we conceal the thoughts and feelings, we deny them!

Last fall we worked with the executive team of an accounting firm. We spent several days in teambuilding exercises and discussions leading to the formation of a set of team agreements. Team members were open about the fact that they had some ongoing relationship issues and expressed confidence that some of those issues could be addressed through the workshop.

During the ColourBlind exercise, several participants became frustrated with one of their teammates. Although the team was making progress, one member thought she could accelerate the problem solving by changing the process. A debate about the pros and cons of the new process ensued with the group prevailing over the dissenting member. The exercise continued and the team successfully solved the problem. During the debriefing discussion, we asked each member to identify the moment of most frustration. As expected, several described the debate over changing the process as the single most frustrating part of the activity. The person who suggested the change acknowledged how she had affected the group and graciously accepted responsibility for the frustration. Upon apologizing, she also asked, "Is everyone okay with me now?" Everyone on the team affirmed they were okay. "Don't be silly. It was just a game." "Heavens yes, I'm fine." "Of course we're okay. It wasn't a big deal." It seemed fine to us, too . . . for about 30 seconds.

During the break, we overheard several members chatting in the hallway. The gist of their conversation bordered on outrage at the person who made the suggestion to change the process. "Can you believe how she tried to take over the entire game?" exclaimed one. "Isn't that what she always does?" said another. "Do you think she'll ever learn?" asked a third.

Even in the face of direct inquiries, many people will withhold or deny true feelings or thoughts that could initiate a deeper conversation and lead to resolution. We believe that this phenomenon is based on the combination of a desire not to put others "on the spot" and to avoid the potential of becoming vulnerable themselves. We also believe that most people don't admit their thoughts or feelings because they believe that their conflict partners "already know how I feel."

In the case just described, if any one of the team members had responded to the original question, "Is everyone okay with me now?" honestly, there could have been a vastly different outcome. Imagine a response such as, "Thanks for asking. I'm not sure I'm completely okay because this isn't the first time I've experienced this." This open, honest response may have led to significant discussion and deeper understanding of the intent and impact of each participant. During such discussions, a framework for future interactions is laid that can lead to more favorable relationships and outcomes. We use an exercise to illustrate the significance and impact of expressing thoughts, feelings, and interests. Here's how it works:

1. Ask participants to think of recent conflict they've experienced.
2. The conflict should be one that had some degree of intensity. They felt some level of negative emotion.
3. Next, ask them to consider a specific time during that conflict when they were feeling that negative emotion.
4. Ask them to imagine looking at themselves in a mirror at that moment.
5. Now, ask them whether or not their conflict partner knew what they were feeling or thinking at that very moment.
6. If they answer yes, ask them how they know that their conflict partner knew. If the answer is anything other than "I described my thought or feeling to them," engage them in a playful discussion about mind reading.
7. The learning point of this exercise is that we often assume that others know what we're thinking or feeling. Unless we disclose or reveal our thoughts or feelings, we can't be sure that our thoughts and feelings are being interpreted accurately.

Perhaps the most severe consequence of hiding thoughts and feelings is the appearance of being dishonest to one's conflict partner. In the previous example, when team members made statements such as, "Don't be silly. It was just a game," they were in fact not being truthful. Concealing the truth about thoughts and feelings, regardless of one's intent, can lead to an erosion of trust. When trust is damaged, the ability to overcome conflict is significantly damaged. On the other hand, when conflict partners share thoughts and feelings honestly, especially when doing so results in heightened vulnerability, trust is significantly enhanced. And nothing supports conflict competence more than working from a base of trust.

Searching for Collaborative Outcomes

The biggest misstep in searching for collaborative outcomes is arriving at this point too quickly. While we advocate treating most conflicts as problems to be solved, rushing to solutions often results in agreements that only superficially address the issue or satisfy only one partner. That's why in our model, this set of behaviors occurs most frequently in the latter stages of conflict discussions.

The three previous components of constructive engagement are necessary steps that prepare conflict partners for true collaborative problem solving. In addition, these three components are frequently interwoven during the search for collaborative solutions. Based on our work with the Conflict Dynamics Profile, we believe three interrelated behavioral components of searching for collaborative outcomes include adapting, reflective thinking, and creating solutions.

Adapting   *Adapting* refers to an optimistic outlook, flexibility, and a willingness to consider all the possibilities. People who are willing to consider many alternatives give themselves and their conflict partners more opportunities for satisfactory outcomes. Adaptability also includes acknowledgment that conflict is natural and inevitable. Conflict is not an unfair consequence that just happens. It is instead an opportunity to see an issue from different perspectives. Even in the most volatile circumstances, effectively adapting means holding out hope that resolution is possible.

Adaptability is often associated with personal styles or psychological preferences. We are avid proponents of assessment tools such as the Myers Briggs Type Indicator (MBTI), Kirton Adaptive-Innovative Survey (KAI), the California Psychological Inventory (CPI), and the Change Style Indicator (CSI). These assessments provide clear evidence of different styles and preferences while illustrating the vast diversity of approaches to creativity, problem solving, and pattern recognition. Such knowledge is powerful when acknowledging differences. This awareness makes it easier to accept that a variety of ideas and possibilities exist for resolving conflict. But awareness alone doesn't address one's ability. That's why we use exercises and activities to enhance participants' willingness to search for multiple solutions and consider a variety of possibilities.

MULTIPLE USES EXERCISE

This exercise is adapted from many classic brainstorming activities. It is fun, engaging, and most important illustrates the ability of individuals to create multiple ideas and solutions for consideration. It generally takes 20–25 minutes to complete. It can be used with two individuals or with an entire team.

1. Assemble several common household or office items. Some of our favorites include paper clips, binder clips, clothes pins, and pillow cases.

2. Assign each person or small group one item.

3. Instruct them to come up with two lists for each item. The first list includes all the "normal uses" for the item. The second list includes all the "creative uses" for that item. Provide a time limit for creating the lists (10 minutes is usually plenty).

4. Call the participants together and ask them to present their lists and demonstrate a variety of their suggestions.

5. Once each list is presented, seek additional suggestions from the other participants.

6. When all lists have been presented, conduct a debrief discussion. Some sample questions for this discussion include:

   • What is your reaction to the sheer volume of ideas?

   • Which ideas and suggestions were your favorites? Why?

   • How many of the ideas and suggestions were wrong or unacceptable? What do you make of this?

   • How can you apply a similar approach for considering possibilities for resolving conflict?

When the parties involved in a conflict bring a sense of optimism and adaptability to the discussion, the potential for collaboration rises substantially. Finding ways to encourage optimism and adaptability, therefore, becomes a very useful strategy for coaching conflict partners and facilitating sessions for teams experiencing conflict. Exercises and activities that demonstrate these concepts are valuable tools for developing conflict competence.

Adapting includes:

- An optimistic mind-set that views conflict as an inevitable part of the workplace (and life in general)
- A willingness to entertain a wide variety of alternatives for resolution
- An awareness of changes or opportunities that signal the potential for engaging in problem solving and conflict resolution

Reflective Thinking   Reacting in the moment is an integral part of our human condition. The stimulus-response process occurs as a function of our "wiring." As we've discussed in previous chapters, when exposed to certain stimuli such as pain or fear, we have an almost instantaneous reaction. *Reflective thinking* is a practice that enables us to slow down our immediate reactions, consider possible alternatives, and reengage later in more fruitful discussions for resolution.

In Chapter Three, we discussed a variety of approaches and techniques for managing our emotions. These included:

- Understanding and assessing our personal hot buttons
- Practicing cognitive reappraisal
- Using processes for establishing improved mindfulness
- Centering and controlled breathing
- Analyzing core concerns
- Delaying our responses

The application of these approaches and techniques can enhance our ability for reflective thinking, as they buy us time for separating the stimulus from the response. (Refer back to Chapter Three for suggestions on how to practice these techniques.)

Reflective thinking is uniquely related to the search for collaborative solutions in that it is an individual ability. The act of reflective thinking is not a collaborative or group activity. It happens only within the confines of our personal thoughts and feelings. It happens in our own heads. But without the ability to do reflective thinking, participating effectively in finding collaborative solutions may be impossible.

Reflective thinking is characterized by:

- Noticing one's own reactions and the reactions of others during conflict; then taking the time to consider and reflect on those reactions

- Being aware of the immediate and ongoing impact of the conflict on oneself and all other parties involved

- Thinking through alternatives for responding to the conflict

Heather Brown, who teaches conflict management in the Washington, D.C., area, shared the following story with us. We believe it demonstrates the power of reflection for choosing appropriate responses even in the most difficult circumstances.

REFLECTING WITHOUT RUMINATING

An attractive, professionally dressed woman, whom I will call Jane, came up to me after a training program and asked if I had a minute to talk to her about a problem she was experiencing concerning what I had taught on the concept of reflection. I agreed to talk with her, and we found a quiet corner in the training room to chat as the rest of the class networked and began leaving for the day. She explained to me that she had started her career as a secretary after a long period of working as a stay-at-home mom and then a divorce that forced her back into the business world for economic reasons.

She told me that her first position upon returning to the business world was a nightmare. Her job was to provide clerical and administrative support to several high-level professionals, and they were abusive to her. She indicated that this was particularly difficult for her because she had left an abusive marriage for a new start, only to land in a workplace where she was again being abused. Her supervisors would yell at her when she made an error. They would berate her in front of others at meetings, and they would call her names in front of customers. One of her supervisors even wrinkled some of her work that they were not happy with and threw it at her! She had tried for a long while to get out of that position unsuccessfully when she found out that they were giving her unfairly poor references. She felt trapped!

Obviously, these were unstable individuals in a dysfunctional work environment! I have found in my years of consulting that "birds of a feather do flock together," and often when one dysfunctional professional is doing the hiring, they hire others who have the same dysfunctional values, communication style, and interpersonal flaws as they do themselves. This helps them to feel better about themselves because they can say, "Well at least I am not as bad as . . ."

Jane went on to explain how she returned to school at night for her BA degree. This was done clandestinely because she feared her bosses would not be supportive and might even try to derail her goal. She began applying for entry-level management jobs after completing her degree, and after sending out dozens of applications she landed her first supervisory position. She vowed that she would never treat others like she was treated—and she didn't. She was such a strong, caring, and competent leader that she excelled quickly in her new organization and moved into midlevel management. At the time we talked she had applied for her first senior-level position. Thinking that Jane was done with her message of bootstrap success, I said, "Thank you for sharing that inspiring story with me; it is so nice to hear about individuals who are able to overcome difficult odds and forge a new life and career for themselves." She thanked me for my kind words but informed me that her story was not yet complete.

As she began to talk, I noticed that her friendly, girl-next-door smile began to fade and her physical posture began to stiffen. The tone of her voice changed to a harsh rusty sound that I found disturbing. Her face turned red, and her eyes were fiery with anger. By this time the training room had cleared out, and I was beginning to get uncomfortable and wondered if I had made a mistake by agreeing to talk privately with Jane.

With anger and venom in her voice, she told me that not a day went by when she did not reflect about getting revenge on her early, abusive supervisors. She said that she often reflected about trying to hurt them in passive-aggressive ways like deliberately misfiling their papers or putting something distasteful in their coffee. She admitted that for a while she even had daydreamed about hurting them by putting a laxative in their beverage or using some other form of nonlethal food poisoning. Then she would think about ways she might berate them in front of customers or make them look bad. However, she proudly told me with the same dark countenance in her facial expression, body language, and tone that through the art of reflection, she had decided not to harm them but vowed to find a constructive way to get back at them. She said that after reflecting on this for some time, she had decided to find out where each of them was living or working today and bring her check stub and job description and tell them that she had become successful in spite of what they had done to her and how they had tried to hold her back. She said, "That is what I wanted to ask you about; don't you think it is a good idea for me to go show them that they were not able to hold me back; I am successful in spite of what they did to me!"

"How long ago did all of this occur?" I asked while trying to think of a tactful way of telling her that her plan was one of the most ridiculous plans for revenge I had ever heard.

"I worked there ten years ago," she said.

"Ten years ago?!" I replied in dismay.

I was shocked that this woman had spent ten years trying to "get revenge" on her former abusive supervisors. What a waste of energy, time, and brain power.

After I overcame my shock, I began explaining that the scenario she described to me was not reflection, it was rumination. *Reflecting* is the skill of taking the time to stop and think about what happened so that you can mine lessons, process your emotions, and formulate a positive strategy to move past the issues you are experiencing. Many people never take the time to stop and think about the conflict issues they are encountering; they just react. Reactive responses without reflection are almost always destructive and escalate issues. We are operating out of emotion over logic, and our emotions have a tendency to initiate unproductive responses to conflict if we don't take time to reflect. Reflection is a positive, constructive process that allows you to produce quality responses and solutions to issues that arise.

Rumination is defined in Merriam-Webster's dictionary as going over an event repeatedly in one's mind. It comes from the Latin word *ruminari,* which means to chew one's cud. A cud consists of regurgitated, partially digested food. When you ruminate on a conflict or issue, you never really settle it; you just keep bringing it back up and going over it. This is not constructive, and it can lead to very unhealthy mental states.

Reflection is careful, serious, considered thought. Reflection also has a component of enlightenment to it. The verb *reflect* means "to throw back light." When we reflect, we think about something in a manner that allows new ideas and solutions to illuminate. When we ruminate on something, we just keep chewing on it, digesting it, and bringing it back up again, because we cannot find closure. The issue remains unsettled in our mind, and it usually festers and infects other thoughts. Ruminating can result in destructive responses like Jane's ideas of retaliation. In contrast, reflection usually results in positive ideas and emotional stability.

I explained to Jane that at this time, it no longer matters what her former supervisors think of her. She has moved beyond them and met success. Each time she brings them up again in her mind she is allowing them to diminish her success. I told her that she should be proud of what she accomplished and that should be enough. I further explained that her thoughts, reflections, and ideas should be geared toward her future goals, not her past tragedies. I told her that it was time for her to move beyond them and spend her time reflecting on more productive things. Essentially, it was time for her to let go and give closure to that phase in her life. Her former supervisors could hurt her now only if she let them by continuing to mull over what happened ten years ago. That kind of negative thinking spills over into our current situations, often sparking new conflicts.

Reflection can happen in all three phases of conflict—before, during, and after. *Before* a full-fledged conflict emerges can be one of the most productive times for an individual to reflect. Often a conflict can be diffused early if the right strategy is contemplated and executed. Reflection *during* conflict is difficult. Usually in the midst of conflict, we are too busy defending and protecting ourselves to recognize the need to stop and reflect. Our strong emotions during conflict tend to block constructive reflection. Additionally, reflection takes time, so it is very difficult to reflect in the midst of a conflict. However, reflection can be a very powerful conflict resolution tool used in the midst of conflict because it forces you to stop and think. Reflection can be very constructive *after* conflict because it focuses on what went wrong and what can be done about it in the future.

REFLECTION QUESTIONS

Here are some questions to help facilitate the constructive process of reflection before, during, and after conflict.

Before an impending conflict:

1. Why do you think a conflict is imminent?
2. Is there something that can be done now to defuse the conflict?
3. Did you initiate or contribute to the conflict?
4. What can be done differently, in the future, to avoid this situation?
5. What is the best solution for both parties?

During a conflict:

1. Do you have to respond now or can this wait until you have time to reflect on the issues and potential solutions?
2. Are emotions in control enough to continue conversing or do you all need some "cooling off time"?
3. Are your tone, body language, words, or stance contributing to the conflict?
4. Is it likely that a constructive solution can be negotiated now?
5. Is there any way for you to defuse the conflict?
6. Can you choose not to respond at all and tell the other party you need time to think about it before you respond?

After a conflict:

1. What was the primary issue in this conflict and what alternative solutions existed?

2. How well did you communicate during the conflict, and is there anything you wish you had done differently?

3. Is there any follow-up you would like to initiate to reduce the impact of something you wish you hadn't said?

4. Is there any follow up action you would like to initiate to get a better understanding of the other person's position?

5. What do you wish you had done differently before or during the conflict?

6. What can you do now to try to resolve the conflict and minimize any further damage?

Before, during, and after a conflict, try to focus your thoughts on these questions to force your thinking into a positive, reflective form of thinking rather than a negative ruminating thought process. Constructive, positive, reflective thinking is the foundation for effective conflict resolution skills.

Creating Solutions Adapting and reflective thinking are the individual components of searching for collaborative solutions. *Creating solutions* is the more interactive portion of this critical behavioral aspect of conflict competence. Descriptively, this is the problem-solving aspect of conflict management and resolution.

Organizations embrace and reward those of us who are adept at spotting problems and finding solutions to them. This is especially true when we do so quickly and repeatedly. This valuable ability, often honed over time, can also work against finding the most effective, agreeable, satisfying solutions to conflict. Creating solutions within conflict not only means finding acceptable resolution, it requires the identification and exploration of multiple possibilities that enable the selection of the best solution.

There are many ways to create solutions. Brainstorming techniques have been used for decades, even centuries. Accessing and engaging others is a preferred technique for many. Careful individual contemplation and consideration of ideas is preferred by others. Reflecting on historical or past solutions to similar challenges is a valuable approach. Encouraging novel and innovative ideas can lead to groundbreaking solutions. The common denominator among all these approaches, and what makes creating solutions so critical, is *not stopping* after discovering a viable solution.

Finding one solution to a problem or a conflict is just doing your job. Anyone worth his or her salt should be able to find a single solution. Seeking multiple possibilities is the key to conflict competence. Once multiple solutions are imagined, each possibility can be considered. The more potential solutions, the more likely an effective agreement can be found.

The Multiple Uses Exercise described earlier is a good example of an activity to use to create numerous possible solutions. There are many other problem-solving exercises that do the same. When using exercises and activities for practicing creating solutions, remember to keep the focus on coming up with multiple solutions. It's easy to get side-tracked when participants discover unique or interesting approaches to the problem.

One of our favorite exercises for practicing creating solutions is one originally designed for exploring process improvement. With a few minor adaptations, we've found it to be especially useful for encouraging the creation of multiple solutions in a collaborative way. In other words, it's appropriate for illustrating the entire concept of searching for collaborative solutions. It's got a memorable title: Four-Letter Words.

FOUR-LETTER WORDS EXERCISE

This activity works best with 6–8 people. It's possible to adapt it for use with as few as two, but we prefer it for group or team situations. It requires a complete set of Scrabble game tiles for each small group participating. If Scrabble game tiles aren't available, make a set of materials using index cards cut into small pieces and labeled with letters of the alphabet in approximate concert with Scrabble guidelines. (*Note:* The scoring numbers on the Scrabble tiles are not important for this exercise. If making your own materials, you need not include these numbers.)

1. Divide participants equally into several teams, with no more than four members on each team.

2. Announce that the goal of the exercise is to form as many four-letter words as possible in a 60-second time period.

3. Teams will have a planning period (we recommend 4–6 minutes) prior to implementation, during which they can strategize

4. During the planning period, complete words cannot be formed and set aside.

5. Before implementation, the tiles must be "shuffled" so partially preformed words are not available. All tiles can remain upright, though.

6. Upon implementation, each word formed is counted by a recorder appointed by each team. In order to qualify as a four-letter word, the word must be completely formed and visible to the recorder, be spelled correctly, and be used only once per round.

7. At the end of 60 seconds, each team reveals how many words they formed.

8. Multiple rounds can be used. Artificial targets can be set by the facilitator to provide challenge and encourage more creativity. Natural competition among the teams will usually suffice.

9. A thorough debriefing discussion will provide insight into the value of creating multiple possibilities and the search for collaborative solutions. We suggest using questions such as:

   • What was your first reaction to the objective?

   • What enabled you to produce more words than you originally thought possible?

   • How did you manage divergent ideas for creating the words?

   • Describe the way you worked to achieve the best solution.

   • How did you decide among all the ideas for producing the most words?

- What connections can you make for creating solutions for resolving conflicts?

When adapting this exercise for use with just two people, we recommend the use of three rounds. Planning in the first two rounds is done silently, with no interaction between the two participants. The first round is conducted with one person creating the words and the other recording the total number. Round two is conducted the same way, with the roles reversed. Planning and word creation is done collaboratively for round three, with the facilitator serving as the recorder.

Creating solutions comes naturally for many of us. Human beings are problem solvers at heart. As a component of searching for collaborative solutions, creating solutions focuses on the interaction among conflict participants for identifying possibilities. Key characteristics of creating solutions include:

- Identifying multiple potential solutions and ideas; never stopping after identifying only one possible solution
- Analyzing and discussing the viability of all the possible solutions
- Agreeing on which solutions to try

Finding agreeable solutions to any problem can be a challenge. When the problem is a conflict, the challenge often intensifies. In addition, because so many of us tend toward avoidance, we often rush to use the first possible solution that comes to mind. The key for successfully searching for collaborative solutions lies in having patience for creating multiple potential solutions. Once multiple ideas are generated, careful reflection and consideration can lead to agreements that are satisfying and successful.

DESTRUCTIVE BEHAVIORS TO AVOID AND CONTROL

The single biggest problem with conflict lies in our all-too-often terrible responses to it. The actual conflict, the differences of view or opinion, can serve us well if only we choose our responses better.

In Chapter Two we presented and described eight categories of destructive conflict behaviors, originally developed by our good friends Sal Capobianco, Mark Davis, and Linda Kraus (1999), in association with the Conflict Dynamics Profile. These include:

1. Winning at all costs
2. Displaying anger
3. Demeaning others
4. Retaliating
5. Avoiding
6. Yielding
7. Hiding emotions
8. Self-criticizing

Each of these destructive behaviors can be prevented or controlled simply by learning and applying constructive responses as we've discussed in the first half of the chapter. However, we can learn much by understanding our mistakes and considering how to limit similar mistakes in the future. In this spirit, we briefly address each of the destructive behaviors and make suggestions for improving our choices.

Winning at All Costs

Who doesn't like to win? In today's highly competitive world, success is measured by winning. The world celebrates winners. Whenever there are winners there must also be losers. Who likes to lose? Therein lies the issue. In the scope of interpersonal, team, and organizational conflict, when one party is perceived as consistently attempting to win *at all costs,* rest assured the conflict will worsen.

Winning at all costs encompasses a wide variety of behaviors. Some are much more overt than others. Some behaviors are valuable when used in other contexts or circumstances. What makes this category of behavior so destructive is the impact it has on one's conflict partners. Presented next is a list of ten behaviors and descriptions to consider. With as much honesty and objectivity as possible, check those that are characteristic of you in conflict. The more you check, and the more frequently you exhibit these behaviors, the more likely it is that others perceive you as attempting to win at all costs.

"Winning at All Costs" Checklist

- ❏ Stand my ground steadfastly
- ❏ Show tenacity for my ideas and suggestions
- ❏ Defend my actions
- ❏ Make excuses for my poor behavior
- ❏ Create rationale for ideas or behavior even when I know better
- ❏ Rationalize my behavior based on good results
- ❏ Blame or accuse others (especially my conflict partner)
- ❏ Argue for the sake of arguing
- ❏ Never admit mistakes or shortcomings
- ❏ Deny responsibility

Overcoming the tendency to win at all costs is no easy task. The most frequent advice we give is to replace this behavior with more constructive behaviors. Many of us can improve by simply adhering to the "cool down, slow down, engage" principles we've discussed throughout this book. Here are a few specific suggestions for exerting more self-control in this area.

Conflict competence involves finding outcomes that are mutually satisfying. Although this isn't always possible, approaches that are perceived as winning at all costs insure outcomes that satisfy only one party. This also sets the stage for more destructive conflict between the parties in the future.

CONTROLLING THE URGE TO WIN AT ALL COSTS

1. In a heated discussion, be very careful when asked to "defend" your actions. For instance, when your conflict partner says, "How could you say such a thing?" or "Why would you do that?" resist the temptation to provide any rationale immediately. If you do, it will very likely sound like excuse making or blaming someone else. Instead, first respond to the emotion behind the question. Lead with something like, "That must have really bothered you." You'll come across as much less defensive.

2. Being confident in your views or positions is great. During a conflict, make sure you acknowledge the other parties' views and positions. Even though you disagree, you'll look less demanding when you can summarize the other side's views.

3. When you feel attacked in a conflict, "fighting fire with fire" is not the only tactic available. Consider responding by calling for a brief time-out or simply pausing for several moments. As in our first tip, you might also consider responding to the feeling or emotion of the speaker with empathy. For instance, "You must be very upset . . ."

Displaying Anger

Classic "fight" behavior is most often expressed through fear and anger. It manifests as raising one's voice, yelling, use of profanity, intimidation, and threatening gestures, posture, and/or facial expressions. It's probably the easiest of the destructive behaviors to describe and understand. When demonstrated by one party, the response of the other party can range from withdrawal to equal or more vehement displays of anger. The result is always a conflict unresolved.

The biggest problem with displaying anger is not just the immediate damage it causes, but the often extraordinarily long-lasting impact on the relationship. The damage can last for years. Another more insidious issue with displaying anger is that the offender may genuinely not realize his or her actions have been perceived as angry. Finally, individuals, organizations, and cultures have varying degrees of tolerance for anger that may not be fully understood or appreciated, therefore exacerbating the situation.

We often hear people attempt to explain this type of behavior away. "Oh, he's just hot tempered," or "She's just having a bad day," or "I'm not angry, I'm just fired up. Everybody knows how passionate I am." All of these explanations may be true. But the truth doesn't matter in the eye of the beholder. The damage is done, and it takes more than a brief explanation for recovery. In a perfect world, prevention is the best course of action. Unfortunately, we don't live in a perfect world. Here are a few tips for preventing and recovering from displays of anger.

The bottom line here is to take notice whenever anyone suggests that you looked or acted angry. It does no good to rationalize this feedback away. Even though your intent may have been different, if the impact was perceived as displaying anger, the conflict will most certainly be negatively affected.

TIPS FOR MANAGING YOUR ANGER

Prevention

1. When you feel your emotions rising during a conflict, acknowledge them immediately. In your mind, say, "I'm feeling upset." This simple act causes you to pause momentarily and takes some of the steam out of the growing and potentially harmful emotion.

2. When you feel your emotions rising, say so out loud to your conflict partner. Describing the feeling almost always prevents acting out the feeling. Saying, "I'm starting to feel angry," provides your conflict partner an opportunity to empathize. In addition, as we've said before, it's a great display of trust to admit an emotion to the person with whom you're in conflict.

3. If you think you may look or sound angry, say so immediately. Catching it early is almost as good as preventing it entirely. And even if your partner says she didn't perceive you as angry, you show good will by bringing it up.

Recovering

1. There's nothing like a genuine apology. Admit it. Take responsibility for your actions. Assure that you'll behave differently in the future.

2. Apply some perspective taking and empathy. Try to see how you sounded from the other's point of view. When you show empathy to someone you've offended, you demonstrate an understanding of how they feel or were affected.

3. Thank your conflict partner for bringing it to your attention and for giving you a chance to show that you can handle the conflict without anger.

Jan McKenzie, head of training for a major corporation in Atlanta, offers the following example about dealing with anger when it occurs. She suggests that often the greatest learning opportunities occur in the heat of the moment.

IN THE HEAT OF THE MOMENT

Your best coaching opportunity when helping someone to develop conflict competence is in the heat of the moment, when the person you are coaching is faced with an uncomfortable situation, no apparent solution, and a real need to deal with his or her problem. Let me explain.

It was Tuesday night and I was prepared. I had an agenda, I had interactive exercises, and I was pretty sure where the night would lead. There should be no surprises. The content was simple and the topic was relevant. The women began to file in, taking their usual places at the table and chatting easily with each other. This group was special—ten women recovering from marital abuse and homelessness with the help of a dedicated staff and comprehensive life recovery program. My role as a volunteer was simply to show up every other Tuesday night and share some guidelines for positive parenting. Just as we were getting ready to begin, the final two participants arrived.

This didn't appear to be the good news it should have been. Something had happened to upset both women, and it showed. The first one's face was red and her fists were clenched as she noisily took her seat. The other woman was shaking her head back and forth and muttering, her eyes narrowed into small angry slits on an otherwise open face. The other women were turning toward the two new arrivals, their own faces beginning to mirror the anger they saw in their teammates. This was a group familiar with and quick to anger.

As the first woman began to tell us what had happened, she angrily tossed a pen and hit another participant on the arm with it. Both women were surprised at the result, and the woman who had been hit stood up and walked out of the room. The woman who had thrown the pen also got up and left. We had one angry woman remaining, and I asked her what had happened. To make a long story short, she had been given a "demerit" for breaking a program rule and felt it was unfair. It occurred to me that we had a moment of opportunity unveiling right in front of our eyes. In that instant the agenda changed and I waded into unfamiliar territory, armed with a skill set that I hoped would make a difference.

"Tonight we're going to talk about the fact that somewhere in between stimulus and response there is a moment when we can choose our response," I said.

It was a bold statement to a group that had been victimized in many ways, but it is a tried and true one. We had been focused on it at work lately as well and, with the help of Stephen M. Covey's training team, we had been learning that we always had a choice, even when it appeared we didn't. It's habit 1 from the *Seven Habits of Highly Effective People,* and it's based on the idea that when something happens to us, we don't have to react—we can choose to act instead.

Asking the woman what she had thought right after she'd received her demerit, I was surprised to hear her say, "I do so much right and no one seems to notice." She had decided to break a rule in the program in order to secure something at her job and felt justified in her decision. In the meantime, she felt that her hard work doing the right things at other times went unnoticed. Those two thoughts—"I had to break the rule" and "No one appreciates my hard work"—had led to her mini-meltdown.

Once we got to this point, we were able to show the participants that our reactions are the children of our thoughts—often born in the heat of the moment. By recognizing when our hot buttons have been pushed, slowing down the process, capturing the thoughts that come from the stimulus, and challenging them, we can choose another thought.

The group began to catch on, and it wasn't long before our conversation went to all the choices we had—including forgiveness, taking responsibility, and more. The women calmed down and were busy challenging other recent reactions by the time I left.

My tip? Don't be afraid to switch agendas, wade in, and work during a time of conflict. Your best results are waiting to grow out of those moments.

Oh, by the way, I went home that evening and saw that my brand-new neighbor was pouring bags of dirt into giant, crooked, coffin-like plywood rectangles on her front lawn. She gladly informed me that she was going to create an organic garden there because there wasn't enough sun in her backyard. No amount of reasoning on my part seemed to encourage her to do otherwise. Now, every time I look out my front window, and when I leave in the morning and arrive home at night, I get to practice what I preach.

"Somewhere between stimulus and response, I can choose," I tell myself. The good news is that I only chose to keep the front curtains closed for one day before I decided to see things differently. When the garden ripens, even though it's an eyesore and a little creepy, I am going to hope for a home-grown tomato or two.

Demeaning Others

Many instances of demeaning others, just like displaying anger, are unintended. The most common instances occur when a person feels unfairly criticized or perceives an attempt at humor as underhanded or mean spirited. Sometimes, even a fleeting glance or gesture can convey a damaging, demeaning message. Of course, there are also times when a comment or action is purposefully demeaning. If you're honest with yourself, you can remember a wisecrack or joke you made at somebody else's expense that went beyond funny and had specific intent or message. Regardless of the intent, demeaning behavior during a conflict is toxic.

Perhaps the most common of demeaning behaviors is sarcasm or misplaced humor. We love laughter. Jokes, funny stories, and quick-witted repartee are common in our workplace and in most every healthy relationship and organization. During conflict, though, the use of humor comes with a risk. What was intended as "just joking or kidding" to the speaker can be received as critical or embarrassing by the listener. Such demeaning behavior is certain to prolong or worsen the conflict situation.

So what is a fun-loving, good-humored person supposed to do? Here's what we suggest.

Actions that demean others are among the most costly behaviors within conflict. These inflict immediate harm in the form of embarrassment or criticism. And the impact can linger for a very long time. The best policy is to avoid demeaning displays altogether. Once committed, however, quick action and sincere apologies are necessary. Otherwise, the conflict is likely to continue without hope of resolution.

MANAGING POTENTIALLY DEMEANING BEHAVIORS

1. During conflict, resist the temptation to offer feedback or advice to your conflict partner. Instead, focus on perspective taking and listening for understanding. Save your feedback for well after the conflict has been resolved. Better yet, wait until you're asked to provide it.

2. In a conflict, relationships are often strained. This creates greater potential for attempts at humor to be misperceived. At the same time, humor can be a great tension reliever. The best kind of humor for conflict situations is of the self-deprecating type. If you must poke fun, poke fun at your own expense.

3. Monitor your nonverbal signals carefully. You might consider asking a colleague for specific feedback on your nonverbal actions during challenging meetings or conflict discussions. Research has shown that even slight mannerisms at the wrong time, such as eye rolling or head tilting, can have a tremendously demeaning impact on others.

Demeaning behavior affects not only the person who is "targeted" but often all those within earshot. The following story contributed by Don Albert underscores the often debilitating effect of a demeaning leader.

THE IMPACT OF A DEMEANING BOSS

In the mid 1990s I was working in a training and development department with a total staff of twelve employees. A new director, Tom, was hired to manage the department. He was hired because of his perceived management skills and success in other settings. Unfortunately, Tom was also quite abrasive, blunt, and demanding.

One day Tom was in the administrative assistant's office, loudly reprimanding her about a perceived mistake. I couldn't help but overhear even though my office was three doors down. When he finished, she was in tears. I met him in the corridor. I said, "You know, Tom, that's not the best way to help an employee improve performance. For gosh sakes, we teach this stuff." Tom replied, peering over his half–reading glasses, "Don, I know all about that leadership stuff. I just chose not to use it today."

At that point I decided that I needed to coach my boss. I started doing my homework by writing in a legal pad the behaviors I had witnessed in similar interactions. After filling approximately thirteen pages in my legal pad, I felt ready to speak with Tom. However, my "gut" wasn't quite ready. After all, Tom was my boss and he was responsible for my performance review.

One fateful day at the end of a one-on-one meeting Tom asked, "Well, Don, do you have anything else we need to talk about?" I was sitting in my office, behind my desk, with the legal pad in my top drawer. I knew it was now or never. I said, in what I hoped was an upbeat manner, "As a matter of fact, I do. Let's discuss your leadership style." He looked over those half-glasses once again and said in an arrogant tone, "Oh really?" Still trying to be upbeat and informal I replied, "Yes, if you have a few minutes."

I began by suggesting that his leadership style was perceived as somewhat abrasive and blunt. He responded, in an angry tone, "Oh yeah, well give me an example." I opened my drawer, pulled out the legal pad, and leafed through the pages (avoiding his half-glasses stare). I found the incident about him and the administrative assistant. I relayed the information to him with specific dates, the situation, his actions, and the impact it had. As I was finishing, he interrupted, waved his hand, and said, "Okay, give me another example." I then reminded him of an incident during a staff meeting when he verbally and publicly reprimanded Debra, our instructional designer, about a perceived lack of progress on a course she was developing. "Any other examples?" he asked.

Our discussion lasted for two and a half hours. I was very glad I had completed extensive homework with regard to specific situations and behaviors that Tom had exhibited, as well as the impact it had on others. When Tom left my office, he did so in a quiet and reflective manner. I would like to tell you that he improved dramatically. He didn't. He improved incrementally. He no longer reprimanded people publicly, and his approach seemed a little less abrasive. To Tom's credit, he never let our discussion influence my annual review.

Unfortunately, lasting damage had occurred. Not only had Tom's demeaning interactions affected individuals with whom he spoke, in nearly every case others in the department overheard or witnessed the behavior. The entire climate was affected and Tom's reputation forever tarnished. Eventually, Tom left the organization. But many of us have scars and memories that will last a lifetime.

Retaliating

By far, the most common types of retaliatory behavior are associated with unexpressed or poorly expressed emotions or beliefs. When a person believes he's been wronged or embarrassed by another, the stage is set for retaliation. The stakes grow higher when that person silently imagines a payback toward the offender. The "eye for an eye" adage grows attractive and getting even takes on more importance than resolving the issue at hand. Obviously, assumptions and attributions also play an important part in the retaliatory cycle.

The problem is that what is seen as "getting even" in one person's mind is perceived as a provocation by the other. What was once a misunderstanding is suddenly a full-blown relationship conflict impacting not only the two principles, but all those in proximity.

Retaliation can take many forms. Physical retaliation is the easiest to spot but probably the least frequent to occur. Instances of workplace violence are relatively rare. Verbal retaliation is more obvious and much more frequent. In the workplace, passive resistance is probably the most common form of retaliation. The length of time between the event and the retaliatory action varies widely. Immediate retaliation occurs within seconds. Delayed retaliation may appear within a few minutes or days or weeks later.

As with each destructive behavior, our advice is to use constructive approaches so consistently that there's little time or room for destructive behaviors. For yourself, or when coaching others, whether you believe there's a pattern of retaliatory behavior or just an occasional slip, here are some tips for avoiding retaliation.

AVOIDING RETALIATION

1. Assume positive intent. Much too often simple misunderstandings lead to ugly confrontations and severed relationships. If you perceive that you've been slighted by someone, and it's an out-of-the-ordinary occurrence, choose to believe that there is an explanation devoid of malice.

2. When you find yourself imagining a way to "get even," stop immediately and examine why you're feeling this way. Allowing yourself to step into the moment, assess your thoughts, and consider your motivations slows everything down. At the worst, you delay taking any action. At the best, you give yourself a chance to reconsider.

3. If you find yourself resisting someone else's idea or suggestion (often associated with passive resistance), take a moment to ask yourself why you're resistant. If you're resistant because of the source or person, you should take even more time for your assessment. You must confront the reason for your resistance to the person, then take steps to address the underlying resentment or issue.

Retaliatory behavior can only lead to deeper, longer-lasting conflicts. In many cases, assumptions and attribution are the only sources of conflict. Substantive issues may not even exist. When you feel or believe that you've been unjustly treated, it's better to address that belief head on rather than via passive action or guerilla tactics. When you deal ineffectively with your emotions or act on assumptions, conflicts will result or deepen.

Avoiding

When we ask people about how they generally deal with conflict, the overwhelming response is that they try to avoid or deny it. They readily admit that this does little to solve the problem, as the conflict festers and usually flares up at a later time. Even knowing this, they still prefer to avoid dealing with it. It is a natural response—aversion to an unpleasant thing—but in the case of conflict it provides at best temporary relief, usually at the cost of more pain later on.

Since so many people tend to avoid conflict, in our workshops we regularly work on helping them learn how to lessen avoidance and increase their ability to engage constructively. Avoidance is one aspect of the "flight" response and is a natural and valuable part of our survival responses in truly life-threatening situations. It worked great thousands of years ago when we might have been faced with a dangerous animal or other threat. The same instinct kicks in when we are faced with less than life-threatening issues like conflict in the office, and unfortunately it does not work well in these changed circumstances. Yet, the flight instinct is hard-wired into our system, which can make it an easy default behavior when we feel threatened.

So the question is, how can you overcome this hard-wired response? Tim Ursiny, author of *The Coward's Guide to Conflict*, shared an approach that he uses effectively with his clients (Ursiny, 2003). He calls it a pain/pleasure analysis. He asks people a series of questions that helps them examine the relative value that avoiding or engaging conflict has for them. He says that the exercise is particularly effective for people who are experiencing conflict with their boss and are afraid to deal with it (conversation with Craig on June 4, 2009).

Ursiny first asks the client to think about the pain they might experience if they face the conflict. In the case of an employee dealing with a conflict with his boss, the potential pain might include getting reprimanded or in the extreme getting fired. He then asks the person to reflect on the likelihood of these things actually happening. There are certainly situations when the boss may truly be mean, vindictive, or retaliatory, and in those cases it may be best to avoid or eventually to find a new job. Fortunately, in most cases these things are not likely to happen even though our thoughts about them contribute heavily to our desire to avoid.

A second step is asking the person to think about the pleasure he or she would get from avoiding the conflict. Usually in the short term, there is some relief that comes from not having to face the other person, although it is often accompanied by a nagging feeling that the issue is still there or that his or her interests are still not met. An employee may put off asking for a raise because he doesn't want to face a conflict with the boss. There may be relief in not having to face the boss, but at the same time the employee isn't getting his raise.

In the third step, Ursiny asks the person to think about the pain that would be caused by not facing the other person. Avoidance usually creates some pain, but we often overlook this at the moment in favor of the temporary relief of not having to engage the conflict. The employee might forgo his raise, and he might also get down because he didn't stand up for himself. In other cases, we avoid but know that at some point we'll probably have to deal with the issue, and it hangs over us like a cloud.

In the final step, Ursiny has the person think about the pleasure that he might derive from dealing with the conflict. In addition to getting it over, perhaps he'll get the raise. In other contexts, he won't have to carry the dread around for so long. He may achieve a breakthrough and come up with a good solution to the problem and a better relationship with the other person.

Ursiny says that, in his experience, people find this exercise to be helpful in putting their fears in context and in recognizing that avoidance is not their only option. By addressing the pain of engagement and the pleasure of avoidance first, people are more willing to consider the other elements—the pain of avoidance and the pleasure of engagement. The process of examining both components often reveals the right answer for how to move forward.

Developing an Engagement Strategy   Avoidance comes from a fear of engaging conflict. It is a natural response, but one that does not work well in most cases. When conflict arises, it stirs up people's emotions. It can produce fear, anger, and other feelings. If a person doesn't have a strategy for how to deal with these situations, her emotions can lead her to default into fight-or-flight behaviors, the latter of which leads to avoidance.

In addition to helping people deal with their emotions, in our workshops we help them develop strategies they can use to respond to the conflict more effectively. We do this in advance of future conflicts because it is very difficult to do this in the heat of the moment.

We talk about the specifics of engagement strategies later in the chapter; these approaches become critical in providing a person with a framework he or she can use to move forward to deal with the conflict issues rather than feel overwhelmed and run away. While he may still not like conflict, he will have a specific set of behaviors and approaches he can use that will enhance his ability to engage the other person, discuss the issues, and develop solutions that lead to mutually beneficial outcomes.

Engaging Conflicts in Performance Management   Clients tell us that it is particularly difficult to deal with confrontations during performance management discussions. It is difficult for managers to give subordinates bad news, so they often don't. Yet, a sugar-coated review does not help resolve problems, and in the end it lets the employee down as well because he fails to receive feedback that can help him improve. Our colleagues, Rick Voyles and Carol Rice at the Conflict Resolution Academy in Atlanta, describe an approach they have successfully used to help clients effectively address performance management issues.

The workplace is a breeding ground for misunderstanding, resulting in disputes that have the power to destroy teams, undermine the mission of the agency, and lead to lower productivity and poor morale. That's the bad news. The good news is that there is a way to deal with these issues that can help manage and/or prevent potential destructive conflicts.

While consulting for a large Atlanta firm, we learned that the firm's situation called for managing conflict between the principals of the company. This high-level conflict, based on performance issues, called for a systemic approach if any resolutions were to be effective, long-term, and stable. The company was stalled, and it was clear something had to change. We initiated several techniques as part of the Collaborative Skills System that we developed at the Conflict Resolution Academy. In this instance, we employed the collaborative feedback technique using our Performance Documentation Instrument assessment tool.

The collaborative feedback technique is designed to create a collaborative document that looks at the individual performance of the employee. It helps develop an action plan with accountability and serves to support the parties involved in the review. It also includes measurable outcomes. Managers and supervisors who are trained in the use of this form benefit from the skills introduced when it is necessary to have a difficult conversation.

The collaborative feedback technique is mission driven. A series of specifically designed appreciative inquiry questions are asked in four areas: response, options, commitment, and action items. Each question is to be answered by both the manager/leader and the employee/volunteer.

Response includes questions designed to determine what is working well and what needs improvement. Building upon information gathered in this first section, *option* questions brainstorm ways to maintain what is working well as well as potential corrections for what needs to be done differently. *Commitment* questions define specific actions and timelines for who will do what, when it will be done, how it will be done, where it is going to be done, as well as what to expect if commitments are not kept or what recognition there will be when commitments are kept. Specific, detailed accountability is the goal of the *action items* section of this collaborative endeavor. Dates are set for specific actions, accomplishment, consequences, and recognition. Signed commitment cards are distributed to both the manager/leader and the employee/volunteer.

The result of our consulting and employment of the Collaboration Skills System was a change in the decision-making process in the firm and communication that led to improved exchanges and more productive conflict between the leadership of the firm. Each person became more accountable for the responsibilities and outcomes assigned to her for the growth and development of the business, and she began to look at conflict as a positive opportunity for change.

The fact is, performance-based reviews can create possibilities for more disagreeable project and/or annual reviews. Feedback on performance must be available in clear, concise, and concrete terms so that accountability is evident both on the part of the employee and the manager. The Collaborative Skills System is designed to promote a performance culture based on feedback, communication, and results, encouraging dispute resolution at the lowest level.

While they must deal with the overarching mission objectives of the organization, managers must also clearly communicate performance expectations and hold employees responsible for accomplishing them, make meaningful distinctions among employees based on performance and contribution, foster and reward excellent performance, address poor performance, create action plans, assure that employees are assigned a rating of record when required, adhere to merit system principles and prohibited personnel practices, and ensure continuing application of, and compliance with, Equal Employment Opportunity (EEO) laws, regulations, and policy.

Yielding

The second of the passive destructive behaviors measured in the Conflict Dynamics Profile is *yielding*. This occurs when a person responds to conflict by giving in to the other person just to avoid having to deal with the conflict. It is different from avoiding in that the person does not stay physically away from the other person but rather capitulates to or accommodates the other person. This is another type of the flight behaviors.

Yielding is not always a completely destructive behavior. You might give in to the other person on a point that is not important to you in hopes of getting a concession in return. This tactical approach can be helpful in certain cases. The problem with yielding comes from consistent patterns of this behavior. When a person regularly gives in to others in order to avoid addressing conflicts, problems arise. In practice, you can spot yielding behaviors when you hear people say with somewhat resigned voices, "Okay, we'll do it your way," or "Whatever you want is fine with me."

A habitual pattern of yielding can cause people to become dissatisfied with themselves. They feel disappointed that they have not stuck up for their principles or interests. They can also get a reputation as a pushover. Other people may begin to take advantage of them.

When we ask about the downsides of yielding, people in our programs usually note the issues just raised. They also point out big downsides of yielding for the organization. One of these is that the person who yields may have had a better idea. If he gives in before his idea is seriously considered, his solution can be lost and the organization loses out on a potentially valuable idea. This lack of open, honest debate leads to lowered levels of innovation and poor decision quality.

A number of organizations we have worked with display cultures of yielding. We often find this in contexts in which employees characterize their company or agency as "a nice organization." In these cases, people typically mean that they do not like to challenge one another, so they quietly go along with someone who has a strong agenda. By "go along," they mean that they do not challenge the person in the meeting, but it does not mean that they support the person in implementation. While it appears that the person received consent from others for his idea, when he starts to move ahead on implementation, there is little or no support from the others who appeared to give their consent.

Moving Beyond Yielding   When working with individuals or groups who have a habit of using yielding behavior, we first try to help them explore why they find conflict so discomforting. You can use similar techniques to those discussed in the section on avoiding. While there are differences between these two behavioral patterns, they are both driven by either fear of or discomfort around conflict. People may be concerned about hurting someone else or being hurt themselves. They may be scared of the emotional aspects of conflict or the uncertainties it brings.

We find that it helps for people to talk about their concerns, especially in safe contexts. This is somewhat easier if the people in a training group do not know one another or when people work in the same area and have high trust of each other. Clearly, discussions of this sort must be of a voluntary nature, and that is why it is so important for a trainer to make sure the context is safe for sharing. As people talk about the concerns that lead them to yield, it can be helpful to ask individuals how they feel about using this behavior. Some people are completely comfortable yielding and find this an appropriate strategy for themselves. Others feel fine about using the technique but only in specific situations. Most people, though, have some regrets about giving in to others when they don't believe the other person's solution is best. When you find people who are dissatisfied with their general pattern of yielding, you can ask them about how they would prefer to handle conflict situations. This inquiry can typically lead to new insights about alternative behavioral approaches.

Hiding Emotions

One of the destructive behaviors on the Conflict Dynamics Profile (CDP) is *hiding emotions.* This is closely linked to the constructive behavior of expressing emotions, only in a negative manner. The inclusion of both behavior patterns on the CDP emphasizes the importance that the emotional side of conflict plays in our models.

Hiding emotions is essentially the same thing as suppressing, which almost always results in negative outcomes. Indeed, researchers have found that suppressing emotions is the worst strategy for emotional regulation (Gross, 1998). When people suppress emotions, it can even affect their health. It also makes it harder for other people to understand what's truly going on in the conflict. Suppressed emotions typically fester and oftentimes emerge as some form of active destructive behavior, such as an outburst of anger or perhaps demeaning remarks to another person.

When we work with individuals who have high scores on hiding emotions, they often have low scores on expressing emotions. The techniques described in the expressing emotions section of this chapter are those that we use to help people overcome the inclination to hide their emotions.

Self-Criticizing

When people obsess over the ways in which they've mishandled a conflict, they're engaging in the CDP behavior of *self-criticizing*. While reflecting on ways in which a person could have handled a conflict better can be positive, when one thinks over and over again about the things she did that were wrong in a conflict, it can sap her energy and prevent her from moving forward productively. It is okay to learn from your mistakes, but to run yourself down for every small mistake you made in a conflict setting is counterproductive. When we work with people who have high scores on self-criticizing, we often find that they have a number of high scores on hot buttons as well. That's because often people with high standards can get irritated when the standards are not met—either by others, which is the case in hot buttons, or by themselves, which can be the case in self-criticizing. We encourage people to reflect on why they are so self-critical and whether or not this is a behavioral pattern that works for them or against them. When we find that people view it as counter-productive, we then help them think about how they can lessen their use of this behavior. One of the approaches we use is similar to the techniques described in the section on mindfulness in Chapter Three. This involves becoming aware of the self-criticizing behavior and thinking patterns while they're occurring. Once awareness of the pattern arises, the person steps back and just observes the thoughts or feelings he's having that are of a self-critical nature. The key here is observing the thought in a nonjudgmental manner. It does no good to look at the self-critical thought and then become self-critical about having the thought. That just fosters further rumi-nation about one's inadequacies. The idea is to merely observe the thoughts and/or feelings until they pass. And indeed, they do pass when less energy is given to them. This can be difficult if you've had a pattern of self-criticizing for many years; it is like a habit. Yet, slowly and surely, it is possible to break that habit by observing, in a dispassionate manner, those thoughts as they come and as they go.

You can ask trusted associates to help you with this. If you start running your-self down or talking over and over again about how poorly you handled a situa-tion, your colleague can suggest that it looks like you're being overly self-critical. It may be time to step back and just observe those thoughts and let them pass.

And while you step back, you needn't analyze the correctness of your thoughts, or whether or not you indeed were overly self-critical, but just observe the thoughts and feelings, nonjudgmentally, and allow them to slowly dissolve and work on thinking of more positive things. When people are able to overcome overly self-critical behavior patterns, their energy for moving forward after conflicts is markedly improved.

ORCHESTRATING THE USE OF CONSTRUCTIVE BEHAVIORS

There is obviously a lot to consider when confronted with conflict. We've spent a significant amount of time reviewing its cognitive, emotional, and behavioral aspects. One additional consideration in addressing conflict is its severity or intensity. In our previous books, we introduced a scale of intensity. We've included a brief review of our intensity scale as a prelude to an orchestration exercise we use to bring the entire notion of constructive engagement together.

Intensity

Most of us tend to recall conflicts that rank among the most painful or awful moments in our lives. And many of our clients come to us during those very moments. As the intensity of conflict rises, so do the stakes, and so does the challenge of finding resolution. As a consequence, we often hear about conflicts that border on being virtually irreconcilable.

There's no doubt that the intensity of conflict can escalate rapidly. That's why we so passionately recommend that conflict be addressed early and often. To emphasize this concept, we have compared the intensity levels of conflict to the intensity scale used to describe the five intensity levels of hurricanes. Just as weather experts recommend different ways to prepare for and recover from storms of various strengths or intensity, we believe it's important to consider the intensity levels of our conflicts as a factor in shaping our responses. With this in mind, we offer a brief review of the five intensity levels and some suggestions on how to prepare or respond during each.

The Intensity Levels of Conflict

Level 1: Differences   We define this level as times when two or more people see a situation differently, understand the other parties' positions and interests well, and feel no discomfort regarding the difference.

The vast majority of people probably don't consider differences to be a form of conflict at all, let alone being an intensity level. On the contrary, we contend that differences contain the very essence of healthy or constructive conflict. When individuals and teams can deal with conflict while it's low in intensity, conflict becomes an asset.

The essence of this lowest level of conflict intensity rests in two or more people having different perspectives. The recommended response to differences is to embrace and explore them! What better time to debate, compare, and analyze than when no animosity exists. Such differences can ultimately lead to better outcomes.

When conflict exists at this lowest level of intensity, we suggest that listening for understanding and perspective taking are the best tools for exploring the possibilities. Use this as an opportunity to investigate deeply, express wonder, demonstrate curiosity, and challenge with gusto.

Level 2: Misunderstandings   We define misunderstandings as times or situations when what is understood by one person is different than what is understood by others.

Misunderstandings are normal and commonplace. They happen all the time in our lives. In most cases they are relatively innocuous. They appear as minor "speed bumps" on life's highway. We experience it, take care of it, and move on. The challenge occurs when misunderstandings cause problems or issues that take time to resolve. Tension rises when misunderstandings result in embarrassment or inconvenience. In the workplace, intensity rises to this level when misunderstandings lead to missed targets, opportunities, appointments, commitments, and obligations. Attributions form, accusations follow, and soon you have a significant conflict on your hands.

Most misunderstandings are handled quickly and easily. This happens when they are addressed as early as possible. Other misunderstandings can lead to higher levels of intensity. We categorize misunderstandings as level 2 primarily because of their potential to morph quickly to higher levels. We believe that the longer a misunderstanding goes unresolved, the greater the likelihood that it will grow to higher intensity levels. In addition, the more critical the misunderstood issue is to those involved, the more potential there is for escalation.

Reaching out and making an apology if you are responsible for the confusion is especially important. We also recommend a healthy dose of listening for understanding and sharing thoughts and feelings when misunderstandings occur.

If misunderstandings happen frequently, it may be a sign of issues related to poor communication. When the frequency is high, we recommend regular checking for understanding and summarizing to help ensure shared comprehension. In other words, slowing down the speed of delivery and discussions may aid in improving the communication.

Level 3: Disagreements   We define disagreements as times when two or more people see a situation differently and, regardless of how well they understand the others' positions and interests, feel discomfort that the other parties disagree.

This is the midpoint of the intensity scale. It's also a very delicate balance point between constructive and destructive avenues. Because emotions are engaged at this point, there's a heightened potential for the conflict to go poorly.

On one hand, a disagreement can be a signal to slow down and examine differences that may lead to new ideas or creative solutions. It's critical in moments like this that all views are fully considered. On the other hand, a disagreement can indicate emotional or relationship issues that are in need of attention. If ignored, these kinds of issues most certainly can lead to more intensity and/or destructive results.

The key to handling disagreements effectively is to not ignore them. We suggest a balance between expressing empathy and demonstrating understanding of the position of one's conflict partner. These two skills comprise both elements of perspective taking. Taking care of the relationship or emotions first is recommended. In addition, one must also remember to clearly and honestly express one's own thoughts and feelings.

Level 4: Discord   We define discord as situations where the conflict causes difficulties in the relationship of the people involved even when the people are not dealing with the original conflict.

Once a conflict reaches the level of discord, serious damage to relationships can result if the conflict is not addressed effectively. Discord is characterized by chronic tension and strain among those involved even during routine interactions. In other words, the parties involved begin to experience consistent, ongoing difficulties with their interactions. This "carryover" effect makes discord especially complex and challenging to address.

Discord most often results from differences, misunderstandings, or disagreements that have been mishandled. The participants must engage in constructive dialogue to have any chance of cooling the intensity enough to enable resolution. We coach the individuals involved to first reach out to one another in order to reestablish a discussion. Once reengaged, we recommend that the parties spend considerable time listening to the others' views, acknowledging the others' perspectives, and summarizing the thoughts and feelings of their conflict partners. Only through persistent demonstrations of understanding can the intensity of discord be reduced. Unaddressed, discord can easily escalate to the most intense level of conflict, polarization.

Level 5: Polarization   We define polarization as conflict situations characterized by severe negative emotions and behavior with little or no hope for reconciliation.

Two common themes arise during this most severe level. One theme involves the active recruitment of others for supporting one's position. The other is an unwillingness or inability to attempt perspective taking. The chasm is so great that accusations and attributions become the norm. Neither side is willing to reengage. Attempts at resolution are considered futile if not impossible. For comparison, when a marriage is at the polarization level, the couple is likely proceeding toward divorce. When countries arrive at this level, they may be on the brink of war.

This level of intensity is obviously damaging and painful, but it is not impossible to address. The one absolutely compulsory step for progress is communication. Those involved must agree to meet, listen, and talk. Quite often third party mediators are necessary. Through them, ground rules can be established for listening, perspective taking, expressing thoughts and feelings, and eventually reaching collaborative solutions. Nothing about this is easy. Through constructive communication, though, there is hope.

Understanding the intensity of conflicts can enable conflict participants to gauge their use of constructive behaviors. Clearly, the lower the intensity, the easier it is to overlook the opportunities. The higher the intensity, the harder it is to ignore the obvious concerns. Simply acknowledging the fact that conflict exists at different intensity levels and understanding what it takes to address the various levels can be extremely helpful. Rather than succumbing to the inclination to avoid or lash out, conflict participants can consider instead ways to constructively engage in behaviors that provide hope for progress. We do not pretend to have a linear, sequential model for engaging in constructive conflict behaviors. Conflicts simply do not occur in simple, easily definable ways. Consequently, what it takes to address conflict competently is as complex and challenging as the conflict itself. This doesn't mean that conflict competence is unattainable. On the contrary, with a combination of self-awareness, understanding, and practice, anyone can improve his or her conflict competence.

CONSTRUCTIVE COMMUNICATION EXERCISE

We have devised an exercise for two (or more) people in conflict to use that offers both an opportunity to practice constructive communication and discover potential solutions to their conflict. The participants will examine one person's conflict at a time. The other person will play the role of the conflict partner.

Step 1: Describe the Conflict

Each participant writes a paragraph describing the conflict as it currently exists.

- Encourage participants to state clearly how the conflict began.
- Tell them that they will share this statement with their conflict partner.
- Direct each participant to write a second paragraph describing a solution to the conflict. (*This statement is not used until the end of the exercise.*)

Step 2: Planning for Starting and Maintaining Communications (Reaching Out)

- Participants craft a statement they can use to reach out to their partners.
- Encourage the use of "I statements."
- Encourage taking responsibility.
- Encourage an apology if warranted.
- Statements should include clear desire to make progress.

Reaching out can be difficult for people, particularly for those who prefer to avoid conflict. Spending time developing an approach for doing it can help ease the anxiety. Part of the process involves becoming clear about the issue involved. When you go to the other person to request that you talk about the issue, it is important to be able to state it in a clear, concise manner. It is also important not to get into the issue until you have set some ground rules for how you will proceed. It is too easy to fall into an argument at this point, so it may be best to schedule a later time to talk.

Step 3: Participants Engage in Reaching Out

- One participant reads or says her prepared statement to the other.
- The listener simply nods and says, "Thank you."
- The second participant reads or says his prepared statement.
- The listener listens, nods, and says, "Thank you."
- No further discussion is allowed.

Step 4: Planning for Perspective Taking (and Listening for Understanding)

- Participants write two statements.
- One statement summarizes one significant content point or view she thinks is held by her partner.
- One statement describes an emotion or feeling she believes her partner holds and the reason for that emotion.
- Encourage participants to see the conflict from their partner's perspective.

When we work with participants in our programs, we have them prepare for discussions about conflicts. Part of the process involves thinking about how the other person may be seeing the conflict. This helps prevent surprises and starts the process of becoming curious about how the other person understands the conflict and feels about it. It makes it easier to then listen and ask clarifying questions when engaging in perspective taking with the other person.

Step 5: Participants Engage in Perspective Taking

- One participant reads or says his statement regarding a significant content point held by his partner. Then he asks, "Do I have that right?"

- The other responds openly.

- If a correction or restatement is warranted, the original speaker makes it.

- The other participant reads or says her content statement, then asks, "Do I have that right?"

- The other responds openly.

- If a correction or restatement is warranted, the original speaker makes it.

- The process is repeated for the statements of emotion or feelings.

- Steps 4 and 5 may be repeated until both parties are satisfied that enough perspective taking and empathy have been demonstrated that progress can be made.

We encourage people to spend significant time on this process. The key is to deeply understand how each other sees and feels about the conflict. This does not mean you agree with your partner about the issue, just that you understand them. Sometimes people rush through this part of the process because they are uncomfortable with perspective taking, but the facilitator can play a role in making sure that sufficient listening is done. One way to test whether enough listening has been done is to ask each party to state the way the other thinks and feels about it. If the conflict partner agrees that the other person has a good understanding of him, then they are ready for the next step.

Step 6: Planning for Sharing Thoughts and Feelings (Expressing Emotions)

- Participants write two statements.

- One statement is a clear expression of his feeling or emotion about the conflict.

- One statement is an expression of a key thought or idea he has about the conflict.

- Encourage participants to be honest and open about their thoughts and feelings.

Conflict communications involve talking and listening. We believe that conflict competent people generally listen first because it helps them learn more about what is involved and it also helps reduce tensions. After you have heard the other person out, there comes a time when you need to share your views and feelings on the conflict. Reflecting on these in advance can be helpful because it allows you to order your thoughts for more effective presentation.

Step 7: Participants Engage in Sharing Thoughts and Feelings

- One participant reads or says her statement regarding a feeling or emotion.

- The other responds by demonstrating understanding and empathy.

- The other participant reads or says her statement regarding a feeling or emotion.

- The other responds by demonstrating understanding and empathy.

- The process repeats for the statements of thoughts or ideas.

- Steps 6 and 7 may be repeated.

We encourage the facilitator to make sure that the person sharing talks about both thoughts and feelings. People are more comfortable talking about thoughts and will often leave out a discussion of how they feel. This is important information.

Step 8: Planning for Collaborative Problem Solving (Reflective Thinking, Creating Solutions, Adapting)

- Each participant writes a paragraph describing how progress can be made.

- Each participant writes three questions to ask his or her partner.

- Each participant writes a second paragraph describing what he or she could do differently.

- Encourage the use of specific words and actions.

Once the parties have heard each other, they are in a position to look at how to solve the problem in ways that address the concerns of each. Successful resolutions come from addressing those elements that are important to each party. So being clear on the interests of each person is the starting point. Coming up with possible solutions comes next. Considering options in advance can help this process. Encourage the participants to think about a number of possible solutions. We often find people settle for simple compromises at this point and often overlook better options.

When creating questions to ask their partners, suggest they request feedback on how to improve different aspects of possible solutions. We also suggest asking about how the solution looks from the other person's perspective.

Step 9: Participants Engage in Collaborative Problem Solving

- Participants take turns reading their descriptions of how progress can be made.

- Each is encouraged to comment on the other's description.

- Participants take turns asking their prepared questions and responding.

- Participants share their statements of what they could each do differently.

This stage is where breakthroughs take place. As in step 5, we encourage spending enough time on this step. When participants comment on each other's descriptions and answer questions, we suggest that they point out something positive and add another point that might also be helpful. When participants share statements about what they could do differently, we recommend they build on one another's suggestions. Rather than critiquing the other person's suggestion, acknowledge some good about it and then add one point that could improve it.

Step 10: Compare Beginning and Ending Solutions

- Participants take turns sharing their original "solution" to the conflict.

- Participants are encouraged to comment on the differences between the original solutions and their comments during step 9.

This exercise takes at least 90 minutes to complete. It can be used for real conflicts or as a practice activity in a training program. It is admittedly more "step by step" than a real conflict conversation. However, it effectively slows down the thinking and emoting processes of the conflict participants so they have time to consider the other's perspectives. It also allows each party to cool down when their emotions run high. Finally, it provides the opportunity to plan, then engage in constructive behaviors that can lead to progress, resolution, and ultimately satisfactory outcomes to conflict.

One of the most significant learning outcomes during the activity is the comparison of the solution prepared at the start of the exercise with the potential solutions generated at the end. All too often participants in conflict rush to solutions. This results in outcomes that are seldom truly mutually agreeable, satisfying, or successful. Rather, when practicing the "cool down, slow down, engage" process within the framework of constructive communication behaviors, the conflict is more fully examined. Both the emotional and content aspects are carefully addressed. Participants are often surprised at the new options they created for making progress and reaching resolutions.

If you have time, you can run through the exercise a second time. In the second round allow the communications to flow more freely, as in a normal conflict context. People can complete steps 2, 4, 6, and 8 ahead of time. They then work in "real time" on reaching out, listening, expressing, and collaborative problem solving. The sequence may begin the same as the first round, but it is likely that there may be deviations. After reaching out, discussion might start with emotions. If things get too hot, there may be a need for some cooling down time. The participants may jump ahead to problem solving only to have to fall back to the listening and expressing steps. One thing the facilitator needs to watch for is the participants jumping to the solution stage before discovering adequate understanding of the issue from both parties' sides. Allowing people to practice these constructive behaviors in safe contexts will help them develop the skills that they can then use in real-life settings. You may want to have periodic follow-up sessions to enable people to reflect, adjust, and continue to practice.

Below, Denise Pearson at the University of Denver shares her experience using principles of conflict competence, the Conflict Dynamics Profile, and her own unique blend of constructive approaches.

CONFLICT AND APPRECIATIVE INQUIRY

The Conflict Dynamics Profile 360 coupled with the organizational development process of appreciative inquiry offers organizational leaders a unique opportunity to engage in collaborative problem solving, employing reflective practices and strengths-based dialogue. Combined, these two approaches are particularly useful in mitigating conflict resulting from organizational change efforts.

More than two decades of consulting and partnering with organizational leaders in the fields of health care, nonprofit administration, higher education, public administration, and business on organizational conflict and change management supports claims that the only guarantees in workplaces around the globe are the inevitability and omnipresence of conflict, change, and the increasing value of leaders who can navigate these complex and dynamic environments.

Observed through organizational downsizing, reengineering, and mergers and acquisitions, change is continually unfolding on an international level—commonly triggering organizational conflict. Consequently, organizational leaders are compelled to equip themselves with the knowledge and skills necessary to mitigate ensuing conflict while keeping change initiatives on track for achieving organizational goals and objectives. The process of change can be wrought with conflict, for personal grounds ranging from fear for economic well-being; fear of the unknown; fear of losing important social relationships; and individuals' inability to recognize the need for change. Organizations, too, often foster resistance to change through support of structural inertia, which creates the perception of stability and work team inertia supported by the development of strong social norms. Threats to existing balances of power and recall of previously unsuccessful change efforts further serve to obstruct change initiatives.

The challenge to successful change is further complicated when transition management is neglected. Bridges (2003) and others have written extensively about this organizational phenomenon, emphasizing the difference between change and transition. While *change* is generally doctrinaire in nature, *transition* represents the internal journey through which people confront and process change. Given its principally personal nature, transition presents additional challenges and opportunities for organizational leaders, which too can be supported by reflective practices and creative problem-solving activities—the Conflict Dynamics Profile (CDP) 360 and appreciative inquiry (AI), as suggested here.

The CDP 360 and change management are natural concepts to discuss concurrently. The CDP 360 offers leaders an opportunity to participate in a nonevaluative development process that engages members from across the organization. Runde and Flanagan talk extensively about this; I use this in my consulting practice to help leaders identify constructive and destructive conflict behaviors that can advance or hinder their effectiveness (Runde and Flanagan, 2007). The CDP 360 complements reflective leadership practices, which further promote the importance of a leader's need to create vision, motivate, inspire, and empower individuals to think and behave in ways that are aligned with organizational mission and goals.

CDP 360

The CDP 360 has proven to be highly effective in my work illustrating leadership blind spots, one of the four quadrants represented in Luft and Ingham's Johari Window (1955). The Johari Window consists of four quadrants that help facilitate understanding of what one knows about oneself, what one does not know about oneself, what others know about oneself, and what others don't know about oneself. The "blind spot" is located in the quadrant that contains those things one does not know about oneself but are known by others (Luft and Ingham, 1955).

The CDP 360 can help leaders identify those blind spots relevant to their conflict behavior—before, during, and after an episode. The critical process of reflection that follows data analysis provides the opportunity for leaders to increase their capacity to motivate and inspire members of the organization to achieve both organizational and personal goals. Based on the work of Schön (1996), Harris (1998), and others, reflective practices encourage continuous development and improvement—a must for twenty-first century leadership. When combined with the cooperative, strengths-based process of appreciative inquiry, the personal and reflective nature of the CDP 360 represents a powerful and energetic approach to change management.

Appreciative Inquiry

Appreciative inquiry (AI) as a collaborative reflective process is quickly becoming this consultant's organizational development tool of choice. The key principles illustrate its potential to build organizational capacity for change and conflict resolution. Derived from the work of Cooperrider (1986), the five principles of AI are summarized as follows by Reed:

1. *The constructivist principle.* People develop ideas about the world through interpretation and construction, which leads to different views.

2. *The principle of simultaneity.* Inquiry and change occur together at the same time.

3. *The poetic principle.* As people develop stories about their worlds, they try out different "plotlines."

4. *The anticipatory principle.* The way people think about the future influences the way they approach it.

5. *The positive principle.* Positive inquiry can create deeper engagement. (Cooperrider, 1986; Reed, 2007)

In essence, AI allows organizations to engage in the process of construction, in the telling of their stories about the past, present, and future. It recognizes that inquiry encourages reflection, which has the capacity to lead to change. AI furthermore supports individuals and groups in the telling of their stories through a process that is engaging and easily reached. Recognizing the relationship between how people think about their future and how they move toward it, AI emphasizes what presently works well as a foundation for building a stronger future.

To summarize, as leaders seek to develop conflict competency throughout their organizations, the CDP 360 has been utilized effectively in combination with the four-phase process of appreciative inquiry. The four phases of this structured inquiry process (discovery, dream, design, and delivery) are built in part on the assumptions that every organization can find things that work, and the act of asking the right questions has the potential to positively influence the future thoughts and actions of organizational members. The task becomes that of fully leveraging the best of the rediscovered past, characterized by reflective practices, on behalf of future visioning, innovative organizational design, and sensitivity to the human dimension of implementing change.

Team Conflict Competence

When we work with teams, we ask the members if they encounter conflict in their work. They almost always say yes and readily agree that they will face it again in the future. When we probe further to see if they have developed processes for handling conflicts when they emerge, they almost always say no. This is why we believe teams have such a difficult time dealing with conflict.

Team conflict is both natural as well as inevitable. It emerges from many types of differences that the members bring to a team such as education, experience, values, culture, personality, and interests. These differences can sometimes lead to people feeling threatened. They can also create expectations about how others should respond. This, in turn, leads to conflicts when people do not respond in the desired manner.

In Chapter One we talked about two kinds of conflict—task and relationship. *Task conflict* occurs when people have differences and they work to solve the problems and issues caused by the differences. This kind of conflict can result in creative solutions, good decisions, and improved implementation. *Relationship conflict* is typified by focusing on whom to blame as opposed to how to solve problems. It leads to divisiveness and poorer outcomes in teams. When teams experience more task conflict than relationship conflict, they tend to perform better. So, how do teams engage in task conflict?

Significant research has examined this issue over the past ten years. The key question is whether team members are able to openly and honestly discuss difficult issues in a constructive manner. While this sounds straightforward, it clearly is not easy given the degree of difficulty that most teams experience around conflict.

In *Building Conflict Competent Teams,* we reviewed the research and provided a framework for what teams need to do to foster robust discussion of issues and keep communications moving in a positive direction. There are two critical steps that teams can take to improve their chances of making the most out of the conflicts they experience. The first involves creating the right climate for discussions, and the second deals with using effective communication strategies to explore issues and develop solutions to problems. However, even when the right climate is established and teams employ effective communication strategies, teams may still experience conflict challenges. In the pages that follow, we suggest ways to create the right climate and communicate effectively. We'll also provide recommendations for staying on track, handling conflict on virtual teams, and meeting the challenge of cultural differences among team members.

THE RIGHT CLIMATE

Creating the right climate means developing processes for handling conflicts when they emerge. While there is no single right way to do this, there is one clearly wrong approach and that is to do nothing. We recommend teams discuss their current attitudes as well as new ways of looking at conflict. We also suggest that they develop norms for developing and maintaining trust among team members so each person can feel safe sharing their opinions with the others. Developing a sense of "teamness" in which each member feels that everyone is working for the good of the team enables everyone to give others the benefit of the doubt when conflicts emerge. Finally, the emotional side of team conflicts is particularly important. Negative emotions can spread among team members and complicate working toward solutions. We look at each of these areas and suggest approaches teams can use to create a more effective climate for managing their conflicts. The various components are shown in Figure 5.1.

Improving Attitudes

In Chapter Two we talked about processes we use in our workshops to help individuals think about the ways they currently view conflict. These same approaches work well in team settings. People usually find it quite interesting to hear how their teammates view conflict. If most people on a team view conflict negatively, it becomes easy to see why teammates would prefer avoiding it and why the team might not have procedures in place to manage it. This is true even when

Figure 5.1
Team Conflict Competence Model

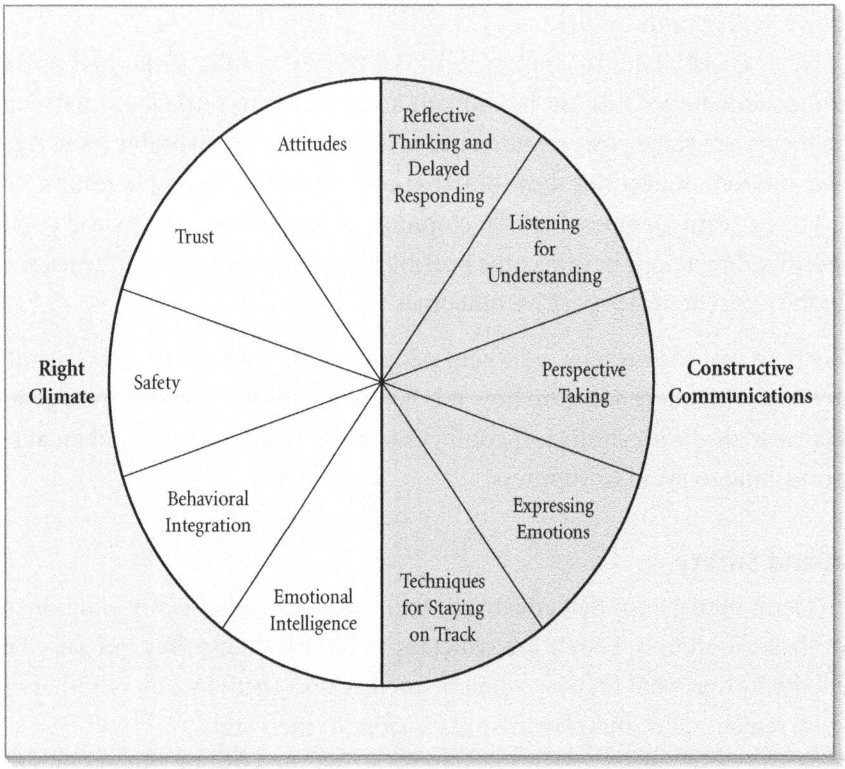

all or most of the members admit that conflicts inevitably arise. It is even true when most people agree that a total lack of conflict would lead to stagnation and mediocre outcomes.

We also find it helpful to have teams talk about how they have managed conflicts in the past. This can be uncomfortable in the beginning, but with encouragement from a facilitator people are usually able to share insights that can both explain why it has been difficult to address conflict and what steps a team may need to take to handle it.

Perhaps the best exercise is one we described in Chapter Two. It involves talking about conflicts that went well. It is so effective; here's how to adapt it to team settings.

1. We ask the team to select a conflict they experienced that turned out well—in other words a constructive conflict.

2. We then ask them to talk about how they handled the conflict and what seemed to lead to the positive outcome. We have them note down the actions they took that were helpful.

3. Next, we ask them to come up with additional conflicts that had positive outcomes. Sometimes this can be difficult and one has to settle for situations in which there were some positive outcomes as well as some unfavorable ones. Again, participants look for actions they took that contributed to favorable results.

4. Finally, team members look for common factors that seemed to lead conflict in a positive direction. These become possible behavioral norms that the team can use in the future to foster positive outcomes.

The power of the exercise is to help people realize that conflict can result in positive outcomes depending on how it is handled. This helps overcome a general reluctance to deal with conflict. If conflict is seen only as a bad thing, then at best it is something to avoid or suppress.

Trust and Safety

When teams manage conflict effectively, their members talk openly and honestly about their differences. People are reluctant to do this unless they feel safe. They need to know that what they say won't be used against them by others. Otherwise, they will remain quiet and play their cards close to their vests.

Trust and safety play a central role in fostering the kind of climate in which people feel comfortable talking with one another about difficult issues. So what do teams need to do to be able to create and maintain trust? In *Building Conflict Competent Teams*, we reviewed the research around trust and psychological safety and found:

- A critical element of trust is having confidence that others have your best interests in mind and won't use what you say against you.

- Getting to know more about other team members through structured disclosure (discussed later in the chapter) can help build trust.

- Acting with integrity, being honest, demonstrating courage, showing respect, being dependable, caring about others, and giving others the benefit of the doubt all help build trust.

- Trusting in others involves being vulnerable; it is helpful when team leaders can show their own vulnerability.
- Using constructive communication behaviors requires risk and is easier to do in high-trust situations.
- Trust can be challenging when team members have different values or come from different groups because stereotypes can emerge that cause suspicions and negative attributions.
- Breaches of trust can be damaging; people will often forgive one breach but rarely will they forgive a second one (Elangovan, Werner, and Szabo, 2007). Therefore, team leaders need to address breaches quickly.
- Psychological safety involves taking risks with the entire team (like telling others how you honestly feel about a situation) and requires both individual trust and mutual respect for one another (Edmondson, 2004).

Our research also led us to talk with Drs. Dennis and Michelle Reina, who have developed an elegant model for developing and regaining team trust. Their model is presented in their book, *Trust and Betrayal in the Workplace* (Reina and Reina, 2006). It includes an analysis of several different types of trust and what can be done to enhance them. The three types are:

1. *Contractual trust (trust of character),* which develops confidence in the intentions of others—it involves managing expectations, establishing boundaries, encouraging mutually serving intentions, and doing what you say you are going to do
2. *Communication trust (trust of disclosure),* which includes sharing information, telling the truth, admitting mistakes, giving and receiving feedback, and maintaining confidences
3. *Capability trust (trust of capability),* which builds confidence in others' ability to deliver on promises by acknowledging abilities, allowing people to make decisions, seeking input from others, and helping people build skills

The Reina trust model also looks at how trust is eroded through betrayals and how it is rebuilt. Betrayals are apparent or real breaches of trust. As Dennis says, "Betrayal comes with trust; it is part of the human condition" (Reina and Reina,

2006, p. 110). So rebuilding trust after breaches becomes as important as creating it in the first place. It is an ongoing effort.

The Reinas' model envisions a number of steps in rebuilding trust, including:

1. Observing and acknowledging what has happened

2. Allowing feelings about the breach to surface

3. Getting support from a friend or trusted colleague to address the feelings

4. Reframing the experience to look for lessons that can come from it

5. Taking responsibility for your part in the matter

6. Forgiving yourself and others

7. Letting go and moving on

We're very pleased that Dennis and Michelle were able to share the following selection from their work.

DEVELOPING COMMUNICATION TRUST: LAYING THE FOUNDATION OF SAFETY TO DEAL WITH CONFLICT

At work, I cannot always honestly share my thoughts and feelings. I'm afraid of what will happen if I do. I have developed a tendency to say what I think they want me to say rather than how I truly feel. This isn't the way I want to be or how others generally see me, but this is how I feel safest in my current work environment. As long as I am professional and considerate in expressing my opinions, there shouldn't be any negative consequences, but unfortunately, this is not always the case.

I would like management to provide a process where people can voice their concerns, feelings, and needs safely. Recognize the need to openly talk about the issues and work them through. Allow employees to speak with supervisors and with one another without retribution. People listening and talking with one another without prejudging or overreacting—this is what creates trust in the workplace!

Do we communicate openly and honestly? Do we create safe forums or work environments in which people are encouraged to express their concerns or voice their feelings without our prejudging them, making assumptions, or overreacting? Can employees speak the truth without fear of retribution? Particularly in times of change, people yearn for straightforward communication and need it from their leaders and one another. If people don't tell the truth, trust can't grow. This is particularly important in today's global economy, where honesty is highly valued worldwide.

Experience shows that when the truth goes by the wayside, trust diminishes. People's natural openness is replaced by sarcasm and cynicism. Regardless of how savvy we may be in spinning the truth, others detect when they are receiving anything less than the full truth. Partial truth creates a betrayal that may take a great deal of time to overcome.

Truth telling is the foundation for trust in an organization, and it is essential for resolving conflict. Telling the truth often takes courage, and employees look to their leaders to create a safe environment in order to have those "courageous conversations." Especially in times of change, employees need their leaders to scrupulously and unflinchingly tell the truth—and nothing but the truth.

Because trust and honesty go together, a leader's behavior is crucial in building trust and fostering honest communication. Through their behavior, leaders can facilitate discussion of problems and concerns and work toward resolving conflict by responding in a nonjudgmental and engaging way. In so doing, they role model this behavior for employees. Having the straight story and accurate information helps employees make better decisions, take the initiative to assume responsibility, be more productive, and make a strong contribution to the organization.

Individuals demonstrate a commitment to their relationships when they express their true thoughts and feelings about each other in a timely and appropriate manner. As one production worker on the shop floor of a northeastern manufacturing plant exclaimed to another, "If you ever get teed off at me, I want you to tell me. I'm a big boy. I can handle it." Or as an office worker exclaimed in a one-on-one communication session, "I don't know how to read you at times, and if I get upset with you, I shut up. That's not good. We need to talk things through with each other as they come up. We need to build on the trust we have had and keep building on it!"

Giving each other effective feedback contributes to developing and maintaining trusting relationships that directly affect performance. To give feedback effectively, we need to be willing to receive it in return—nondefensively. When receiving feedback, we need to listen to the intent of what people are saying rather than think of a comeback or response. We need to make an effort to show genuine interest in what we are hearing. Leaders support building this environment of trust around feedback by giving and receiving it themselves consistently.

In receiving constructive feedback, people may find it difficult to trust themselves and others. They may not trust the messenger because of their low readiness to trust or because they are not convinced that the messenger is genuinely interested in their well-being. (For example, their manager tells everyone he has an open-door policy and that anything can be shared in confidence, but then takes punitive action against anyone who complains about anything.) Another problem might be that instead of hearing the issues presented, they cloud their perspective by consciously or unconsciously revisiting their past or bringing up prior mistakes they have made. They have difficulty separating the past from the present, possibly because they have unresolved issues.

Trust develops when people feel comfortable and safe enough to share their perceptions regarding one another's behavior without negative repercussions. They trust that they will not suffer the consequences of retaliation because they spoke the truth.

Working constructively with feedback helps develop our readiness and willingness to trust in ourselves and in others. From this perspective, feedback is a gift—to those giving it and to those receiving it. Either way, when given with positive intentions and practiced skill, honest feedback helps us grow and develop, and nurtures communication trust.

Application Exercises

The following exercises are designed to develop, measure, and monitor trust within your team. When practiced with conscious positive intent, they create a foundation of psychological safety (trust) that will facilitate team members' ability to discuss and deal with conflict issues as they arise in the workplace.

Pretest/Post-Test: Team Communication Trust Quiz The Reina Team Communication Trust Quiz is intended to facilitate dialogue within a team. Reflect on how you and your teammates practice each of the behaviors that create communication trust. The quiz is presented as Exhibit 5.1. Rate each question on a scale of 1–5 (1 = low, 5 = high).

Note: This quiz was excerpted from the statistically valid and reliable Reina Team Trust Scale®. While the quiz is not the equivalent of this rigorously proven instrument, it will give you a starting point for dialogue within your team.

Exhibit 5.1
The Reina Communication Trust Quiz™

HOW WELL DOES YOUR *TEAM* PRACTICE BEHAVIORS THAT BUILD TRUST?

TAKE A FEW MOMENTS TO EVALUATE

LEGEND:		*1*	*2*	*3*	*4*	*5*
(1) Almost Never (AN)		*AN*	*O*	*ST*	*F*	*AA*
(2) Occasionally (O)						
(3) Some of the Time (ST)						
(4) Frequently (F)						
(5) Almost Always (AA)						
1.	Do we willingly share job-related information with one another that is pertinent to getting the job done?	❏	❏	❏	❏	❏
2.	Do we openly and honestly tell the truth with each other?	❏	❏	❏	❏	❏
3.	Do we openly admit and take responsibility for the mistakes we have made?	❏	❏	❏	❏	❏

(continued)

4.	Do we give each other constructive feedback to help each other grow in our jobs?	❏	❏	❏	❏	❏
5.	Do we speak our minds even when others disagree?	❏	❏	❏	❏	❏
6.	Do we receive constructive feedback from each other without getting defensive?	❏	❏	❏	❏	❏
7.	Do we appropriately maintain confidential information?	❏	❏	❏	❏	❏
8.	Are we able to bring up concerns and talk through issues with one another without fear of retribution?	❏	❏	❏	❏	❏
9.	Do we discourage gossiping or participation in unfair criticism about other people?	❏	❏	❏	❏	❏
10.	Do we speak directly to the person with whom we may have an issue or concern?	❏	❏	❏	❏	❏

SCORING

Add up all your scores for the above questions to come up with your score of the team.

The highest possible score is 50, and the lowest would be 10. The higher the score, the greater you perceive your team practices trust-building behaviors, and the greater the likelihood the team has effective working relationships.

Your team practices trust-building behaviors . . .

10 . . . Almost never. There is serious room for improvement!

11 to 19 . . . Occasionally, which damages trust within the team.

20 to 29 . . . Some of the time, which does not build sustainable trust.

30 to 39 . . . Frequently, and most likely has effective working relationships.

40 to 50 . . . Almost always, and is probably viewed as a highly effective team.

Source: Excerpted from the *Reina Team Trust Scale*® ©1995–2009 Dennis S. Reina, Ph.D., and Michelle L. Reina, Ph.D. The Reina Trust Building Institute, Inc. www.ReinaTrustBuilding.com.

One-on-One Team Communication Trust Meetings   This exercise is intended to facilitate communication trust within a group or team. This process is effective in dealing with interpersonal issues that impede communication and performance within a group. Construct a matrix of all the participants in the group so that every person has an opportunity to have a one-on-one meeting with everyone else. Set up one- to two-hour meetings. (Refer to the communication matrix in Exhibit 5.2 as a sample.)

Have participants speak candidly to one another about how they interact and work together. You may use the following sentences to add structure to the meeting. Have each person reflect on these in preparation for the meetings with each of their teammates.

- What I appreciate about you is . . .
- What works in our relationship is . . .
- What doesn't work in our relationship is . . .
- What I need from you is . . .
- Let's brainstorm together ways in which we can work together better.

This exercise works with groups as small as four individuals or as large as twelve. For larger groups, you might want to divide the participants into subgroups to expedite the process.

If there is low trust or antagonism within the group, it is advisable to lead these sessions with a skilled facilitator who does not have a relationship with any of the participants. It is important to conduct the sessions in a confined time frame to achieve optimum results. We strongly suggest that team members contract with one another before the sessions start to keep these conversations confidential. Establish working agreements ahead of time to ensure the psychological safety of the participants.

Team Reflection/Dialogue Exercise   The following questions are intended to facilitate dialogue as a team after conducting the one-on-one Team Communication Trust Meetings. Reflect on the following

Exhibit 5.2
Sample Matrix for Team Communication Meeting

Communication Matrix

Purpose: To facilitate the logistics of everyone participating in this communication exercise

Participants:

1. Harry	5. Rachel
2. Maria	6. Jackson
3. Carlos	7. Joanne
4. Lee	

Process: The participants will speak to each other in the prescribed rounds during the following weeks:

	May 7–9	May 12–16		May 19–23		May 26–30	
Rounds	**1**	**2**	**3**	**4**	**5**	**6**	**7**
Participants:	1 and 7	1 and 6	1 and 5	1 and 4	1 and 3	1 and 2	2 and 7
	2 and 6	2 and 5	2 and 4	2 and 3	6 and 5	6 and 4	6 and 3
	3 and 5	3 and 4	7 and 6	7 and 5	7 and 4	7 and 3	5 and 4

Example:
During the week of May 7–9, the following people talk with each other:

Harry and Joanne
Maria and Jackson
Carlos and Rachel

behaviors that create communication trust. Share those thoughts with your teammates. Notice the attitude and tenor of teammates toward one another.

1. *Share information.* How willingly do you share information with others? Do you receive the information you need? What happens to your communication trust when you don't? What can you do in the future to share information at a high level and encourage others to share with you?

2. *Tell the truth.* Do others tell you the truth? What happens to your level of trust when you question the truthfulness of others? What can you do to encourage more truth telling both by you and by others?

3. *Admit mistakes.* Are you willing to admit your mistakes? What happens when you do admit mistakes? What do you do when others admit their mistakes? What can you do to support the admission of mistakes within your organization?

4. *Give and receive constructive feedback.* How do giving and receiving constructive feedback contribute to communication trust in your organization? What can you do in the future to encourage constructive feedback?

5. *Maintain confidentiality.* How do you decide what to share and what to hold back? How do you balance this behavior with the need to share information?

6. *Speak with good purpose.* How do people speak of each other in your organization? Do they speak respectfully of others, or is there a lot of gossiping and backbiting? What can you do to promote speaking with good purpose in your organization?

TRUST NOTE

Trust influences communication, and communication influences trust. The two are very closely related. Leaders who readily and consistently share information and involve employees in the running of the business not only build trust within the organization but also boost productivity and profitability.

TRUST TIP

When we gossip, criticize, and shun others, we destroy trust between individuals, within a team, and throughout an organization. The consequences are devastating to relationships, morale, and performance. Conversely, when we speak with good purpose, speak constructively and affirmatively, and stand up for each other, we build trust, strengthen relationships, boost morale, and improve performance.

Trust Norms

During a presentation about team conflict competence, Tim and I were discussing the importance of developing norms around the various elements of creating the right climate. When we came to trust, one of the participants said, "You can't legislate trust." He was right!

Trust is something that has to be built and maintained. At the same time, it is important to recognize its importance, and we believe that this can be a part of a team agreement. It might look like, "Trust plays a crucial role in enabling our team to openly and honestly discuss issues. We work on building trust among team members."

Perhaps more important would be the inclusion of norms about how to handle breaches of trust. They could include something like, "When trust is betrayed among team members, it becomes more challenging to talk about difficult issues. Therefore, we agree not to use what one of our team members has said against them either inside or outside of the team. If we have a problem with what someone said, we will talk directly to that person about it. If someone hears a colleague talking behind another team member's back or using what they have said against that person, they will approach the colleague about it. This applies to the team leader and all team members."

The team norms could also address how to rebuild trust after breaches. They might say, "If there has been a breach of trust, team members will discuss the matter and work on rebuilding trust among the team members. They will also talk about how to prevent the problem in the future."

Once norms are established, they need to be periodically reviewed, and they should be shared with new members as they join the team.

Collaboration (Behavioral Integration)

When team members work together collaboratively, they not only increase their chances of success, they also build a sense of "teamness" that can help them deal with conflict more effectively. Researchers describe this process of mutual and collaborative interaction as "behavioral integration." Behavioral integration consists of three key elements, including high degrees of information sharing, collaborative behavior, and collective decision making (Hambrick, 1998). It has been shown to improve decision-making quality and to improve a team's ability to deal with conflict (Carmeli and Schaubroeck, 2006; Mooney, Holahan, and Amason, 2007).

When team members know teammates well and feel that the group is truly working together toward a common goal, they can give others the benefit of a doubt when conflicts emerge. While differences may occur, they remain confident that everyone has the team's best interests in mind, rather than just their own.

So how does a team become more behaviorally integrated? We recommend starting by helping the team get a sense of its current level of "teamness." We ask the team questions like:

1. How well is information shared among team members? There are a number of components of this inquiry. Does the team leader share information with all members of the team? Is information shared with members of subgroups but not with everyone? Are some people purposely kept out of the loop?

In behaviorally integrated teams, information is shared widely. All team members are kept in the know. This heightens trust and enables everyone to participate on an equal information footing when important issues are discussed. If information is not shared, cliques can form and suspicions can be raised.

To improve behavioral integration, the team should adopt a norm that encourages processes that ensure that team members are brought up to date on new information and that efforts are made to keep everyone in the loop on key information. When in doubt, assume that the information should be shared.

2. Does the team discuss issues in depth? Is input sought from all members of the team on common issues? Collaborative decision making is a hallmark of a behaviorally integrated team. Team leaders should make efforts to get everyone's input on key issues. This can be difficult especially when some members are introverted or shy away from conflict. It may require individual discussions or even asking for comments in written form.

When one asks for input, it is certainly possible to encounter conflict because people can have differing opinions. Yet, as long as communications can be kept constructive, these kinds of differences can lead to helpful debate and better-quality decisions. Seeking input does not mean that the team leader has to abrogate decision-making responsibility. Rather, the leader needs to get team members involved in thinking issues through and working toward consensus. In terms of norms, a team should look at its decision-making processes and incorporate methods for ensuring input from all team members. The norms should also encourage respect for differing opinions, even when there may not be agreement on the substance of them. When people feel that they have the opportunity to present their opinions and have them heard by their teammates, they are more likely to go along with whatever final decision is made.

3. Do team members work interdependently with one another? The essence of behaviorally integrated teams is that people work together and feel that they are "in this together." If team members have little interaction with one another and operate independently from one another, there is a risk that when conflict arises they will not have confidence that they will be able to work through it. When they work closely with one another, they get to know one another better and can see that they are working toward a common end. This may be why teams with high levels of behavioral integration can outperform other teams with technically more talented members who lack a sense of togetherness. It is also why "All-Star" teams often fall short of their potential.

We also have teams look at other elements that can contribute to behavioral integration such as team identity, team makeup, and reward structures. Something as simple as giving a team a name can help create a sense of identity. If this were the only step, it would fall short, but it can be a helpful addition. Teams need gradual turnover to keep things fresh, but if done too frequently or rapidly it could disturb the cohesion that has developed. When reinforcing performance, there should be an emphasis on collective rewards and celebration rather than a focus on the individual. If more emphasis is put on individual performance and rewards, people may feel suspicious of others' motives when conflicts arise, and this can complicate their resolution.

When developing norms related to behavioral integration, teams should emphasize that team success is of paramount importance. Specific norms support this premise and emphasize information sharing, working together collaboratively, making decisions together by seeking everyone's input, and sharing both responsibilities and rewards. When conflicts emerge, team members agree to share information with one another (and not withhold important points), listen carefully and respectfully to everyone's input, and make decisions that are in the best interests of the team and that also try to reconcile the interests of the team members.

We talked with Professor Ann Mooney, from Stevens Institute of Technology, whose research includes the field of behavioral integration. According to Professor Mooney, one of the key benefits of behavioral integration to team conflicts involves improved attitudes toward one another among team members. When people recognize through experience that the other members of their team indeed have the interests of the team ahead of their own personal interests, then they're willing to give the others the benefit of the doubt when conflict arises (Craig, conversation with Ann Mooney, May 19, 2009). They're willing to put aside suspicions and negative attributions more easily. This, in turn, leads to more willingness to listen to the other person, understand where he or she is coming from, and collaborate to find solutions to the problems.

In virtual team settings, behavioral integration becomes even more important because the opportunities to speak face to face are fewer. It often requires more work on the front end to develop norms for how the team will work together in virtual team settings. In particular, teams need to develop norms around communications processes that enhance their ability to share information and work more closely together to build behavioral integration.

Teams can enhance their behavioral integration by promoting open exchange and developing norms that enable all members to participate equally—ensuring equal airtime. This includes making sure that leaders don't assert too much authority or presence in meetings in which joint decision making is the goal. Sometimes the use of external facilitators can help in this process (Craig, conversation with Ann Mooney, May 19, 2009).

Emotional Intelligence and Team Conflict

In Chapter Three we discussed the importance of being able to regulate emotions in the context of individual conflict competence. Emotional intelligence also plays a crucial role in team conflict competence. Emotions affect individual members of a team and can spread to other members as well. The term *emotional contagion* describes the phenomenon in which the feelings of one person can be "caught" by others. One part of our brain called *mirror neurons* enables us to read other people and feel similar kinds of emotions (Hotz, 2007). This happens automatically and typically occurs outside our normal awareness (Goleman, 2003).

Emotional intelligence in teams includes the components of individual emotional intelligence plus norms that help govern the social interactions of the team (Rapisarda, 2002). It also helps reinforce other aspects of the right climate, including trust and behavioral integration (Rapisarda, 2002; Prati and others, 2003). When people are able to regulate their emotions in team settings, they can prevent outbursts that lead to suspicions and divisiveness.

We particularly like the work of Marcia Hughes and James Terrell in this field. Their book, *The Emotionally Intelligent Team* (Hughes and Terrell, 2007), describes a number of elements or skills that are important for developing emotional and social intelligence in teams. These include:

- *Developing a team identity*: Having a common purpose, commitment, and pride in the team
- *Motivation*: Creating and harnessing the drive that enables teams to execute
- *Emotional awareness*: Ability to read one another and respond to how others feel
- *Communications*: Being able to talk and listen effectively to one another
- *Stress tolerance*: Building strong relationships to overcome challenges
- *Conflict resolution*: Developing capabilities to address the inevitable conflicts that teams face
- *Positive mood*: Cultivating happiness about today and optimism about tomorrow—encourages a can-do attitude, curiosity, and hopefulness

Marcia and James have developed an assessment instrument called the Team Emotional and Social Intelligence® Survey (TESI®) that measures these seven areas and provides valuable insights to teams about their current strengths and areas for improvement. We are happy that Marcia was able to provide the following story and tips that help illustrate the significance of team emotional intelligence.

USING EMOTIONAL INTELLIGENCE TO RESOLVE TEAM CONFLICT

A woman I'll call Sandra became the team leader and member of the senior team at a nonprofit foundation. Sandra is accomplished and committed to doing her work well. She is inclined to be task oriented and reserved; Sandra loves to analyze, strategize, and make good plans. These skills have served her well in the past, and she has repeatedly been successful. However, she walked into a Trouble Team, truly with a capital T, when she took on her new role heading this team. The organization was only a decade old, and at the beginning all staff had had a fairly strong role in making hiring and policy decisions. That changed over time, and the staff is asked to fulfill their team roles but they no longer have a role in top decisions. This loss of power caused considerable resentment among the people who have been involved from the beginning, and they willingly spread that resentment to any new hires. The team had managed to get their last two leaders fired, and Sandra could see that they were aiming for her to be the next one on the firing block.

It was time for intervention, so we were brought in to work with the CEO, Sandra, and the team. We had every team member take two assessments at the beginning, the EQ-I, an individual measure of emotional intelligence skills, and the Team Emotional and Social Intelligence® Survey (TESI®). The results provided good data to support the intervention. We created the TESI at Collaborative Growth in order to help teams self-assess and understand how well they function in seven behaviors required for team success: team identity, motivation, emotional awareness, communication, stress tolerance, conflict resolution, and positive mood.

We worked to open the team members' eyes so they would recognize the costs of their conflict and revise their engagement. This team's function is to help give away money to excellent causes and support the recipients in using the money successfully. Thus they have strong motivation to do a good job. The team members were feeling many emotions: passion for their work, love for their clients, jealousy that they had lost some of their job functions, and annoyed and resentful that a new team leader was coming in when many of them had been there from the start. This manifested in gossip and an overall negative spirit.

Sandra was a good match for the team with her intellect, connections, and organizational skills. However, her reserve and straightforward intellectual approach alienated many team members who thought focusing on the human side was most important. As a result, she was accused of favoritism; team members kept information from her and just weren't good team players. She was quickly on her way to her first career failure.

The team's TESI report showed they were very strong in positive mood and motivation, and they were struggling with emotional awareness and conflict resolution. They decided to start building their skills by using their strengths to guide their interactions. Taking time to stop and be grateful for their great jobs and the tremendous results they help facilitate opened the door to finding the flexibility to shift their behavior and expand their skills in other areas. They took time naming all that they appreciate and then moved on to developing their emotional awareness, one of their challenged skills. They knew expanding their skills in being aware of one another and intending to be sensitive and responsive would provide a good foundation for being able to resolve conflict better.

They worked on building their demonstration of emotional awareness in several ways. One was to drop notes in a community bowl throughout the week whenever they saw someone doing something well. Sandra then pulled the notes out and read them at the beginning of the weekly team meeting. This concrete positive engagement changed the tenor of their meetings, creating a much more open environment that supported creative problem solving. It diminished the conflict and helped the team resolve disagreements more readily when they did arise.

Another key contribution to the team's progress is that Sandra realized she needed to change her limited and moderate engagement with the staff if they were to connect with her and build trust. She practiced using this formula several times a day: "I feel ___ because ___." For example, Sandra might say, "I feel worried because our grantees are so stressed in this economy. And therefore, we need to take on more support roles." The difference in using both sentences instead of just telling the team to take on more jobs was equivalent to the difference between night and day. When they heard that she cared, they knew they were sharing a common purpose. They immediately began to creatively find ways to provide that additional support.

After several months of committed work, telling the truth to one another, and everyone taking responsibility for his or her engagement in the team, the team made substantial progress. They took the TESI again, and we ran a pre/post comparison of their results. Every area showed significant progress, which motivated the team to keep up their good work.

Practice Tips and Information

- Good data from the team members themselves helps them quickly take an honest look at what is happening. Excellent assessments to use are the Conflict Dynamics Profile, www.conflictdynamics.org, and the Team Emotional and Social Intelligence® Survey (TESI®), www.EITeams.com. The individual measurement of emotional intelligence through the EQi® adds in strong additional data, www.mhsassessments.com.

- Plan on conducting pre- and post-analysis with the team so they know their progress will be measured. It builds motivation and accountability.

- Emotional and social intelligence is data—trying to operate without taking advantage of that potent information hurts success and sustainability of any results accomplished. The root word for emotions and for motivation is the same Latin word—*emovare*—and it means "to move." To resolve conflict, teams must know how they are feeling and why at the individual and at the team levels if they are to get to the root cause and effectively find the way to move forward. When they do move, they are successfully using their emotional data along with the other data and are on their way to sustainable results.

Norms and Team Emotional Intelligence

Organizations usually ignore emotional aspects of conflict. It is as though they have a large sign on the front door that reads, "Leave your emotions outside." Of course, people don't leave their feelings outside, and when conflict emerges so do their emotions. Unless teams have spent time talking about how they want to address emotions as they arise, they will be unprepared to deal with the consequences. We believe that team agreements should expressly address how the team wants to deal with emotions. An agreement could include some of the following:

- Expressed acknowledgment that team members will experience emotions around conflict and that this is normal

- Recognition that suppressing or hiding emotions does not work well, because they will fester and usually come out later in harmful ways

- Appreciation that emotions convey important information about conflict, including the degree to which people care about certain issues

- Learning to regulate emotions so that individuals do not act when they are in the grip of negative emotions

- The right to call a time-out to let things cool down before proceeding

- Encouragement to share their thoughts *and* feelings about conflict issues and to listen for the thoughts and feelings of others

- Creating and maintaining a positive mood in the team as a helpful antidote to negative emotions when they arise

An interesting norming application related to group emotions can be found in the works of Buddhist monk and author, Thich Nhat Hanh. During a conversation with Fred Eppsteiner of the Florida Community of Mindfulness, Fred mentioned Thich's Peace Treaty, which was originally used to help manage conflicts in monastic settings (Thich, 1992, 2002). In this agreement (or set of norms), people are encouraged to not suppress anger and at the same time refrain from acting on it until there is a chance to talk with the other person in the conflict. There is a call for using mindfulness techniques like those described in Chapter Three and self-reflection to recognize one's own contribution to the conflict. This is then followed by apologies where appropriate and conversation about the conflict when emotions have sufficiently cooled. Although the principles mentioned in the Peace Treaty were developed for monastic settings, we find that they are adaptable to workplace settings.

CONSTRUCTIVE COMMUNICATION

The components of constructive engagement we discussed in detail in Chapter Four are applicable and useful in both individual and team conflict situations. However, when focusing exclusively on team conflict, we emphasize some of the constructive communication behaviors in a different way than when we focus exclusively on individual conflicts.

Most obviously, in team conflict the number of perspectives grows with each additional member on the team. In addition, the complexity of relationships skyrockets on teams. For instance, the way two people interact when alone may be very different from the way they interact when they are around teammates or other people. The relationship between every pair of teammates becomes a study in complexity depending on which other teammates are around. Add a vast diversity of situations and context to the mix, and soon you have a recipe for an extraordinarily complex soup!

In our model illustrating the components of building conflict competent teams (Figure 5.1), we identify five discrete aspects of constructive communications:

1. Reflective thinking and delayed responding
2. Listening for understanding
3. Perspective taking
4. Expressing emotions
5. Techniques for staying on track

In our model illustrating the behavioral components of engaging constructively (see Figure 5.2) we identify four discrete behavioral categories:

1. Reaching out or initiating contact
2. Perspective taking and listening for understanding
3. Expressing thoughts, emotions, and interests
4. Searching for collaborative solutions

There's no surprise that there is significant overlap across these components. The differences are illustrative of the nuances of addressing conflict between two people versus conflict among team members. For instance, the use of techniques for staying on track is much more compatible with teams than for individuals.

We shall briefly review each behavioral component of constructive communication covered in Chapter Four as it applies to team conflict. Later in the chapter, we provide a comprehensive description of techniques teams can use to stay on track. In all cases, the focus is on how to best utilize these approaches and behaviors in a team context.

Reaching Out or Initiating Contact

Reaching out involves an overt attempt to begin or resume communications with a team member once a conflict has arisen. It includes the intent to repair emotional damage caused during the conflict. It may also include an apology, taking responsibility, or making amends.

Figure 5.2
Engage Constructively Model

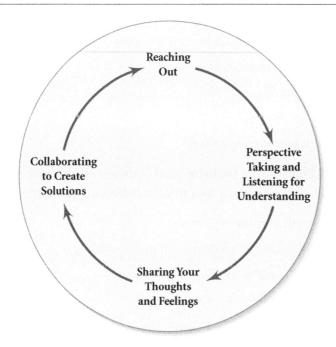

The act of reaching out in a team may carry even more weight than when used between two individuals. This is especially true when the act of reaching out occurs in the presence of the whole team. Once a conflict has occurred on a team, every member of the team is affected, not just those directly involved. In the same way, when a team member reaches out effectively, there is a clear impact on every team member. Sometimes one person's acknowledgment of the issue or issuance of an apology is all it takes to initiate a veritable avalanche of similar sentiments from other team members.

Our colleague, Dan Dana, suggests an effective process for reaching out. When conflict has turned dysfunctional and people stop talking, Dan recommends setting up a time to hold a meeting to talk about how to resolve the conflict. This sounds easy enough, but it can be tricky. This is where having a framework can be helpful.

Setting up a meeting consists of several steps. These include getting the other person's attention, identifying the issue that you want to talk about, asking the other person to join you in talking about the problem, addressing any objections they may have to talking, setting a time and place for having the meeting, and agreeing to some ground rules for the session.

Identifying the issue entails creating an unbiased, objective, specific, resolvable, and concise *statement* that can be shared with the other person. When people articulate effective issue statements, their efforts to reach out are greatly enhanced. The components of such a statement are as follows:

- *Unbiased* statements are impartial to both parties and *objective* ones refrain from blaming either person. Once people have cooled down sufficiently, they are usually able to craft unbiased, objective statements of the issue, although it can be difficult to present them in an unbiased and objective manner.

- *Specific* statements with clear language are critical. People seem to have difficulty actually describing the problem in terms that the other person understands. The circumstances typically contribute to this challenge. People have stopped talking because they are upset with one another and generally blame the other person for the difficulties they are experiencing.

- *Resolvable* relates to issues that people have the authority to fix by themselves. If the problem is one that the parties cannot resolve on their own, the participants may need to reach out to a third party for help.

- *Concise* statements are brief ones that address the other elements. One risk of having a long statement is that it can get into so many facts that it makes people want to start arguing about the conflict at a time when they are just trying to set up a later time to talk.

While the elements of an effective issue statement are easy to understand, they can be quite difficult to master. When we work with people on reaching out, we frequently have them create and test out issue statements. We present Dan's model and then use sample conflict scenarios to allow the participants to practice. The steps we use include:

1. Choose a sample conflict scenario. We suggest that you work with your client to develop sample situations. This is particularly helpful when your client feels that their workplace has unique challenges.

2. Have everyone in the small groups start by developing their own issue statement related to the common conflict scenario, emphasizing that it exhibit the five characteristics: unbiased, objective, specific, ability to be resolved by the parties, and concise.

3. Ask the participants in each group to share their individual statements. The group then picks one statement to use as its starting point. From there the group works collaboratively to improve the statement, again checking it against the five qualities.

4. Once all the groups are finished, have each one present its statement and write it down on a flip chart so that they are visible to everyone. The whole group comments on the effective aspects of each statement. Afterward the whole group makes suggestions about how the various issue statements could be improved.

5. Repeat the process for a second time using a different conflict scenario. You should find that all of the groups do a much better job of creating issue statements the second time around.

If participants are able to develop effective issue statements, they usually get better responses from their conflict partners. People involved do not feel attacked or blamed. They may still have objections, but they will be less likely to feel attacked.

A good issue statement does not guarantee success, though. The other parties may still harbor negative emotions about the conflict and may blame the person who is reaching out. The prospect of rejection is one of the challenges of reaching out. If you experience rejection, we suggest trying again. This involves addressing objections to talking and continuing to try to "make the sale" of going forward with a meeting to try to work things out. This includes acknowledging the other person's objection, showing why going ahead with a meeting would benefit both parties, and making the request again.

Perspective Taking and Listening for Understanding

Perspective taking and listening for understanding are very simply the most critical behaviors for handling conflict competently. The descriptions and suggestions made in Chapter Four are very useful for addressing conflict on teams. Again, because the sheer number of possible perspectives rises dramatically with the number of team members involved, so too does the potential for more complexity and confusion. But with more perspectives also comes the potential for a greater variety of solutions.

We often use synergy or consensus-seeking exercises in our workshops or interventions with teams. The purpose of these exercises is to demonstrate the power of collaborative problem solving. Tim has created an exercise specifically for use with teams experiencing conflict titled "Last Gasp Gorge." Others are available in the public domain or for purchase through a variety of vendors. (See the Resources section for suggestions.) Each challenges participants to consider a list of items or steps and place them in a rank order based on a level of importance or the sequence necessary to address a particular issue or challenge. Next, the participants form groups and try to reach a consensus rank order for the same items. The debriefing discussion upon completion highlights the ways the team interacted with specific focus on the use of constructive and destructive behaviors.

When we wish to emphasize perspective taking or listening for understanding during these exercises, we closely monitor the way groups elect to share information or use processes to guide their interaction. For instance, when teams simply agree on processes that focus on the ranked items ("Let's agree on the top three first, then go to the bottom three, and finish by focusing on the items in the middle"), they often produce an orderly, polite discussion and seemingly agreeable solution. However, when teams decide on a process that invites each person to share their rationale for approaching the challenge as a first step, perspective taking is immediately enhanced. The resulting discussion is often more animated and deep. Participants appreciate being heard. More possibilities are debated. And in many instances, the final decision is described as a commitment, not just an answer.

In cases where you wish to provide practice at perspective taking, include the presentation of each person's rationale in your directions to the team. Then include specific questions during the facilitated debriefing discussion upon the conclusion of the exercise. Some sample questions:

- How did the presentation of each person's rationale in the very beginning influence the nature of your decision-making process?

- What was your reaction to the variety of rationales and perspectives?

- When there were differences of opinion or approach, how did the group proceed?

- Did you change your mind during the exercise? Why? What caused you to change?

- What learning can you apply from this exercise when difficult challenges or conflicting views arise on your team?

In our estimation, there is virtually no limit to the amount of practice one can provide to teams for perspective taking. Time after time, teams that demonstrate effective listening for understanding and perspective taking are the teams that find the greatest value in the natural conflicts they encounter.

Expressing Emotions, Thoughts, and Interests

One way to think about the effective expression of emotions, thoughts, and interests on a team is to imagine a continuum of behaviors (see Figure 5.3). On one end is displaying anger and winning at all costs. A team member behaving like this is relentless in trying to get his or her own way. He may raise his voice, be prone to angry outbursts, swear, and threaten. On the other end is avoiding and hiding emotions. A person behaving this way withdraws or yields. He may become silent or detached during the conflict discussion. Sometimes she simply nods in veiled agreement just to put an end to the conflict. In between these extremes is expressing emotions, thoughts, and feelings effectively. The key to effectiveness is in the expressing.

We often describe this behavior as open, honest communication. While this may seem much too simple a definition, for many individuals it is anything but simple to accomplish in the midst of a conflict on a team. When team members are skilled at expressing their emotions, thoughts, and interests effectively, the discussions of conflicting ideas and issues can become spirited without resulting in hurt feelings. However, when dealing with difficult issues, many of us often hide our true feelings from our teammates. Unfortunately, this can lead to unexpected surges of emotion in the form of lashing out, shutting down, or demeaning others. Before we know it, the entire team is at one end of the continuum or the other, demoralized in silence or embroiled in argument. At either extreme, the conflict is left unresolved and the team climate is at least temporarily in shambles. A far better choice is for team members to develop skills to effectively express their emotions, thoughts, and interests.

One common suggestion we make to teams involves legitimizing such expressions when conflict arises. In other words, we encourage teams to discuss how they will handle conflict as they establish team agreements or norms. Unfortunately,

Figure 5.3
Continuum of Behaviors

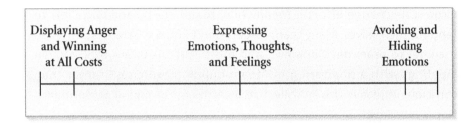

| Displaying Anger and Winning at All Costs | Expressing Emotions, Thoughts, and Feelings | Avoiding and Hiding Emotions |

our experience is that most teams do not have these kinds of process and expectation discussions early enough in their existence. So when conflict does occur, they are often ill equipped to handle it.

In the section "Getting and Staying on Track" later in the chapter, we present a variety of exercises and activities that lend themselves to competency in sharing emotions, thoughts, and interests. As good as these are, exercises and processes are just vehicles for expression. The key to being able to express thoughts, emotions, and interests is that the trust level on the team supports and enables it. Only when the right climate exists can team members be expected to willingly express themselves in ways that may make them vulnerable.

Common Vocabulary Aids Dialogue   In addition to trust, a common frame of reference for discussing conflict helps. Mark Nevins, a consultant and coach in New York, shares his experience using the CDP instrument as a means for promoting dialogue.

Our work with executive and senior teams usually goes well beyond typical "team-building events." We approach team building not simply as a time-out to talk about and fine-tune interpersonal dynamics (though those do matter), but as a holistic opportunity to improve the team's overall alignment among its members and in the context of its specific near-term business goals as well as its longer-term mission and purpose. We see the team as the fundamental social unit of any organization. Ironically, however, most of the investment (time and money) in organizations is spent on *individual* development (executive education and coaching) or *organizational* initiatives (transformation projects and large-scale change efforts). Meanwhile, teams are by and large left to fend for themselves. Many team leaders don't know where to start when it comes to team development, and most "off-sites" are topic-driven meetings with a smattering of "team-building exercises" rather than conscious objective-driven collective investments in taking performance to the next level.

Most of our team alignment engagements take place via a series of team activities over the course of six to nine months, in situations when a new leader is on-boarding, when some significant change (organizational or strategic) has taken place, or when a team decides it has reached a sticking point or state of inertia that it needs to push through. Team alignment sessions challenge teams to take a close look at where they are, where they need to go, and how they can best get there. The teams discover if they share the same priorities; they assess their current state, for good and for bad; they create tangible action plans to improve performance; and they make meaningful commitments to critical issues, including better focus on execution, improving decision making, a more disciplined development of talent, and more effective communication and collaboration with stakeholders.

In the context of our work with teams, we have found the CDP a powerful tool not just for improving conflict resolution but also for enhancing fundamental team functionality. Used as part of a team alignment program, the CDP can create self-awareness and openness that foster a more productive working-through of the issues at hand. But we also encourage the participants to use the CDP feedback to think more broadly about improving their ability to foster more effective *dialogue.* We believe that the ability to foster dialogue is one of the most critical skills for any leader or manager. However, this skill is not effectively taught in universities or business schools and rarely gets meaningful attention in executive development programs. An unwillingness or inability to foster dialogue—and, in turn, to engage the necessary range of stakeholders, effect collaboration, and make people feel as if they are partners—is a significant "derailer" for many executives. Indeed, if one examines the careers of leaders who have failed, often it was an insufficient degree of dialogue that led to their downfall. This lack of dialogue manifests itself as not appreciating the needs of constituents; failing to see the broader strategic landscape; shutting down critical feedback or input; mistaking collaboration opportunities for competition; and projecting a hubristic persona of not needing others in order to succeed.

We use the CDP (either CDP-I or CDP-360, depending on the situation and development objectives) as a means to engage leaders and team members in the arts of asking questions, listening, and building relationships. While there are many models and theories about what makes teams effective, all of them have in common the fact that good teams have open and honest communication, and good leaders (and followers) seek continually to improve the level and quality of dialogue with those around them.

Searching for Collaborative Outcomes

The essence of effective teamwork is displayed when teams tackle tough problems together. When teams apply to their conflicts the same problem-solving skills and processes they use to deal with their work-related challenges, collaborative outcomes are not only possible but expected. Unfortunately, many obstacles appear when teams experience conflict. The application of even the greatest problem-solving processes and skills too early in the process is almost always a recipe for failure. That's why searching for collaborative outcomes appears as the final part of our model. Teams must be fully prepared, having addressed many of the potential obstacles before beginning their search.

As we described in Chapter Four, we suggest that searching for collaborative outcomes is made up of three discrete but interrelated components. These include adapting, reflective thinking, and creating solutions. These focus primarily on the approaches and skills utilized by each team member. (The suggested exercises and activities in Chapter Four can all be used with teams. In fact, the Four-Letter Words Exercise is best used with teams and is one of our favorites for working on this competency with teams.)

When assessing a team's readiness for searching for collaborative outcomes, consider the following questions. The more "yesses," the better.

1. Do team members think of conflict as an inevitable part of being a team?

2. Are team members willing to consider a wide variety of approaches to problem solving?

3. Does the team welcome change?

4. Do team members demonstrate an awareness of the reactions of others?

5. Are team members cognizant of both the immediate and longer-term impact of conflict?

6. Do team members show an affinity for considering many alternatives?

7. Does the team regularly create multiple possible solutions to problems rather than finding the one best solution?

8. Do team members engage in open, honest debate of issues?

9. Once several possibilities are established, can the team objectively analyze each possibility?

10. Do team members willingly "put themselves out there" when discussing issues and problems?

One of the true tests of "teamness" is the team's ability to reach critical decisions in ways that not only result in good outcomes but provide a sense of satisfaction for the team members. In today's world full of ambiguous situations, impossible deadlines, complex issues, and ever-expanding technologies, teams must more than ever be comfortable with disagreement and conflict. At the end of the day, we advise teams to evaluate their performance not just on the "what" or the outcome, but also on the "how" or the ways in which they interacted to find collaborative solutions.

Expanding Participation Leads to Better Outcomes   When more people are involved in the search for solutions, creativity can be enhanced. When people feel involved and empowered, they are more willing to participate in implementation of decisions. The process can also reduce destructive conflicts that occur when people feel decisions on which they had no input are being forced on them.

Amanda Pace, an ombuds working in Atlanta, illustrates this point in her story.

It involves a department that was being restructured. Traditionally, decisions had been made by managers with very little input from employees. This approach had caused conflicts and made employees feel undervalued. So this time around, efforts were made to enable employees to take responsibility for aspects of the restructuring. In particular, team associates:

1. Defined the ground rules and procedures for their meetings
2. Outlined the process to get others' views of their ideas and suggestions
3. Sought to gain early approval from the more outspoken associates before presenting their final work to the department as a whole

Inside each team, the focus was on hearing each person's point of view and generating alternatives when agreement was an issue. All ideas and suggestions would have to be linked to the vision and goals. This approach helped to minimize conflict. Brainstorming sessions were held as well to build on a particular concept or idea. This allowed for every idea and suggestion to be explored, and no one person felt they were not being heard. Because the foundation of this department rests on "good communication skills," the associates used those skills to avoid personal attacks or judging each other as they offered ideas. People listened to each other with a high level of cooperation. Being part of the decision-making process gave the associates a level of engagement in the work and cooperation that propelled the work forward. The result of the work done by the teams contributed to a successful restructuring.

GETTING AND STAYING ON TRACK

The tools and techniques we review in this section represent a sampling of some of our favorites. We review them in a sequence related to the time they may be most useful. As discussed, we see conflict as an unfolding process that includes before, during, and after stages. The lines between each stage are admittedly rather blurry. Nevertheless, as we review each tool, we believe you'll see the progression and come to appreciate the unfolding nature of team conflict.

Before Conflict

The first three tools we describe are associated with "before conflict begins" or "as it is just beginning." In our experience, most teams never discuss in advance how they will handle conflict. In some ways this is surprising, as nearly everyone agrees that conflict is inevitable. Why not prepare for it? Perhaps the most common method for dealing with conflict is avoidance. Failing to create agreements or set norms for dealing with conflict is just another expression of our avoidance.

Teams that do take the time to establish norms or team agreements, especially early in their existence, are much better positioned for meeting the inevitable conflicts that emerge. We hope the following tools help you and your team take some proactive steps.

Reaching Team Agreements   We responded to a request from the executive team of a medical billing firm for "a day or two of team building." After a series of discussions, it became apparent that "team building" was code for "We need to learn to talk with each other when the stakes are high and we don't agree." Team members knew they needed help, but they didn't know what kind. A major portion of our intervention involved a review of the team's mission, key priorities, and agreements. The team was quite articulate about their mission and purpose. They were in almost complete agreement. Key priorities were equally clear and understood. When we asked about team agreements, it's fair to say that team members' faces went blank. It had simply never occurred to them that a discussion about standards of conduct, interaction, and behavior was needed. The process we used with this team to establish a set of team agreements is one we've used with great success. It's simple, thorough, and "tailorable" to fit almost any team's needs.

THE EIGHT-STEP METHOD FOR TEAM AGREEMENTS

Step 1: Review the Team's Mission and Context

- Ask the team to gather or create written statements regarding the team's charter, mission, and priorities.

- Seek mission, charter, and priorities information from the team's sponsor and/or customers.

- Share, discuss, and clarify all information with the team.

Note: This step may not take long, especially if there is general agreement among team members. It is, however, a mistake to assume shared, clear understanding of mission and priorities.

Step 2: Discuss the Desired Climate

- Ask team members to independently create "wish lists" consisting of words and phrases that describe the nature of the interactions they'd like to experience on the team.

- Ask team members to share their lists while one team member records the words and phrases publicly using a flip chart or computer with the screen projected and visible to all.

- If necessary, clarify the "why" behind descriptions that seem misunderstood or unclear.

- Encourage the team to create a comprehensive list.

Note: Sometimes we ask team members to comment on their most satisfying experiences on other teams. If the team has difficulty or seems reluctant to share, it can be helpful to ask for examples of the most successful teams they've seen and the climates they've noticed.

Step 3: Brainstorm Suggestions and Ideas for Creating the Desired Climate

- Post the descriptions of the desired climate (from step 2) in clear view of the participants.

- Remind participants of brainstorming guidelines (give everyone opportunities to be heard, record all items, resist debate and evaluation, and so on).

- Suggest that ideas and suggestions be phrased in behavioral or process terms. For instance, it's better to suggest that "team members shall assume positive intent of colleagues during discussions and debates" rather than "Be positive."

Step 4: Combine Similar Suggestions

- Invite participants to analyze all the ideas.
- Encourage the combination of suggestions to improve the efficiency of later steps.

Note. Caution team members not to "force" combinations. It's better to err on the side of keeping items distinct rather than collapsing discrete ideas together.

Step 5: Prioritize Suggestions

- Describe the goal or outcome of this step as reducing the length of the list to those items necessary and sufficient to support the desired climate created in step 2.
- Utilize appropriate classic brainstorming techniques for this step, such as each person gets *X* number of votes, and so on.
- Recommend a final list of between five and ten items.
- Display the description of the desired climate created in step 2 and refer to it often.

Note: During this step, we always encourage the creation of statements that specifically address how the team will handle conflict.

Step 6: "Behaviorize" the Remaining Items

- Remind participants that this step is about fine-tuning and bringing clarity to the agreements.
- Suggest the use of behavioral language and actionable descriptions.
- Simple, clear, concise agreements are best.

Note: When team members have difficulty using behavioral language, ask questions such as, "How would that look?" and "What would someone say or do to demonstrate that?"

Step 7: Record and Distribute the Resulting List for Review

- Set a time for the team to meet again to finalize their agreements.
- We recommend at least an overnight break for team members to review and reflect (this isn't always possible).

Step 8: Review and Finalize Agreements

- Each of the final draft agreements are posted and read aloud.
- Team members are asked for amendments or revisions to each.
- As each agreement is finalized, ask team members to verbally signify their commitment.
- Distribute final copies of the agreements to all team members.

Note: We recommend that teams periodically review their agreements. It is also helpful to establish a process for revising the agreements if/when circumstances warrant. Examples of these circumstances include the addition of new team members, significant changes in the organization, changes to the team's mission and priorities, and so on. A sample list of team agreements is presented as Exhibit 5.3.

Exhibit 5.3
Sample List of Team Agreements

1. We will demonstrate respect for each member of the team by being on time for meetings and completing projects on time. We will give advance notice if we cannot attend or complete projects.

2. We pledge to share thoughts and ideas openly during team meetings.

3. Whenever we have disagreements with other team members, we will address our concerns directly with our conflict partner. We will not talk behind our team members' backs.

4. During team meetings, all cell phones, BlackBerries, and other electronic communication devices will be turned off (or silenced in the case of emergency situations with the knowledge of all team members).

5. Sidebar conversations during team meetings are rude and distracting. We agree that sidebars and other similar interruptions are prohibited.

6. We will support team decisions in public even when the decision was not our personal best choice.

7. We will review these agreements at least twice a year and make revisions as necessary.

The establishment of team agreements doesn't guarantee anything. In our experience though, this process is the single best proactive step teams can take for developing conflict competence. The process we've outlined provides a simple and thorough way to establish clarity and a shared vision among team members. It enables the team to discuss the ways they expect to handle interactions in good times and tough times. Perhaps most important, the process allows discussion of how to handle the inevitable challenges they'll face before those challenges appear. When teams establish agreements and norms, they are in effect practicing preventative medicine: like health professionals, teams administer vaccinations in advance rather than wait to treat the symptoms of disease when they occur.

Structured Disclosure   We are often surprised at how little team members know about one another. This isn't to suggest that the only successful teams are comprised of team members who have deep, intimate relationships. However, there's little doubt that openness goes a long way in the establishment of high-trust team climates.

Over the past few years, we've been honored to play a small role in the transformation of the New York–Penn Baseball League. The New York–Penn League is the premiere short season minor league baseball association in the country. When Ben Hayes became the league president, he wanted to change the way league members worked together. Now this may sound a bit strange. Aren't the teams in the league competing against each other? Of course they are—on the field. Otherwise, in Hayes's mind, much of the success of the league depended on cooperation and collaboration among the general managers (GMs) of the sixteen teams. Slowly and methodically, over a number of years, Hayes instituted a number of steps to encourage exactly that. He organized the first-ever spring GM meeting at which participants were encouraged to share their approaches to marketing and fan experience. The now annual league meetings occur in Florida prior to the beginning of the season. League committees were established to address marketing issues, community outreach, and other common issues.

Hayes also provided a series of leadership development sessions for the GMs. This is where we became involved and used the process of structured disclosure to expand the GMs' comfort with one another. In short, during introductions we asked each GM to share a unique fact about themselves with the rest of the group. The one rule was that the information had to be something that no one else in the room knew.

We promised that we wouldn't share any of the specifics of the structured disclosure session in this book. Suffice it to say, though, that the laughter was infectious. The GMs, even though many of them had known one another for years, discovered a myriad of previously unknown similarities, experiences, and interests. The significance of these meetings and the techniques employed has not eluded Hayes. As the GMs established closer, more open relationships, disputes between and among teams diminished, and disagreements were handled without third-party intervention.

The keys to using structured disclosure are timing and choice. Typically, this technique works best during introductory activities or when the team is socially active. For instance, it can work as an icebreaker prior to a team dinner meeting. Providing team members with the choice of how to participate is also a good idea. We often use a disclaimer suggesting that team members can choose their level of participation. In other words, the depth of their disclosures is entirely up to them, as is their decision to participate at all.

Some of our favorite structured disclosure categories:

- Share something unique about yourself (that nobody else in the room knows).

- Share an experience that you found absolutely exhilarating.

- What's a nickname you've had or nickname of another person that you'll never forget?

- Who's one person you'd love to interview (that will probably never happen)?

- What was your favorite game as a child?

- Share a special skill or ability that you possess.

- What's your favorite guilty pleasure?

The power of this technique exists in the contagious level of sharing that occurs. We love it when participants begin to try to "outdo" each other. The laughter, amusement, insights, and revelations lead to improved connections, heightened trust, and a willingness to engage—all invaluable traits for effective teams.

Preliminary Perspective Sharing   This technique is recommended when a team knows they are about to enter into a serious discussion in which differing views are anticipated and the stakes are high. We don't claim to be the originators of this idea, but we do believe we've witnessed the evolution of its applicability and impact. It works because all team members are given an opportunity to be heard from the outset. There's a sense of fairness to the process and a level of acceptance for diverse views that sets the stage for a debate of issues. Here's how it works:

- The potentially hot topic for team discussion is introduced.

- Each team member is invited to share their initial view in a specified brief period of time. For instance, each member is given 60 seconds to state their preliminary perspective.

- Each member has exclusive rights to the floor for the time period with no questions or interruptions from others.

- No discussion occurs until after each member completes their "air time."

- As each person shares his or her view, a scribe records the essence of each perspective.

- When all participants have been heard, the scribe reviews the perspectives.

We've found that when teams begin discussions of hot topics with this brief bit of structure, they nearly always have more satisfying interactions than when they simply dive into the debate. In fact, the debates are often more spirited when this technique is used than when it's not. We believe this is due to the enhanced sense of safety that's created when everyone has been heard in advance of the debate. In addition, we believe that the sooner teams engage in perspective taking and examination of their differences, the more likely they are to fully explore all the options available to them.

During Conflict

The next several tools are most useful in the "during" stage of conflict. We review more techniques here than in either the "before" or "after" stage. We are strong advocates of proactive rather than reactive processes and tools. We highly encourage teams to take the time to discuss how to deal with future conflicts at any point.

As with any set of tools, it's important to select the right one for the job. If you're drilling a hole in the wall so you can hang a picture, you'd choose a hand-held drill with a very tiny drill bit. If you're drilling for oil in the Persian Gulf, you would select mammoth pieces of equipment that can pierce through layers and layers of rock, soil, and sediment. In a similar way, think carefully about the depth of the conflicts you're addressing when selecting tools to use in these situations.

Summarizing Techniques The wisdom of summarization is that it acknowledges the significance of what others have previously stated. During conflict, such acknowledgments are powerful factors in keeping the intensity low. When participants in a conflict feel that their views are heard and valued, there is a much greater chance that the debate over those views will be constructive versus destructive. We review three kinds of summarizing that are useful during team conflict.

Conversational Summaries This type of summary is very common in group interactions. Once a number of ideas, suggestions, views, or opinions have been stated, any member of the discussion can summarize what's been said.

For instance, a team member might say, "So several of us think we need to start immediately, some want to have another meeting with our sponsor before starting, and a couple of others believe this isn't within our charter and we shouldn't even consider beginning."

Structured Summaries We often refer to this technique as "summer before fall." Just as the summer season precedes fall, the idea is to summarize another's view before falling into a description of one's own view.

Any team member can suggest the use of this tool. The idea is that teammates summarize another's view before stating their own. It's most useful when team members have varied and passionate viewpoints.

Have you ever observed a team meeting that deteriorated into a series of "taking stands"? This is a situation in which it seems like everyone has an opinion and wants to share it. In many cases, there's actually more agreement among the opinions than is apparent because everyone is so focused on standing their ground. This is the perfect opportunity for someone on the team to suggest structured summaries. All they have to say is, "Hey folks, I think we need to make sure we've got summer before fall here. Why don't we summarize what we've heard before sharing our thoughts and see if that helps us slow down and make better sense of our discussion?"

Power Summaries Power summaries represent a highly structured process that is most useful when teams find themselves deadlocked or believe that they must simply "agree to disagree." The process involves slowing the discussion to "idle speed." This is accomplished by asking each team member, one at a time, to state his or her view. When the person completes his statement, each remaining team member's only job is to summarize that person's view. Once everyone has provided a summary, the speaker either acknowledges that her view has been accurately summarized or clarifies what she believes is missing. The process continues until each team member has had a turn to express his or her view and all views have been summarized.

At the risk of sounding like Tim "the Toolman" Taylor on the long-running television show *Home Improvement*, we have a way of adding even more power to this technique. As each person provides his summary, he must also add a comment about what he appreciates about the view he is summarizing. This approach, even though highly structured, provides a sense of value for each person's view that goes beyond a simple demonstration of hearing the other's view. We recommend this "power added" technique especially for situations in which views have been openly criticized. Here's how it works:

1. One person begins by stating her or his view of the situation or issue under discussion. Depending on the complexity of the situation, a time limit may be established.

2. One by one, all team members summarize the view of the first person. In large teams, limiting the number of "summarizers" can help manage time. We suggest three summaries for most cases. (When using the "power added" technique, summarizers add one thing they appreciate during this step.)

3. The person who stated their view acknowledges the accuracy of the summaries or clarifies any missing or misunderstood points. (When using the

"power added" technique, the person acknowledges what each summarizer appreciated during this step.)

4. At least one more summary is provided if there has been missing or misunderstood information.

5. The process continues and repeats for each view stated.

Time-Outs   When a conflict discussion becomes overly chaotic, heated, or emotional, a well-placed time-out can help restore calm and civility. A team time-out works in much the same way as the tried-and-true advice of "Count to ten when you're angry" helps individuals pause before they say or do something they regret. A time-out can serve several purposes:

- It provides participants a temporary respite from the heat of the moment.
- A time-out enables valuable moments for reflection on what has just transpired.
- Time-outs allow participants a chance to reconsider what they have contributed and how they have affected others.
- Similarly, time-outs provide the opportunity to reconsider what others have contributed, said, or done.
- A pause stops potentially destructive processes and behaviors such as interrupting, blaming, loss of focus, and accusations.

As simple as the act of calling a time-out seems, we advocate several "rules" for team members. These include:

- All team members have the authority and the responsibility to call time-outs.
- Once a team member calls for a time-out, there is no option but to take the time-out. A time-out cannot be overruled.
- Because too many time-outs can be disruptive, we suggest setting limits in advance. For instance, during a single team meeting or discussion, there is a limit of three time-outs allowed. Once the third time-out is called, the team should determine a time to reconvene.

We suggest that teams create their own agreements governing the use of time-outs. Most important, we believe teams should encourage all members to accept responsibility for calling time-outs when the situation warrants.

Devil's Advocacy   This technique is widely used in casual social and business conversations. Most of us can probably recall a time when somebody said, "Let me play devil's advocate . . . " Applied to conflict resolution, it asks those individuals with opposing views to go beyond summarizing their conflict partners' views. Quite literally, the technique asks that conflict partners argue for the opposing view or position.

It sounds easy enough. And most of us have had some practice at it during friendly banter over a movie or a book or a sporting event. As the stakes get higher, though, the degree of difficulty of playing devil's advocate also rises. We see it all the time on teams . . . even when using exercises and simulations in a classroom setting. Consider the following example.

The global strategy team from a highly regarded technical support organization met with us for a three-day team development program. One of the exercises we used is a classic negotiation simulation that almost always causes some level of conflict among the small groups involved. During the debriefing of the exercise, it was apparent that two of the negotiating groups had vastly different views of the situation they had experienced. The conversation between the groups was laced with deflecting comments such as, "We didn't say that!" "You said . . . ," "But you did . . . ," and our favorite, "Yeah, but. . ." In fact, whenever we hear the phrase, "Yeah, but . . . ," we challenge the debating sides to stop using made-up words (like yabutt!). When they say, "Yeah, but . . . ," it's a clear sign that neither side is making sense of the other's views.

True to form, we asked both sides to stop and take a stab at playing devil's advocate for the other side. The first person to volunteer had been arguing passionately for his point of view. He smiled sheepishly and agreed to give it a try. "When you set your price in the third month, you didn't fully consider the other options. You were only trying to make up for the past two rounds." We're sure this person truly intended to play devil's advocate. Needless to say, what he said did not impress the other side as an effective effort. They continued to feel blamed for their decision.

The key to effectively using the technique of devil's advocacy is to speak in first person. In other words, when I'm advocating for your point of view, I get so far into your view, perspective, and position that I speak as if I am you. Even if I don't get the substance 100 percent correct, the fact that I'm speaking in first person removes any perception that I'm being accusatory, because I never say "you." As facilitators of this technique, the most critical part of the process to manage is encouraging the speakers to use first-person language.

This technique is most useful when two or more parties are stuck in advocacy. When conflict partners spend most of the time defending their rationale or restating their reasoning, it's a tell-tale sign that neither side is attempting to *understand* one another's rationale or reasoning. We suggest that teams make it okay to use devil's advocacy by identifying it as one of a set of tools they can access when they are slowed by conflicts. Ideally, any team member can suggest using the technique. We encourage teams not to wait for a consultant's or outside facilitator's advice. Devil's advocacy can help team members practice perspective taking and result in deep understanding and appreciation for opposing views.

Reaching Out   Stated simply, the technique of reaching out involves a team member acknowledging the emotional damage caused by a previous interaction and taking responsibility for resuming communication with a team member or members. It sometimes takes the form of an apology or making amends. Most important, the act of reaching out is intended to initiate a dialogue with a conflict partner or partners at a time when all parties feel inhibited by some emotional pain or discomfort.

There is no specific formula or suggested series of steps to follow for reaching out. For this technique to work, someone has to take a risk or at least take the "high road" to get beyond the emotional distress weighing on the team. An example we often share occurred with a team at a cancer research hospital. A new team leader, Melinda, had been selected to replace the long-standing leader, who retired. The new team leader was highly qualified but was also the spouse of a prominent physician at the hospital. Almost immediately, team members balked at her attempts to change and improve team processes. They questioned her on almost every suggestion. Over a period of several months, team members and the new leader were polarized. Relationships were strained, and the team's results suffered. Human resources attempted to intervene, but nothing seemed to work.

We were asked to help the team work through their issues. After two sessions, we were stymied. Beginning with the third session, we decided to provide some feedback based on our observations of interactions among team members. This seemed to provide a sense of sobering reality for the members. Sensing some motivation to break out of the malaise, we asked team members to reflect on what had been happening and asked what they would like to say to each other specifically about the decline of relationships over the past few months. The dialogue proceeded as follows:

> *Dallas (hesitatingly):* Melinda, I'm really sorry for how we've welcomed you into the team. I suppose "welcome" isn't really the right word for it.
>
> *Nancy:* We didn't really give you a chance.
>
> *Melinda (nodding slightly):* Thank you.
>
> *David:* You must be feeling like a complete outsider around us. What can I do to help you feel more a part of the team?
>
> *Melinda:* I'm really not sure.
>
> *Dallas:* I guess I didn't realize just how tough we've been on you and in some ways on ourselves. We really haven't accomplished much in the past few weeks. Do you think we can move forward from here?
>
> *O'Neil:* I've probably been the worst. Sara [the former team leader] was a good friend of mine. The last thing I wanted to do was deal with a change. It didn't matter who the new leader was. I didn't want anyone else but Sara.
>
> *Nancy:* I actually found myself getting upset with you at times, O'Neil. I know I wasn't easy on Melinda, but I wish I had said something to the team.
>
> *Melinda:* It's been very tough, I admit. And I know I've thought some pretty terrible things about you all, too.
>
> *Dallas (chuckling):* Imagine that. Why would you ever think poorly of us?
>
> *O'Neil:* How can we begin to get back on the right track?

The technique of reaching out was demonstrated first by Dallas. The power of the technique is illustrated not so much by Melinda's response to his apology but by the outpouring of comments by other team members. In teams, once one person reaches out, it often seems as if the fog of depression begins to lift for all team members. The repair of relationship damage, however, doesn't happen in a flash. Reaching out enables it to begin but doesn't result in a magical cure. This team still had to face the challenge of having a new leader who presented a different style. And much more dialogue was necessary to repair and rebuild trust. But the act of reaching out was the beginning of that rebuilding. In cases where emotional damage is evident, reaching out may be just the tool for a team to begin turning things around.

Reframing Questions   We offer this tool with some slight hesitation. In truth, it is probably better described as a skill rather than a tool. Many people describe it as *checking for understanding*. We tend to think it is just a bit deeper than that. It is most commonly used in those moments when a spirited debate suddenly turns into an ugly argument. When used effectively, it is an amazingly beautiful thing. And it happens almost as quickly as the debate morphed into argument.

The reframing technique we prefer is one of inquiry. The "reframer" comments with the sole intent to clarify or understand what was just said or what has just happened. It can focus on the topic, a recent comment, the process, assumptions, or even the current progress of the discussion. Certainly the person doing the reframing must deliver in a nonconfrontational and nonthreatening manner. Done poorly, the reframing can be mistaken for "taking sides" or criticizing.

Here are some samples of questions or statements that can be used for reframing. This is not an exhaustive list by any means. The words you choose will reflect the context and content in the moment.

- What might be the consequences of that course of action?
- What if we found our assumption to be in error?
- Are there more than just these two alternatives?
- What else have you considered?
- What else might we try?
- Please help me understand why.
- You obviously see it differently. I'd like to hear you say more.
- How important is this versus that?
- I misunderstood your point. Can you say it again?
- How does this discussion fit with our main priority?
- If we do that, what are the implications?
- What impact will our decision on this topic have on . . . ?
- Will spending more time now on this pay off on that?
- What would it take to change your or our minds?
- Would it be helpful to revisit what we've already decided or know?

Obviously this tool requires good timing and tact. Not everyone will be especially good at it. That's why we think it's more a skill than a technique. In fact, the more reframing becomes "technique-ish," the less effective it is. The more jargon we hear and the more technique we sense from a conflict partner, the less genuine that person appears. Nevertheless, used effectively, reframing can be the key to defusing a quickly rising conflict or to unlock discussions that have stalled. The key in the heat of the moment is to use inquiry to reframe or clarify rather than advocacy. So rather than asserting, "We have to move beyond this stalemate," it is better to seek, "What are our options given the different views expressed?"

Brainstorming   Most teams engage in some form of brainstorming from time to time, if not routinely. It is a tried-and-true technique for generating ideas and coming up with possible solutions to challenges. The heart of effective brainstorming is its process. Although brainstorming processes can vary, most guidelines share several key characteristics. Among them:

- All ideas are welcome and acknowledged.
- Creative thought is encouraged.
- No ideas are discussed or debated until the idea-generating phase is complete.
- Generating a great volume of ideas is the primary objective.
- All parties are encouraged to participate.
- Violations of these guidelines are immediately recognized and rectified.

When applied as tools for engaging conflicts among team members, these very same characteristics can work wonders.

One common opportunity to use brainstorming occurs when just two or three ideas are "on the table" at once. When the choices are limited, taking sides can happen very quickly. Once the sides become polarized, the chance for a satisfying resolution is greatly diminished. Brainstorming provides a vehicle for staying focused on the challenge, creating a respite from the argument, and generating new possibilities.

The real trick is in knowing the difference between a healthy debate of the issues and polarizing arguments for positions. We are huge fans of healthy debate. Cutting off such dialogue prematurely can do more damage than good.

In this spirit, we offer five tips for distinguishing healthy debate from polarizing argument:

1. Debates feature passion; arguments feature venom.

2. Debates involve emphasis; arguments involve shouting.

3. Debates include critiques of the opposing ideas; arguments include criticism.

4. Debates are often friendly; arguments are seldom friendly.

5. Debates imply civility and have structure; arguments often include neither.

There are also a great many similarities. Debates and arguments can both be won and lost. Both involve persuasion. Both, once resolved, have the potential for resulting in new perspectives. And both feature taking and defending sides.

The most critical decision for utilizing brainstorming as a technique for addressing team conflict is when to call for it. It's a handy tool for many purposes, including problem solving. And with the plethora of challenges facing teams, it's easy to see how it can be overused. With this in mind, we encourage teams and team members to observe carefully and distinguish among the debates and arguments that occur. Replacing an argument with brainstorming is nearly always a useful substitution. Replacing a debate with brainstorming is a misuse of the tool and may hinder the development of future debates.

Intentional Intent   This technique is one of Tim's favorites for slowing things down in the heat of the moment. It's very simple, it doesn't take long, and it nearly always presents an immediate impact on the participants.

When it's obvious to any team member that two or more other team members have misunderstood, misinterpreted, or otherwise misperceived one another, this tool can provide a quick dose of structure and a "reality check" before things spiral out of control. It simply requires that each speaker clearly states his or her intent before making their statement. It sounds so simple that the first reaction of many is to consider the technique absurd. In practice, what it accomplishes is taking the guesswork out of perception.

Recall a time when one colleague mistook the comment of another as a criticism. How did the conversation continue? In many cases, we think the parties quickly recognized the miscommunication and took quick steps to reconcile. In other cases, we suspect the conversation proceeded with one or both parties feeling hurt, disrespected, or unheard. This technique can quickly assist by ensuring that there's no misinterpretation of intent.

We are keenly aware of the impact of the recession on our business in 2009. I remember a staff meeting not long ago when I proclaimed to my teammates that "we had better start generating some new ideas . . ." Almost immediately, all eyes in the room turned to me. Many of my colleagues looked surprised and were doing their best Mr. Spock "one eyebrow cocked" impression. Even before anyone asked me what I meant, I knew my message had not come across the way I had intended. Immediately, I self-invoked the technique of intentional intent, although in this case it was done as an act of recovery rather than prevention. I said, "Can I try that again? What I was trying to communicate was my frustration with the economic crisis and my fear that without significant change our business will be badly damaged." Had I made my intent clear in the first place, the impact on my teammates might have been quite improved.

In its purest form, intentional intent is a technique that asks each speaker to describe his or her intent before making a statement, rather that vice versa. When in use, you'll hear comments such as:

- "What I'm about to say is intended to support the comments made by Lois last week . . . "

- "What I'm trying to communicate here is my curiosity about your idea . . . "

- "I'm hoping to indicate my dissatisfaction with the process we followed, not the result . . . "

When team members use intentional intent, many assumptions can be preempted. As we've seen, most destructive conflict occurs when emotions are frayed or damaged. Even when parties are trying to be as clear as possible, it's our human nature to interpret what's being said. This technique is a way to head off faulty assumptions and misinterpretations. That said, because of its structure, we caution against overuse. Part of what makes our interactions unique and our communications interesting is interpretation. We'd rather err slightly on the side of stimulating interest and intrigue than eliminating all facets of distinction and uniqueness.

Observation and Feedback We use several variations of this methodology in our work with teams. At the core of this tool is observation. The observation can be conducted by a team member, an outside facilitator, or with the use of video recording. In each case, the purpose is to accurately record the behaviors, interactions, and group dynamics of the team. Once recorded, the team can examine their interactions and decide how to alter or improve in the future.

Many teams select a team member to be the observer when using this technique. This method is the easiest in terms of scheduling and there are no costs involved. However, when using a team member as the observer, there are several important issues to consider. First, and most important, the normal team dynamics are disrupted when removing a current member to serve as the observer. The interactions of a team missing one of its regular members will be different than "normal." Second, it may be challenging for the observer to be completely objective. Plus, even the most accurate and objective observations may be perceived as subjective or skewed by other members of the team. Finally, unless the observer is experienced or has special training, they may not be adept at spotting key behaviors and identifying them accurately.

Another option is to use an outside facilitator as the observer. Many organizations have human resources professionals, organizational development specialists, or internal coaches who can assist. There are also many consultants and organizations that can provide this service for a fee. The advantages of utilizing an outside resource rather than a team member are many. Most important, each of the cautions we noted previously can be addressed by using an outside resource.

A third option, growing in popularity, is the use of video recording. We have long been advocates of video recording as a training tool. Using video to record team meetings is a logical extension of this technology. In most cases, there is no need for a full-time camera operator as cameras with wide-angle lenses can be positioned to record the team meeting. A key factor to consider is the sound quality. We have the best results when equipping the camera with an external microphone rather than relying on the camera's built-in microphone. We strongly recommend testing the sound recording quality by using a group of individuals talking rather than the traditional method of one person stepping in front of the camera and saying, "Testing 1, 2, 3 . . . " It is critical that the sound quality can distinguish between and among many voices sometimes speaking at once. A quality check using just one voice will not suffice.

Once you've decided on which observation method to use, there are several techniques to consider for providing feedback. One method simply involves taking notes or using a checklist to track the interactions of team members. (Obviously when using video recording, this is the only option.) When using a team member as the observer, this method works best when teams have had a common experience with training programs or assessment tools that provide a common language. The observer can use the common language to create a list of behaviors or points. Such a list makes it easier for the observer to catch critical interactions and for the team to understand the observations and feedback when reviewed.

A variation on this method involves the team agreeing to take several time-outs during the observed meeting so the observer can provide feedback. This approach is valuable in its immediacy of feedback, but it is disruptive in that it breaks the flow of the interactions. It is essential that all team members agree in advance if the time-out method is to be used. This technique is most useful when team members use the feedback to make immediate changes in their behaviors. It is most effective for use in training sessions rather than team meetings.

Another variation on this theme involves the observer verbally labeling behaviors as they occur. Again, this works most effectively when team members have a common language, such as the fifteen constructive and destructive behaviors associated with the Conflict Dynamics Profile. As the meeting progresses, the observer not only makes note of the behaviors, he or she identifies each behavior verbally in real time. What results is akin to the public address announcer at a ball game. As the action continues, the teams and the fans hear, "Goal by Kyle." In the team meeting, team members will hear, "Summary by Matt" or "Perspective taking by Lindsay." To reduce disruption even more, the observer doesn't identify the source, only the behavior. We have the greatest success with this variation in situations in which teams have floundered with conflict and are ready and willing to try something different. It is a powerful way to identify and acknowledge behaviors that have a significant impact on the effectiveness of team interactions.

Finally, the most common variation of the observation technique includes a specific time period for feedback and discussion after the meeting. When using video recording, the team is gathered to watch the replay of the video, identify key points, discuss the impact of behaviors, and decide how to improve in future meetings. Asking a third-party facilitator to participate can lend expertise and an element of objectivity to this process. When video recording has not been used, this session relies on the skill and thoroughness of the observer. Again, key points and the impact of behaviors are reviewed. Once these are analyzed and discussed, team members can decide what improvements are necessary.

We believe it's a good idea for teams to use this technique periodically whether or not they are experiencing any difficulties with conflict. Just as we schedule routine maintenance on our vehicles, routine "tune ups" for our teams makes just as much sense. When small, sometimes imperceptible behaviors or trends are identified and corrected early, more complex and potentially damaging situations are prevented.

Clearing the Air   Clearing the air requires courage and honesty. It is a technique utilized for times when emotions are running high but are not being expressed effectively. The most obvious situations involve times when destructive, overt displays of emotions, such as displaying anger or demeaning others, erupt. Just as crucial, and perhaps even more risky, are situations when emotions are hidden, repressed, or denied. The technique of clearing the air provides the team a mildly structured way for expressing emotions safely.

The process for clearing involves several discrete steps or segments as outlined here:

1. *Call a time-out.* The team member who calls the time-out takes the first risk by identifying his or her own strong emotions or reactions to the current interactions. The time-out is accompanied by the suggestion that the team uses the "clearing the air" process.

2. *Identify and write down thoughts and feelings.* The simple process of writing down thoughts and feelings creates some time and space between the interactions and the discussion to follow. Emphasis on feelings is key. We recommend writing simple words and phrases to describe the feelings.

3. *Identify sources.* Next to each feeling, participants are asked to identify the sources of the emotion. We highly encourage that the writer take ownership or acknowledge control of at least some of the sources. This eliminates playing the "blame game."

4. *List alternatives.* Each person lists alternative actions, behaviors, or processes for each source that may have resulted in different responses or results. Alternatives must include suggestions for the writer, not just other team members. We recommend that the first suggestion for each source focus on oneself.

5. *Share lists.* Team members take turns sharing their thought and feelings, sources, and alternatives. We recommend that each person share one, then the turn moves to the next team member.

6. *Summarize and reengage.* Once all members have shared, ask for a few thoughts about the process. Ask if the team is ready to return to the issue or meeting. Reengage.

Clearing the air involves a significant degree of risk and disclosure. Admitting strong emotions is not easy. Neither is identifying sources of the emotions or suggesting alternatives. The risks of allowing destructive emotions and feelings to flow unchecked or to go unacknowledged and denied are even greater. The structure suggested for clearing the air provides safety through the process of delaying each person's response and providing time for reflective thinking. Because of the high stakes, we suggest that teams consider the use of a third-party facilitator to manage this technique. As challenging as it may feel, when team members are open and honest with one another, there is great opportunity for trust and respect to grow.

Stop, Start, Continue   We use this process for addressing a variety of team challenges. In general, it is a tool that is most helpful when teams find themselves in a rut, not performing up to past standards. It can also be used for addressing specific challenges such as dealing with significant changes in the team's mission. This technique is among the most thorough for analyzing how the team is handling conflict and what they can do to handle it more effectively.

Although it's called "Stop, Start, Continue," the title doesn't necessarily dictate the order in which the three categories should be addressed. In fact, the most common order we use is Continue, then Stop, and finally Start. We find that beginning with a focus on what's working provides a sense of accomplishment for most teams.

We also recommend that this technique always be facilitated by a third party with expertise in group dynamics and behavior. The process itself is not complex. We believe though, that asking a team member to facilitate alters the team dynamic significantly. It is important that all team members contribute in their normal roles. The process can also be lengthy. Having a facilitator can help manage the process objectively and efficiently.

The process involves preparation and three distinct stages. The following description is meant as a guideline for facilitating. As with any process of this nature, a skilled facilitator must be ready to adjust and alter to meet the needs of the team.

STOP, START, CONTINUE PROCESS

Preparation

Secure the following:

1. A private meeting space with tables and seating to accommodate the team

2. Smartboards, whiteboards, and/or easels with flip charts and markers

3. Notepads and pens for each team member

4. Refreshments

Stage 1

The facilitator and/or team leader welcomes the team members. The facilitator briefly describes the process. Here's a sample opening:

> This session uses a tool called Start, Stop, Continue. It will help you describe how you've been dealing with conflict, analyze the behaviors and processes you've used, and ultimately to agree on how to address the conflict moving forward.
>
> It's critical that each of you focus on sharing ideas and perspectives openly and honestly. Keeping information and views hidden will stifle the process and prevent the team from making progress. Because we're dealing with conflict, some of the discussion may feel risky at times. This is natural and expected.
>
> My role is to manage the process in a way that helps you focus on behaviors and information rather than placing blame. I appreciate your willingness to participate. I anticipate that you'll find the session meaningful, but only if you participate fully.

The process includes three stages. [Insert a description of how long you expect the session to last and whether you plan to extend it over two days.] Are you ready to begin?

Stage 1 begins by seeking ideas and suggestions for what the team should *continue* to do about the conflict. Each suggestion is recorded publicly so that all members can see. We suggest asking team members to do the recording. When teams have trouble getting started, we remind them that suggestions for this category can focus on what they do before, during, and after confronting the conflict. We encourage them not to limit their thinking to only the time when actually embroiled in the conflict. We have found that by beginning with the category Continue, teams are able to consider behaviors and interactions that they consider effective. By focusing on positives first, the team gains a sense of reinforcement and recognition. This also highlights the fact that the team engages in constructive behavior. In other words, even though this technique addresses conflict that is causing a problem, the team can clearly see that they have been doing some things well.

At this point, the process resembles brainstorming in that no suggestions are debated. The key issue is to record as many suggestions about what to continue as possible. The suggestions are simply recorded.

Once the list for Continue is exhausted, the same approach is used to record suggestions for Stop. You can expect this phase to be a bit more contentious. As team members reflect on past experiences that have not gone well, some items may embody perspectives that seem judgmental or focused on individuals. It is essential that the facilitator keeps the focus on observations that describe behavior, not people. The listing continues until the team has difficulty coming up with additional items for this category.

Next, the team considers the category Start. Now the focus is on what the team can do differently or better in the future. Because this category is future oriented, it sometimes takes longer than the first two categories. Once again, effective brainstorming guidelines are followed, with no discussion or debate. It is common to find a significant number of suggestions that are reverse characterizations of items listed in the Stop category. Although this can appear repetitive, we are generally supportive of this practice because it emphasizes the need for change. If the team has difficulty coming up with ideas, the facilitator can suggest that they review the previously created Continue list. This often results in suggestions that build on behaviors and processes already seen as worthwhile.

Once all three categories are addressed, we suggest taking a break. It's not uncommon for this segment to take one to two hours. During the break, the facilitator should organize and display the lists around the room. Once reconvened, team members are asked to silently review each list. They each carry a notepad so they can jot down additional suggestions for each list. After everyone has had ample time for review (15–20 minutes is usually enough), the additional suggestions are sought and recorded.

At this point, we find that many teams experience a feeling of real accomplishment. We encourage team members to gaze around the meeting room so they can see the walls covered with the information they produced. Often the sheer volume of information alone gives team members the sense that they have made significant progress. This leads to optimism and hope that much more is possible. Capitalizing on this sense of hope and accomplishment is the goal of the next stage.

Stage 2

In stage 2, each category (Continue, Stop, and Start) is reviewed. Each and every item is reviewed. The methodology for stage 2 can take a variety of forms and may include a number of process options. The ultimate goal is to discuss each item, clarify it, and determine whether or not it should stay on the list. One option we often suggest is to consider each item as a critical incident. The team provides examples of when the action or behavior was observed and how it affected the team. This practice helps the team verify the item's value and understand its application.

Another important step in this stage is grouping similar items together. This enables the team to compare items and consider the relative value of all the suggestions. This typically results in a methodical reduction of the number of suggestions and items in each category. We find this very helpful as we prepare for the final stage of this technique.

Stage 3

Stage 3 involves a final review of each category and prioritization of the remaining suggestions. The method and outcome for each of the three categories is slightly different. In the Continue category, we ask team members to identify the most important items to continue. One way to do so is by giving each member an opportunity to identify their personal "top three" or "top five" items. A simple method for completing this task is to ask team members to silently review the list and select their top items by placing a mark beside each. As the team members reveal their selections, those items most important to the team become apparent. The facilitator can review the "voting" and circle the top selections, checking of course with the team.

For the Stop category, the process is very similar. The idea is to identify those suggestions that, if stopped, will have the greatest impact on the team's ability to deal with the conflict. The same method of identifying one's "top three" or "top five" seems to work well. Once again, the facilitator reviews the results and circles the top items. This usually results in a very clear list of things the team agrees it must stop doing.

The suggested method for considering items in the Start category is more complex. In this case, instead of deciding only which actions are most important, we encourage a discussion of how each action will be implemented. This discussion is critical. The first step can include the same elimination process used for Continue and Stop. This can reduce the number of suggestions to those deemed most essential. Next, we suggest reaching agreement on four factors for each agreed-upon item: who, what, when, and how. Team members should specify *who* has responsibility for engaging in the behavior (in the vast majority of circumstances all team members share this responsibility). This emphasizes that every team member has the authority to intervene or make suggestions when conflict occurs. The team should also consider *what* should be said or done when accessing each item on the list. Many times this results in the identification of "warnings" or "catch phrases" that signal the team to slow down. Next, the team should consider *when*, or under what conditions, they will engage in the new behavior or process. For example, teams may agree that whenever a team member feels sufficiently uncomfortable, he or she should or must mention it. Finally, the team discusses *how* such interventions should take place. This discussion focuses on how to use respectful, well-intentioned interventions, even when the suggestion may at first appear as an interruption.

The discussions on *who, what, when, and how* comprise the heart of this technique. The team has identified and agreed on specific actions for addressing conflict. This makes it okay to "do something constructive" instead of avoiding or taking action that could be misinterpreted as destructive. When team members agree on new specific behaviors, actions, and processes for addressing their conflict, they are well on their way not only to resolving the current conflict but for confidently handling similar conflicts in the future.

Team Leader or Team Member Intervention   From time to time, team members may violate team norms or rules. In some cases, such mistakes can be handled through the organization's prescribed performance or work habits procedures. We believe taking this kind of formal action is appropriate when warranted. We also believe that the most effective teams find ways to use informal interventions to address the poor work habits or performance of team members.

It's difficult to itemize the many variations and forms this can take. We thought it would be helpful to describe a recent high-profile example of this approach. So, welcome to the world of major league baseball!

The 2008 season of my hometown team, the Tampa Bay Rays, was one to remember. The team had never posted a winning record in a season until that year. Amazingly, in 2008 they not only won more games than they lost, they became the American League champions and made it to the World Series! Although they lost to the Philadelphia Phillies in the series, the way this team developed during the season was one of the best sports stories of the year.

Of particular interest during the season was the way the Rays' manager Joe Maddon handled several situations involving young center fielder BJ Upton. The team had been built on a foundation of outworking and out-hustling other arguably more talented teams. This was epitomized by the team slogan, "9 = 8." Loosely translated, 9 = 8 meant nine players working together for nine innings every game would result in the team being one of the eight teams making the playoffs.

In midseason, Upton failed to run hard to first base on what he thought was a routine groundball, a cardinal sin in the Rays' "out-hustling" climate. Just a few games later, Upton hit what he thought was a sure double. As he rounded first base, he slowed to a trot as he neared second base, unaware that the throw in from the outfield came to the first baseman. Before he reached second base, the first baseman tagged him out from behind. Two incidents in such close proximity demanded action.

Maddon intervened in two ways. First he had a private conversation with Upton explaining his disappointment, reiterating his and the team's expectations, and asserting how important BJ is to the team. Second, he looked to veteran players on the team like Cliff Floyd and Carlos Pena to work with Upton. The veterans "took Upton under their wings," providing invaluable guidance, coaching, and support. Upton stepped up to the challenge to improve his effort. He starred during the playoffs with stellar defense and a team high of seven home runs.

By intervening himself and expecting other team members to intervene, Maddon demonstrated his commitment to team standards and the value of true "teamness." When team members violate standards or agreements, action is necessary. Without intervention, the power of team norms and rules is rendered useless.

Mediation   As we discussed in Chapter Four, mediation is perhaps the most serious kind of intervention or technique for resolving conflict on teams. Mediation is typically reserved for conflicts that have reached the highest levels of intensity (discord or polarization). There are formal mediation processes available and firms that specialize in business mediation services. We focus here on more informal types of mediation. This type of mediation can be provided by team members, the team leader, a respected colleague, or an agreed-upon third-party mediator.

Four basic tenets or guidelines must be present for mediation to be effective:

1. The mediation meeting is conducted in a private, safe environment.

2. The mediator presents ground rules that ensure safety, honesty, openness, and commitment to listening by all parties.

3. The conflict parties agree to air their views honestly and listen respectfully and completely to the other views.

4. The parties agree to continue talking until progress is made.

If mediation is an option, refer back to the section on intensity levels in Chapter Four for a more in-depth review.

After Conflict

Just as teams conduct periodic progress reviews, milestone summaries, and project debriefs, there is great value in reviewing the behaviors, tactics, and processes used once a team conflict has been addressed. We suggest two approaches for reviewing conflicts. Although both can be used periodically as best practices whether or not a specific conflict has been addressed, they are especially valuable once conflict has occurred. Both involve thorough, honest reviews of the behaviors and processes used by the team.

Periodic Peer Feedback   High-performing teams often establish agreements for conducting routine peer feedback sessions. The purpose of these sessions is to share perceptions of what's working or not working in team communication and team member interaction. The more specific the feedback, the more likely team members are to understand and engage in constructive behaviors.

We recommend and use a specific method for conducting peer feedback. It is characterized by a degree of structure and requires the willingness of team members to request feedback from their colleagues. For feedback to be the most productive, it must be welcome. This is possible only when the team climate is right. As we discussed earlier, team climate cannot be legislated. It must be created, established, and nurtured over time. Generally speaking, the better the team climate, the more likely the team is to experience value and productivity during these feedback sessions. That said, even when the climate is not as good as one would like, feedback is a necessary ingredient for improvement. As a facilitator of feedback processes, one must be prepared to guide and intervene more frequently when the team climate is not ideal.

Situation-Behavior-Impact Method   The successful use of this method involves sharing the Situation-Behavior-Impact (SBI) model with team members and asking them to provide feedback to one another by following this simple model. We highly recommend using a third-party facilitator when using this approach. The components include:

Situation: The context in which the behavior or action took place.

Behavior: What was said or done.

Impact: How the behavior impacted the observer or others in the situation.

A technique we recommend for team members when first learning the model involves taking notes. Each team member makes a three-column grid for each of their colleagues on a notepad. The first column is labeled "situation," the second "behavior," and the third "impact." As they work together, team members make brief SBI notes recording their observations of each other. These notes will be used during the facilitated session when members share their feedback.

The feedback session is obviously the most critical portion of this method. The facilitator can ensure the success of the session by providing some process guidelines such as the following:

1. Conduct the session away from potential interruptions and distractions.

2. Set a reasonable time period for the session. Allow ample time. Rushing this session greatly inhibits the value. For teams of five to seven members, two hours is recommended.

3. Team members are expected to come prepared with SBI observations for each teammate. Especially in a team's earliest experiences with the SBI method, keeping notes as described previously is highly recommended.

4. Each team member specifically requests feedback by asking teammates to share their observations.

5. To ensure safety, team members can pass on providing or requesting feedback. Forcing participation only fosters resentment.

6. Each team member takes a turn on the "receiving seat." When a team member asks for feedback, all other team members provide SBI observations. Depending on the time allotted for the session, and the volume of data collected by each team member, we often suggest that feedback is focused on those SBIs deemed most critical or impactful.

7. While receiving feedback, the receiver does not defend or explain. They simply listen and take notes if they wish.

8. If a piece of feedback is misunderstood or unclear, the receiver may ask clarifying questions, again without defending or explaining.

9. The receiver thanks all the teammates and the process continues until all participants have had an opportunity to receive feedback.

Once the SBI model becomes comfortable and the team has effectively used the process several times, an outside facilitator may no longer be needed. This process is an extremely valuable tool for debriefing a recent conflict. We also recommend it as a "routine maintenance" tool for teams. Our colleague Susan Gunn from Richmond, Virginia, uses the SBI method when she works with teams on conflict. As she says, "I find it especially useful in exploring the concept of expressing emotions. For a variety of reasons, it isn't unusual to meet with resistance to the notion of telling others what one is feeling in work situations. Even when individuals get past the resistance and accept its value in resolving the conflict, expressing emotions can feel awkward. Practicing this technique helps get past this discomfort along with gaining clarity and ability to identify and communicate the real emotion at the heart of the conflict" (Craig's and Tim's correspondence with Susan Gunn, July 7, 2009).

The better team members communicate, the easier it is to handle conflicts when they arise. The more effectively team members seek and share feedback, the more they know what's working. And the more open and honest teammates are with one another, the more likely it is that they can engage in spirited debates constructively. When this happens, conflict becomes constructive, expansive, and productive.

VIRTUAL AND GLOBAL TEAMS

In addition to all of the conflict challenges that face traditional teams, new ones emerge when team members work at a distance or come from different cultures. In the case of virtual teams, most communications take place using electronic media, which poses a set of unique issues. It is also harder to build familiarity and trust at a distance. Understanding is impaired because team members lack a shared context and cannot use visual clues like body language and facial expressions as easily as they can in person. For instance, lag times with e-mail and other messaging can lead to misunderstandings when messages pass like ships in the night.

Conflict can be hard to recognize in virtual teams. It is difficult to interpret the meaning of silence in these situations (Armstrong and Cole, 2002). As a consequence, conflict can arise but go undetected until it has built into a serious problem. Billie Williamson of Ernst & Young suggests that it is important to listen for who is being silent and then to make sure to follow up so that everyone is heard (Williamson, 2009).

Virtual teams have a more difficult time developing behavioral integration than do traditional teams. People do not feel as much in touch when their colleagues are at a distance. It is harder to develop a sense of cohesiveness.

Faced with these and other problems, what can a team leader and team members of a virtual team do to improve their chances of addressing conflicts effectively? First, we strongly advocate an early face-to-face meeting where they can begin to build familiarity and trust using the same techniques as traditional teams. This meeting also helps the team develop a shared understanding of team member roles and responsibilities. Even though there are costs associated with this process, the investment is even more important in the case of virtual teams because of the additional problems they face in dealing with conflict.

The face-to-face meeting also provides them with the opportunity to develop a team agreement about the norms they wish to use to manage conflict. In addition to the standard issues related to creating the right climate and employing constructive communications techniques, virtual teams also need to focus on several unique issues.

First, they need to talk about what approaches they want to take to make sure when conflict is happening and the team is not aware of it. Several approaches can be used, including emphasizing the importance of everyone being responsible for raising issues. For people who are uncomfortable doing this, the team could create a method that would let the person bring the issue to the attention of the team leader. If the team leader was the focus of the problem, another team member could be used as a conduit to alert the team about the problem.

The team also needs to agree on what kinds of communications technologies it wants to use to address conflicts once they arise. Usually it is better to use higher-bandwidth techniques (phone is preferable to e-mail, videoconference is better than phone) because they make it easier to see nonverbal cues. Depending on where the team members are located, they may need to develop norms for when they meet. If they are many time zones apart, it will be important to *not* require the same people to always be the ones to take late-night calls.

Cultural Issues

People from different cultures can easily misunderstand one another. This can stem from language differences as well as cultural variations that can lead to expectations being unmet. These misunderstandings and unmet expectations frequently lead to conflict.

Different cultures also have varying approaches for how conflicts should be managed. In some cultures, it is preferable to talk directly about issues—put your cards on the table. In others, such directness is frowned upon because it could lead to a breakdown in the harmony of relationships. The differences are quite real, and each culture's approach is not only authentic but can be effective when used by people from the same culture. At the same time, when you have a conflict with someone from another culture, that person's way of trying to resolve it may be very different from yours. These differences themselves can complicate resolution of conflict and can escalate conflicts by causing frustration.

We recommend that teams with members from different cultures spend some time learning more about the cultural approaches to conflict of its members. For a general background on the subject we recommend the book *Managing Intercultural Conflict Effectively* (Ting-Toomey and Oetzel, 2001). You can also get a better understanding of the cultural conflict styles of team members using the Intercultural Conflict Style Inventory (Hammer, 2005). It examines two key domains: the degree of directness that people prefer to use when addressing conflict and the degree to which they are emotionally expressive or reserved when doing so.

Three of our colleagues have provided us with helpful insights about intercultural conflict. Maya Hu-Chan is a consultant and author in the field of intercultural communications. I (Craig) first met her at a global leadership conference in Shanghai. She was kind enough to share stories and insights that can be helpful when dealing with global teams.

GLOBAL TEAM LEADER ALERT! AVOID CULTURAL DYSFUNCTION IN YOUR WORKPLACE

Is it a social faux pas or a compliment? It really depends to whom you're talking. "You've gained so much weight!" Insulting to most Westerners, this comment is a neutral and even flattering observation in China. On the other hand, the "thumbs up" sign means "A-OK" in the United States but is offensive in Iran and Greece. Even First Lady Michelle Obama took a cultural misstep in London by placing her hand on the queen's back, a violation of royal protocol.

Take these different cultural frameworks, drop them into the international workplace, and you have a recipe for cross-cultural dysfunction on a global scale. Yet this disagreeable dish can be saved with the proper ingredients—curiosity, knowledge, empathy, and adaptability.

Take three examples of global teams I've worked with in recent years. Team A, Asians, South Africans, and Australians, worked together in Asia via e-mail and conference calls with satellite offices. Productivity had dropped and mistrust was growing. People were working at cross-purposes and had stopped communicating. As reflected in the Thomas-Kilmann conflict model, some members verbalized their grievances, others withdrew into an avoidance mode of silence, and compromisers tried to work things out. Cultural differences and virtual distances were creating an impasse.

Team recovery began with talking, the team leader setting the tone by admitting that he could have done a better job. Efforts were made to understand different cultural frameworks and to give others the benefit of the doubt. Some commonsense ground rules and "do's" and "don'ts" were charted. Terms were specified: "open communication" meant "active listening." "Follow up" was described in behavioral terms. A year later, team A reported an 82 percent improvement in productivity, compared to 25 percent growth the previous year.

Team B's dysfunction arose from cultural differences between a Japanese team leader and his American team. Silence, limited eye contact, and deference to his supervisors, all appropriate in a Japanese workplace, served only to erode his credibility as a leader in the United States. Team performance began to suffer.

"He doesn't make eye contact with people, and seems to lack self-confidence," some employees said. "He is so quiet and shy. We don't know where he stands," described another. Receptive to feedback, the leader changed, emerged from his shell, called more team meetings, and initiated team-building social activities. Within six months, the team had turned around and, even in a tough economy, outperformed other teams.

Team C's leader faced similar problems but with a less successful outcome. A high performer in the United States, she expected similar kudos managing a team of workers from Mexico, the Philippines, and the United Kingdom. Yet her direct communication style was not an appropriate fit for her team, and lack of flexibility was her downfall. When approached about the situation, she responded, "I am from New York. This is how I communicate, direct and to the point. That's what I expect from everyone. Indirect communication and hierarchy just don't work for me." The situation worsened.

Culture permeates every part of our lives, whether personal or professional. Women are discriminated against in many cultures, and ageism is a problem in others. While some countries have come to accept certain life events, such as divorce or having a child out of wedlock, these are still taboo subjects for many people. Even socializing after work can trip up the unknowing foreign employee. Evenings of eating and drinking might seem like an optional nonwork activity, when in fact work matters are discussed, important decisions made, and social relations cemented.

Tips and Best Practices

How does the global team leader find the appropriate recipe to avoid such cultural dysfunction? Start with these key ingredients:

- Learn about your team member's culture.

- Be respectful and open-minded.

- Remember that each team member is an individual, as well as a product of his or her culture.

When conflict occurs, remember the DIN model:

D   Describe facts in an objective manner with no prejudgment.

I   Interpret the facts from the other person's point of view.

N   Navigate and search for a different approach that will be satisfactory to both parties.

With these ingredients at hand, the global team leader can steer clear of cross-cultural pitfalls and create instead a productive and harmonious recipe for success.

Curtis Curry is a longtime colleague of Tim. Curtis is fluent in multiple languages and has more than twenty years of cross-cultural training experience.

He gives us a glimpse at how cultural differences around time, individualism versus collectivism, and power-distance can cause conflict and how they can be bridged.

The past twenty years have witnessed a great increase in interactions among individuals of diverse cultures. Globalization, improved communication technology, and an increasingly diverse workforce have led to a rise in conflicts stemming from cultural differences. Such conflicts arise from many differences in expectations of "normal" behavior, including diverse perspectives on how individuals should relate to one another, how authority figures should be treated, and how time is viewed. My time as master trainer and director of the Peace Corps training center for Honduras and Nicaragua was an intense period of learning how powerfully cultural values inform conflict behavior and often serve as a catalyst for conflict. One area of difference is the conceptualization of time. While a common North American saying is "Time is money," a well-known Central American aphorism is *"hay más tiempo que vida,"* or "There is more time than life."

Our weekly senior staff meetings had an official start time, but meetings generally began with a period of informal socializing before turning to the agenda. While formal meetings were occasionally scattered through the week, chatting informally with managers and employees was a more common and productive way of getting work done in Central America. Formal meetings were not as important or as frequent as in the United States.

When we hired a new assistant director from the United States, I noticed that when I would drop in on her, as was my common practice with host country staff, I noticed she seemed a bit anxious to get back to her work. "Curtis, did you need something in particular?" Her reaction reflected a number of values: her U.S. expectation of holding formal, planned meetings to discuss business, her view of time as a resource to be used efficiently, and her focus on completing the task that had been structured for that time slot. Latin American leaders are often expected to postpone scheduled tasks when facing a choice between people issues and task assignments. Differences in time orientation can be a major source of conflict across cultures.

Another important area of cultural difference is power-distance. In high power-distance cultures, such as Colombia, Japan, and Honduras, there is greater deference to authority figures than in low power-distance cultures such as Holland, Canada, and the United States. Differences along this dimension can lead to conflict.

When the Peace Corps established a new training center in Jinotepe, Nicaragua, Doña Norma, our Honduran executive assistant, accompanied our Honduran/American team to help out with the project start-up. When addressing one another, Hondurans primarily use the formal *you* form, *usted,* rather than the highly informal *vos,* which is reserved for lifelong friends. In Nicaragua, *vos* is a much more common way to address colleagues, and *usted* is much less frequently used.

One of the project drivers we had recently hired addressed me using *vos* and was quickly corrected by Doña Norma. "How could you think of using *vos* with the director! What a lack of respect! Don Curtis is how he should be addressed." While U.S. business culture is much less formal than Honduran business culture, I had lived in Honduras for a couple of years, and the driver's use of *vos* initially struck me as a bit disrespectful as well. I soon learned that this informal manner of address did not demonstrate a lack of respect in Nicaragua, but rather a cultural difference between Hondurans and Nicaraguans.

A final critical area of cultural differences that often leads to conflict is individualism versus collectivism. In general, individualist cultures focus on individual goals, individual performance, and "individuality." Collectivist cultures focus more on community, group loyalty, and family goals. The United States ranks high on the individualism end of the spectrum. As an American leader working in Honduras, a more collectivist culture, I learned that a leader's responsibilities in Honduras differed in some respects from those of the United States. Birthdays, Mother's Day, and other significant events marked special occasions that were to be observed by the organization. The director was expected to make a presentation to honor the individual or group. Additionally, the leader is expected to support his or her employees in interactions with the home office and help the employee get through personal rough times. Initially, I was surprised to have an employee ask me for a personal bridge loan, but realized that the leader has obligations to employees in collectivist cultures not generally found in individualistic cultures.

Quick Tips for Communicating Effectively Across Cultures

- Withhold making judgments when working with individuals from other cultures. Instead, focus on trying to *understand* rather than judge differences in behavior. For example, "That Brazilian team member stands close to me and touches my arm a lot while he is talking. Perhaps he's not being aggressive, but rather demonstrating a cultural difference."

- Since many cultures focus first on relationships, then on task deadlines, listen carefully to others. Make time to cultivate relationships. Value the differences.

- Be open to changing your cultural paradigms. In Honduras, we created a hybrid organizational culture in which meetings would start ten minutes after the official start time, and much business was conducted Honduras-style by walking around and chatting. We still got the job done, and to very high standards!

- Learn more about cultural elements that affect conflict such as the importance of hierarchical structure and the relative importance of the individual and collective concerns. You can get more information at http://www.geert-hofstede.com.

- Learn about differences across cultures. *Kiss, Bow, or Shake Hands: The Bestselling Guide to Doing Business in Sixty Countries* (Morrison and Conway, 2006) is a good starter resource.

- A final caveat: Avoid stereotyping. Research shows that while cultures do differ along certain dimensions such as time orientation, individualism-collectivism, and power-distance, there are great differences among individuals within cultures. There are highly individualistic people in collectivist cultures and vice versa.

Creating a Third Culture

Another interesting approach to managing cultural differences around conflicts is to create a new culture. Michael Rawlings, conflict management expert and a senior faculty member at the Federal Executive Institute, has dealt with intercultural conflict in many contexts. His contribution describes what he calls "creating a third culture."

Living in Brussels, Belgium, from 1986 to 1996 was invaluable in learning the importance of developing skills for building effective relationships in the international community. Working at NATO HQ, the Commission of the E.U., in multinational corporations, serving as an officer in the U.S.–European Chamber of Commerce, and teaching at business school presented daily challenges of finding middle ground. Not surprisingly, building long-term personal relationships within the international community presented exactly the same challenges.

As the emerging "Capital of Europe," Brussels is a place like no other, requiring the coming together of business and government, government with government, language to language, culture to culture. It's like London or Paris or Berlin, Washington or New York, Tokyo or Bangkok, Sidney, Mumbai, Cairo, or Jerusalem, taken to an exponential level by a dozen or more intermingled languages and many more cultural differences and nuanced interests. It's a learning laboratory for interest-based problem solving, with the fortunate elixirs of beer and wine coupled with the lubricant of long gourmet dinners, both of which encourage hours of practice in the arts of conversation and relationship building.

Daily life in Brussels presents challenges in how to move toward others and how to guide others in moving toward each other. Year after year I watched, participated, and learned the techniques used for effective interaction and meaningful experience in interpersonal relationships and organizational collaboration.

Perhaps the most important lesson Brussels has taught me about conflict management and collaborative problem solving is the importance of what I call "third culture." True third culture requires learning various methods and creating opportunities for each person within a group to move at will into a space that is native to neither of them but in which they can each function effectively. The components include (1) having a distinct third culture, (2) cultivating an attitude of willingness to step into *third* at any time with anyone, and (3) practicing the development of skills, attitudes, and approaches to support third culture. All three are important, and they build on each other. There is a well-established saying that after one lives outside of one's native culture for more than five years, one is forever a member of the broader expatriate community and culture. I think this is true, and it seems to hinge on the principles of third culture.

The first and second components are a matter of seeing and choosing. The third presents the basis for my preferred approach to conflict management and collaborative problem solving. It is an alternative to assimilation and is arguably more powerful than one person or group stepping into and adapting to the culture of another party. As an example, my boss at the Commission of the European Union was an Italian senior executive. We found it highly effective to communicate in French, a second language for each of us, which formed the basis for our third way. Not only did we work well together, we learned a lot from each other about flexibility, adventure, and humility, each of which built trust.

These experiences have powerfully informed my work with teams. Whether a client request is reactive or proactive, my first question before beginning work with the team is what "languages" or tools members of the team have in common. For example, I ask if members of the team have a working knowledge of Myers Briggs Type Inventory or another Jungian tool; a shared 360 assessment instrument such as Cornerstones, Benchmarks, Hogan, Conflict Dynamics Profile; or self-assessments like Thomas-Killman Inventory or Alexander Hiam's Dealing with Conflict Instrument.

After doing an inventory of the team's existing tools, it is essential to organize a refresher for one or more of those tools as well as ensure that new members of the team are given the same materials. Frequently

I find that one or more of these classic tools are poorly understood or only presented in the abstract; the refresher gives the team members a motivation to anchor the material and an opportunity to internalize it within the context of our approaching work together. If it is a new team or if no investment has been previously made in assessments or tools, I recommend that we administer at least one before beginning our work together. In either case, this step must be both time and cost effective to allow the group to move forward with the conflict management and collaborative problem-solving work.

With executive teams or small- to medium-sized intact working groups, I frequently ask each member of the team to pull together a personal package of their assessments and tools and do some preparatory self-reflection, including journaling:

- "What do I bring to the team that benefits our work together?"
- "What do I bring to the team that might be counterproductive to its work or that I might need to use more or less of to make us more effective?"

Bringing the group together, we go through a norming exercise, review the principles of their existing and new tools—which I refer to as "third languages"—and discuss the benefits of using those tools to help reduce counterproductive emotion or personalization of issues. Whenever possible, I provide groups with their normative strengths and predictable weaknesses or challenges.

Typically, I instruct the group in a consensus-building technique such as the commonly used five-finger model. The Five Finger Method is often attributed to the Society of Friends. It is not only useful for building consensus, it is also the most efficient method I've found of getting feedback from groups of any size and of systematically managing both support and concerns. This simple system is based on a proposal being offered to the group, followed by each person in the group raising the appropriate finger(s) to indicate his or her view on that proposal. Thumbs-up is "strongly agree," two fingers (the V sign) is "agree," three fingers is "can live with it," four fingers is "I have a question, comment, or concern," and five fingers is "No—I block this." Trust must be present for this method to work, yet it's highly effective and will build trust over time when used effectively.

It's only at this point that we are ready to begin the work of interest-based problem solving. It's essential to show the team and then model for and with them—often over an extended period of time—effective and proven collaborative models.

The team learns to use and prove the effectiveness of a classic collaborative problem-solving model and uses this model as their default approach to meetings and challenges. The essential steps include:

1. Identifying stakeholders

2. Refining and prioritizing issues together

3. Hearing their stories and sometimes doing fact finding

4. Sorting out the positions and interests of each stakeholder

5. Exploring options

6. Ground testing those options the group chooses

7. Moving toward workable win-win solutions

My goal in this sort of team intervention has been to work myself out of a job. That is, to help each team see the value of learning, sharing, and internalizing one or more third languages, then providing them with classic interest-based problem-solving methods and modeling these methods for and with them, using their real issues until they become competent at using the models. Teams can then continue to expand their capacity by bringing new members into the language and methods as well as by periodically investing in new languages and tools, thus enriching their team's creativity, productivity, and enjoyment.

Corporate Culture Clash

We often think of cultural conflicts in terms of national differences. Yet, some of the most difficult conflicts emerge when companies merge. Their respective cultural differences can cause suspicions and make it hard for people to work together. This is often exacerbated when a focus on the financial elements of a merger is not matched by sufficient attention to the people elements.

Our colleague Mary Khosh, a psychologist and organizational development trainer, shared an example of how to deal with this phenomenon.

A large, traditional, international pharmaceutical company acquired a smaller innovative informal U.S. pharmaceutical company headquartered in a western state. There was a need to merge the workforce of the giant company with the workforce of the smaller and very specialized drug company without interrupting the work and destroying the innovative culture of the smaller company. Employees were nervous about the impact of the change and worried that what they enjoyed about their work (casual environment and easy communication) would be eliminated. These concerns could have presented significant morale problems and turnover. They were resolved, though, by holding weekly town hall meetings in the western headquarters of the smaller company. Arrangements were made so that every employee could watch live or online. Questions could be asked by anyone companywide. The meetings were archived so employees could watch them again. Everyone was told that all questions would be respected and no questions were off-limits.

An abundance of communications and attention to employee concerns is an excellent step in preventing destructive conflicts from occurring in merger and acquisition contexts. Our advice is, don't wait for conflicts to emerge. Expect cultural differences to cause concerns and meet them head on through communications and constructive conflict engagement.

Norms for Managing Conflicts Involving Team Members from Different Cultures

As with other team conflict challenges, we recommend developing norms for how the team wants to address conflict issues that involve cultural differences. In general, we suggest including norms that recognize the cultural differences as natural and respect the authenticity of each culture's particular approach toward conflict. It is helpful to recognize that intercultural conflict can be complex and that it is important to slow things down when it is recognized. This allows participants time to sort through things and try to make sense of them. We encourage working to understand one another and not try to force solutions too quickly. It should be recognized that language differences can make it more difficult to develop understanding. It may be appropriate to turn to outside help from consultants like Maya, Curtis, or Michael to help sort things out. There is no one right way to handle conflict between people from different cultures. If the team has worked to develop trust and collaboration among its members, team members will be more willing to have faith in the good intentions of other teammates, and this will help overcome misunderstandings caused by the cultural differences.

Organizational Conflict Competence

I n *Becoming a Conflict Competent Leader* we discussed how leaders could champion organizational conflict competence and discussed the basic elements associated with systemic treatment of organizational conflict. In this chapter we look at the subject again through the viewpoint of practitioners. We look at the nature of organizational conflict competence, the benefits that accrue from it, and what it takes to change organizational culture and systems to enable more effective conflict management. We will also look in some depth at one of the finest examples of integrated conflict management systems design and implementation at the Transportation Security Administration (TSA).

In our earlier book, we noted that leaders can have a big impact on corporate culture in general and the way an organization deals with conflict more specifically. When leaders look at conflict as a zero-sum game, their organizations tend to take a more adversarial approach to conflict management. On the other hand, when leaders prefer to seek win-win outcomes, their organizations more often use collaborative problem-solving approaches (Lipsky, Seeber, and Fincher, 2003). We believe that the latter approach lends itself to development of organizational conflict competence and the benefits this competence can bring.

So exactly what is organizational conflict competence? As we mentioned in Chapter One, it involves creating a culture that supports our "cool down, slow down, and engage constructively" model. It also includes aligning mission, policies, training programs, performance standards, and reward structures to reinforce these approaches. Finally, it includes developing systems to support cultural change and for managing conflicts that become too intense for individuals to manage on their own. This enables a "shift to a systematic focus on relationship management, and early resolution of conflict at the lowest possible level" (Lynch, 2005). Deborah Katz, TSA's Director of the Office of Collaborative Strategies, provides an excellent description of its essence: "I cannot stress enough that enabling interests and concerns to surface, be heard with respect and discussed constructively not only supports employees, it supports the entire organization and should be a critical component of any approach to risk management and organizational development" (International Institute for Conflict Prevention & Resolution, 2009, p. 102).

BENEFITS OF ORGANIZATIONAL CONFLICT COMPETENCE

When an organization effectively manages conflict, it can cut down on costs from wasted management time, turnover, absenteeism, presenteeism, lost productivity, lawsuits, vandalism, and violence. It can increase creativity and collaboration, improve relationships and morale, and enhance decision quality and implementation efforts. When interpersonal issues are not allowed to fester and organizational issues are allowed to be aired, employees become more engaged, trust is improved, dialogue and collaboration expand, and people become effective problem solvers. The pain and stress of conflict can be eased (International Institute for Conflict Prevention & Resolution, 2009). In the case of TSA, the overriding need was to manage risk by enabling concerns and issues to be raised and addressed as swiftly as possible. If conflicts kept people from discussing serious security issues, the results could be disastrous. As Katz notes, "Enforcing expectations that executives and managers create an environment that is respectful and open to new or unwelcome ideas is critical to any organization's risk management efforts. Examine virtually any catastrophic organizational failure, and you will almost always find that at least one person in the organization had doubts or concerns that could have averted disaster" (International Institute for Conflict Prevention & Resolution, 2009, p. 91).

An Example of the Benefits of Effective Conflict Management

Cindy Koehn is the director of human resources at the Corrections Corporation of America (CCA). One of her tasks is helping staff at prisons deal with conflicts more effectively. As Cindy notes, "People who work in correctional institutions know that conflict is inevitable and often stressful. They live it every day." She told us a story about a training program she conducted in one of CCA's facilities that involved the warden, department heads, and senior correctional officers (Craig's conversation with Cindy Koehn July 20, 2009). The facility was undergoing expansion, which always brings about additional stress.

The program placed specific emphasis on slowing down and constructive engagement practices. Cindy used the CDP instrument with participants and focused on the behavior of delayed responding as a technique to help people calm down before saying something that could escalate conflicts. Once people had regained their composure, they were then encouraged to use reaching out and perspective taking behaviors in order to engage the issue and better understand the differences that were at the heart of the conflicts.

Before the program, Cindy had been receiving a number of complaints from employees related to different conflicts. Soon after the program was implemented, there was a 70 percent drop in the number of complaints, and the remaining complaints were generally less serious. This example demonstrates some of the benefits that constructive engagement can bring.

ADDRESSING CONFLICT SYSTEMATICALLY

Team conflict is typically more complex (although not necessarily harder) to manage than interpersonal conflict. Creating the right climate and constructive norms is a key to addressing team conflict effectively. When taken to an organizational level, creating the right culture and reinforcing constructive behavioral approaches to conflict remain a key element of conflict competence, but the process for achieving them is more complex still. The use of integrated conflict management systems (ICMS) helps address this complexity and achieve the cultural change that is essential for success. Key aspects of such systems include:

- Provides multiple options for how to raise and address conflicts
- Fosters a culture that welcomes dissent and encourages resolution at the lowest point at the earliest time

- Allows for multiple access points to the system
- Incorporates systemic support and structures that coordinate access to and use of the various options to address conflict
- Supports confidentiality and safety (Gosline and others, 2000)

An ICMS includes alternative dispute resolution (ADR) but it is much more. Indeed, most of its value derives from the parts that serve to prevent destructive conflict and help promote the constructive resolution of differences. The focus in an ICMS is on changing an organization's cultural norms around conflict that shape how people work together, manage their differences, and resolve problems. It promotes surfacing concerns and issues as a means of developing creative resolutions. When these issues are surfaced, it provides leaders with a much better sense of what is going on in an organization than when the problems stay submerged and arise in crises. Systemic issues can be identified sooner. As Deborah Katz says to leaders, "You have a choice. You can be the first to know or the last to know what is going on in your organization. It depends on whether you have created an environment in which issues and concerns can be raised with confidence that they will be received respectfully and responsibly" (International Institute for Conflict Prevention & Resolution, 2009, p. 88).

THE TSA EXPERIENCE

The Transportation Security Administration was created in 2001 and has responsibility for security for all modes of transportation. Among other responsibilities, it provides passenger and baggage screening for 450 commercial airports in the United States. TSA, which is part of the U.S. Department of Homeland Security, has more than 43,000 employees. It began work on its ICMS in 2003. We appreciate the access that TSA has provided us for this book. In addition to Deborah Katz, we were able to speak with Diane Ditzler, Program Manager, and Ruth Britt, Conflict Management Specialist, from TSA's Model Workplace Program Office (MWPO), and with Jennifer Lynch, who served as the key outside consultant during the first few years of the effort.

The key components of TSA's integrated conflict management system can be summed up as skills, structure, and support. The *skills* component involves helping all employees develop conflict management and communication skills, as well as helping supervisors and managers develop a higher level of cooperative problem-solving skills to help them routinely use an interest-based approach to addressing workplace issues. Additional skills are developing internal practitioners across the organization in facilitation, coaching, and mediation, which builds internal capacity that enables TSA to provide internal conflict management services throughout the agency.

The *structure* component of the ICMS refers to practices and processes that allow issues to be raised and addressed either informally or as needed in more formal ways through a traditional alternative dispute resolution system. Employees are provided with confidential and anonymous options for raising concerns. There are also work groups and employee councils that can address group-related concerns. These options are available in local settings as well as on the national level.

The *support* component involves creating an environment that encourages people to raise issues and protects them against retaliation when they do. This includes having leaders model and reinforce the practices and behaviors that are espoused as part of the model. This type of modeling gives leaders credibility to champion widespread adoption of the ICMS within the organization (International Institute for Conflict Prevention & Resolution, 2009).

ICMS support includes providing governance and coordination for system implementation and sustainment efforts, strategic and ongoing communication about the system, and ongoing assessment and evaluation for monitoring progress and planning for continuous improvement.

A major aspect to ICMS support is integrating the core principles of the ICMS so that they become embedded in all organizational processes and practices. The core principles, outlined in a TSA management directive and firmly established as organizational policy, include Prohibition of Retaliation, Voluntary Participation, Protection of Confidentiality and Privacy, Collaborative Decision Making, Impartiality of Neutrals, as well as Qualifications and Training of Neutrals, and Diversity and Accessibility.

As the ICMS has taken hold at TSA, the conflict management practices have begun to be aligned with the TSA mission and its hiring and promotion practices, performance management processes, and reward and recognition structure. This integration of the ICMS into the larger organizational culture marks its transformation from an interesting new approach to a core competency of the organization.

Another principle that is a unique feature of TSA's ICMS evolved through work with the early adopter sites. In ongoing dialogue in the earlier years of development, team members struggled with how to get middle management to routinely think about the need to involve stakeholders to ensure fair processes and open communications regarding decision making. One team member, Scott Lorenzo from Port Columbus International Airport, said, "It is really pretty simple—they just need to remember to be fair, inclusive, and transparent." Diane Ditzler adds, "Thus was born the FIT test," which is now codified in TSA policy with the following definition:

> The FIT Test: TSA expects that decisions will meet the FIT test, i.e., decision making processes and practices will be fair and, to the fullest extent possible, inclusive and transparent [excerpt from TSA Management Directive 1100.00–5].

At TSA, it has become everyone's responsibility to raise concerns. One way this has been accomplished dates back to the original design workshop. As the group wrestled with how to frame and educate others about the ICMS, one team came up with the notion that the ICMS really could be cast as "I C Me in the Solution." This catchphrase embodies several meanings, all reinforcing that it is everyone's responsibility to be a part of the process in dealing with conflicts and issues that arise in the normal span of our workday. Following are the statements that appear on the "I C Me in the Solution" poster sent to all field locations:

> I am responsible for raising concerns, recognizing and resolving conflict and making TSA a Model Workplace.
>
> I alone am not the solution: I am part of the solution.
>
> I have the skills I need to raise and resolve issues and concerns.
>
> I know where to go with an issue or concern.
>
> I am confident I will be listened to respectfully.
>
> I am confident my interests and relevant input will be considered when decisions are made that affect me.

Considering that most people prefer to avoid dealing with conflict, this amounts to a big change. One thing that helped people make this change was a message that simplified what raising concerns meant. It is called the 4R model and includes *recognizing* that there is a problem, *responding* to it with respect, *resolving* or managing the issue, and *reflecting* on what caused it and how it was able to be resolved. Figure 6.1 shows a poster of the 4R model. Since the 4Rs are everyone's responsibility, the model helps interpersonal issues get raised so that they don't fester and become larger problems. It also represents a method of

Figure 6.1
The Four Rs of Conflict Management

The **4R's** of Conflict Management

Recognize

Conflict is normal and may present positive opportunities. We all have the responsibility to recognize common causes of conflict, separating the person from the conflict and respecting differences.

Respond
with Respect

Responding respectfully, constructively and with active listening. We take responsibility to respond to conflict and not let differences become distracting or destructive.

Resolve
and Manage

Using a cooperative problem solving approach. Cooperative problem solving encourages us to uncover interests and consider them when working together to resolve and manage conflict, issues and concerns.

Reflect

Building on and learning from our experience. Benefiting from conflict by stepping back and examining what happened, appreciating what went well, and identifying opportunities for improvement.

Transportation Security Administration

The **Model** Workplace
I *C* Me in the Solution

creating a simplified way of explaining what could have been a complex process. It helps make the approach more understandable and accessible.

The ICMS emphasizes engagement and cooperative problem solving. Collaborative problem solving is encompassed in a collaborative problem-solving graphic that shows the elements of interest-based problem solving in the shape of a wheel. The parts of the wheel include raising the issue, uncovering the interests of the parties, exploring options to resolve the problem, and deciding on a solution. Figure 6.2 shows the wheel with a line between the raising of the issue and deciding on a solution components to help people from jumping too quickly to a solution.

Design and Implementation

TSA leaders provided the initial support that allowed the ICMS effort to begin. The MWPO knew they had to build buy-in and chose to start working with people in the field. They would collaborate with people at airports who had interest and enthusiasm about the concept and leaders whose personal leadership style and approach mirrored that of the ICMS principles. Regardless of the motivation—excitement about dealing with conflict more effectively or pain from experiencing so much dysfunctional conflict—the MWPO went "where the energy was."

Jennifer Lynch, the ICMS external consultant, urged being flexible and inclusive and to model interest-based approaches to problem solving at every step along the way. This approach helped expand buy-in and led to many innovations from field staff, who were experts on their working environments. They didn't look for cookie cutter approaches. Although some core concepts applied to all situations, flexibility was allowed in how they were implemented. The process became the product.

They started by convening an initial meeting with several early adopters. As Katz described it, "We held a design workshop with cross-functional teams from 11 airports that had volunteered to be pilot sites. They proposed a basic design including conflict management training for all, conflict coaching training for some, a communication strategy, a plan for establishing a baseline and evaluating progress, and various options customized to local site needs. The optional techniques included peer review panels to be used in the grievance process, local employees' councils and other work groups, and confidential 'concern forms' to raise issues outside the chain of command" (International Institute for Conflict Prevention & Resolution, 2009, p. 89).

One of the key elements of the design was a half-day course in conflict management available to all employees. We asked Diane Ditzler and Ruth Britt about what seemed to catch people's attention in the course. The first concerned an exercise in

Figure 6.2
TSA's CPS Wheel

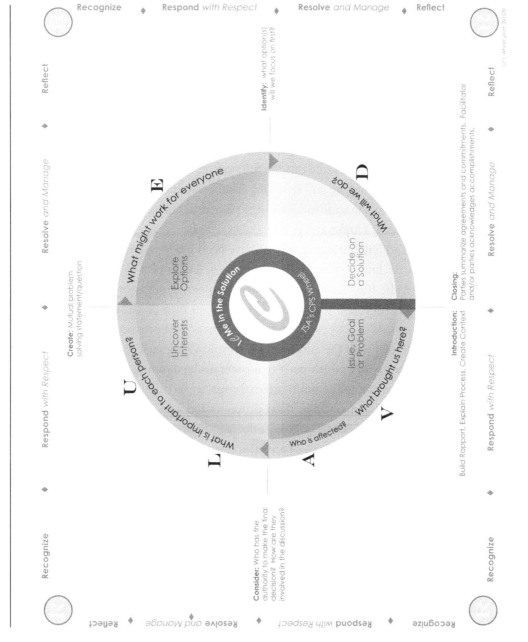

which participants listed conflicts they experienced or had seen in the workplace. They wrote them on Post-it notes that were put on the wall, categorized as individual, group, or organizational issues, and then discussed. The process seemed to free people up and led to a feeling that it was all right to talk about conflict—no small breakthrough! The second element was picking a conflict and using the principles and processes of interest-based negotiations to figure out how to deal with it. Additionally, local coordinators developed a "Top Ten" list of the group and organizational issues, which provided leadership and the new local councils with a place to begin work. Showing some early successes on group conflicts that resonated with a majority of employees provided the initial impetus to get solid grounding for the implementation teams to build out the full system. Once again, it demonstrated a new approach to managing and resolving conflicts that captured people's interest and provided avenues to address major workplace issues in meaningful ways (Craig's conversation with D. Ditzler and R. Britt, July 1, 2009).

In addition to initial training, efforts have been made to reinforce the lessons. In some airports, home-grown visuals have started to appear that underscore the key aspects of the ICMS. At the Milwaukee airport, supervisors now provide a monthly report on ICMS principles they have put into place. These are shared with all supervisors so they can benefit from others' best practices. The reporting process has helped with the adoption of common language to describe conflict management behaviors, which itself reinforces understanding.

Efforts have continued to build internal capacity to train, facilitate, and coach others. Having peers involved in these processes has added credibility. One-shot training is not enough. These ongoing efforts to help people put constructive behaviors into action are critical, as are efforts to maintain a supportive environment for raising and addressing issues.

After a few years, the core team recognized the need to solidify and institutionalize the gains that had been made. While individual responses to conflict had improved, there was a need to enhance the integration of the ICMS into all areas at TSA. They began development of a way to visualize the entire path of implementation and the evolutionary nature of that work. This led to the creation of the ICMS Maturity Model. It spells out in more detail the foundational work needed to build to higher levels of performance and effectiveness in conflict management, issue resolution, and organizational change. The model and accompanying tools provide specific information on observable milestones and activities necessary to achieve different levels of effectiveness in implementing the ICMS (see Figure 6.3). They also provide behavioral indicators for various actions. As such, the Maturity Model becomes a "road map with goals, landmarks, and directions" (International Institute for Conflict Prevention & Resolution, 2009, p. 89). This provides a basis for measuring effectiveness at sites. Assessment and evaluation of the entire program in light of its objectives is also part of the ICMS strategy, and TSA has contracted with an outside third party to evaluate the success of the program thus far.

The process of integrating the ICMS into the overall TSA culture has also begun. Team members appreciate that the base of knowledge provided by the ICMS is helping TSA accomplish its overall mission. When problems and issues are raised and addressed, people feel more engaged and help create solutions that enable the organization to function more smoothly and effectively. Conflict competencies, including behavioral indicators, are reviewed in relation to hiring, promotion, performance management, recognition, and rewards. This alignment represents a transformative stage in the evolution of an ICMS, where it becomes an integral part of an organizational culture rather than a new project or program.

Practical Advice

When implementing an ICMS, it can be challenging to resist the temptations of trying to move too fast or limit the effort to a specific outcome. An ICMS that grows organically has the best chance of success. This requires allowing time for involvement by a wide range of stakeholders, including those who champion and lead implementation, those who use the system and those who own processes within the system or are affected by the system (for example, offices that manage alternative dispute resolution practices, the training department, and human resource process owners). When you are able to get their participation and buy-in to the process, you are able to draw from their experience and insights to develop approaches that will be more readily accepted. These groups will also help devise ways of recognizing and overcoming resistance. The TSA staff found this to be particularly true when early adopters as well as skeptics were included in the design and implementation phases. By listening to the input of stakeholders and being willing to make changes that emerged from discussions, the staff was able to adjust the ICMS so it could be most beneficial to various TSA locations. All this takes patience and a recognition that developing an ICMS is a marathon rather than a sprint. It involves a great deal of ongoing dialogue—both talking

Figure 6.3
TSA's ICMS Maturity Model

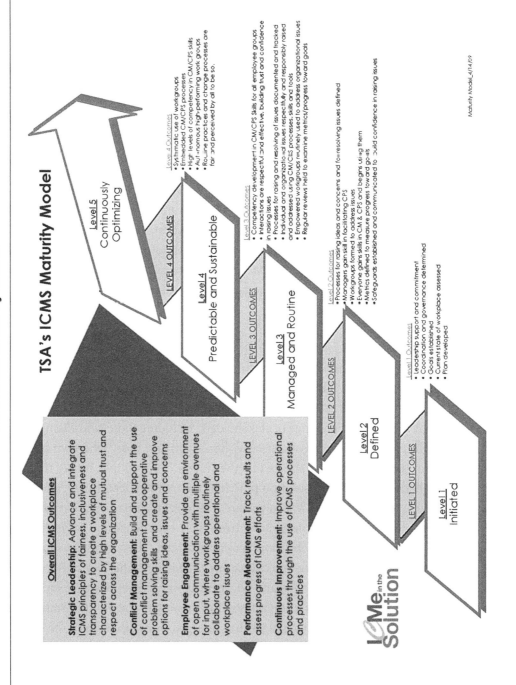

TSA's ICMS Maturity Model

and listening. If not rushed, it can help an organization build a sustainable model for long-term success.

When asked for suggestions to others who are contemplating creating an ICMS, Diane Ditzler and Ruth Britt recommended making the most of one's opportunities. To do this one needs to be open and flexible. Ditzler and Britt cited a session that had become know as the "Lost in Translation" meeting. The session involved the first ICMS coordinators at the pilot sites who were struggling with local ICMS implementation. In particular, team members at the sites were confused about the approach, and the coordinators were having a hard time explaining the system to local leaders and team members. The coordinators expressed a need to reframe the ICMS in simpler language. The MWPO used this opportunity to apply collaborative problem-solving skills, to have everyone at the meetings be open to not knowing the answer and to working collaboratively to come up with one. This enabled everyone to experience the power of the approach and confirmed the validity of what they were doing. It also enabled them to come up with practical and effective answers to the issues they have been facing. Two takeaways from this meeting were that the MWPO had a new model for explaining the ICMS and a valuable lesson in the power of the model: that using these opportunities to practice what they preach, trust in the system, and model the skills inherent in the ICMS model can be fruitful and help in addressing key issues that arise (Craig's conversation with D. Ditzler and R. Britt, July 1, 2009).

While the emphasis in this section has been on TSA's system of dealing with conflict, it is important not to lose sight of the personal impacts that effective conflict management can have. They are nicely put in a statement Eileen Lundgren, a TSA conflict coach, wrote in 2006.

What I Learned from Conflict in 2006

I have learned that conflict is not a bad thing
    and it does not make you a bad person.
I have learned that my unfulfilled expectations are my own,
I can give up my stand of being right,
    and be neutral in the situation.
I reflect back on the beauty of my growth and development of
becoming an extraordinary person through conflict
when I let go of judgment and celebrate that being human we
both want the same things—to feel valued and loved.

I will listen differently and be more present to the words
    instead of allowing my past experience to influence how
      the person is showing up for me.
I will ask more open-ended questions
    to clarify how I perceived the meaning of the words.
I will not react next time but respond.
I will stay in the now, use my active listening skills,
    and let go—it is not personal.

The behavior I want to change is to acknowledge the person that I am in conflict with and let them know that it made a difference in my life.

Eileen Lundgren,
Conflict Coach (DEN)

CHALLENGES OF MANAGING ORGANIZATIONAL CONFLICT

The TSA example represents a success story that is still in progress. TSA staff have had to meet a number of obstacles along the way. The challenges of developing and implementing an ICMS can be formidable. While we believe such systems hold great potential, we recognize that they represent a significant effort that can prevent organizations from taking the first step.

Richard Fincher is a full-time mediator and arbitrator of workplace disputes and litigation. He has a national consulting practice assisting organizations in establishing and evaluating conflict management systems. We appreciate his contribution, which addresses the organizational challenges that ICMS implementations face.

CONFLICT MANAGEMENT SYSTEMS IN THE WORKPLACE: A PROMISE UNFULFILLED

In 2003, two academic researchers (David Lipsky and Ronald Seeber of Cornell University) and a practitioner (myself) published a textbook titled *Emerging Systems for Managing Workplace Conflict: Lessons from American Corporations for Managers and Dispute Resolution Professionals* (Jossey-Bass). The content and observations in the text were the results of research and onsite interviews with a variety of organizational leaders, including CEOs, CFOs, general counsels, and human resource officers.

At that time, numerous large employers—including General Electric, Prudential, Eastman Kodak, Exelon, Shell, Halliburton, FMC, as well as several universities—had implemented various forms of workplace systems. All of these systems provided a multistep conflict resolution model, including mediation. Some models included voluntary arbitration, and most models included mandatory arbitration. From other researchers, there was soft data suggesting that more employees were employed under these workplace conflict management systems than there were employees employed under collective bargaining agreements.

Original Premise

The premise of the book was that progressive organizations were moving "beyond ADR." As described by coauthor David Lipsky, "Organizations weren't simply using mediation, arbitration, or other third-party techniques to resolve disputes, but had developed comprehensive, integrated conflict management systems. These systems put the emphasis on *managing* conflict rather than merely *resolving* conflict. They usually involve elaborate internal procedures to handle conflict before it ever reaches an arbitrator, mediator, or other outsider. In an integrated conflict management system (ICMS), the organization takes a *proactive* approach to conflict within the organization, rather than a *reactive* one."

The tone of the book was optimistic. As ADR researchers, we believed ICMS has the potential to reshape the nature of the American workplace and be part of a new social contract. While acknowledging that employers were motivated to establish workplace systems for a variety of reasons, we were attracted to such expressed motivations as employee engagement, quality improvement, employer branding, and a new cultural norm. We pondered whether these emerging workplace systems had reached the "tipping point" in American business or legal culture.

Acknowledged Barriers

Our research acknowledged several concerns about the future of integrated conflict management systems. One chapter in the text was dedicated to these anticipated barriers to the growth of workplace systems. Three representative quotes from that chapter:

"There is nothing inevitable about the ultimate triumph of ADR in the workplace."

"Without further institutionalization, ADR may prove to be a transitory phase rather than a permanent shift in corporate conflict management."

"Our research demonstrates that dispute management overwhelms conflict management as the dominant mode of corporate behavior."

In this chapter, we noted the potential barriers to growth of ICMS, including that some organizations view conflict as an exception or an aberration and do not buy into the logic of the ICMS; some organizations do not welcome disputes over rights; and while no one denies conflict resolution costs money, some organizations disconnect the cost of resolving employee litigation from the cost of a preventative program. Additional barriers included that some CEOs fear a flood of employee complaints: if you build it, they will come; opposition to workplace systems by some labor unions; and the paucity of hard data research from existing systems, requiring a leap of faith by internal champions. One final barrier was that ADR systems never become embedded in the corporate culture because the organizations selectively embrace ADR for some uses (for example, employment) but reject it for other uses (for example, product liability).

The View from Today

We have not formally updated our data since publishing our text. However, we continue to consult in the field and have a significant amount of anecdotal observation. In hindsight, our original view about the future of workplace systems was overly optimistic. Many of the barriers we anticipated have come true. While most employers who had workplace systems in 2003 still have them (and appear satisfied with their efficacy), there has been no expansion of the movement across the country. Today, there are few articles in legal or HR journals about ICMS for the workplace. Fewer academics are researching the concept. The new focus is on fairness in workplace arbitration, prompted by the proposed Arbitration Fairness Act, which would eliminate mandatory arbitration of employment disputes.

What Has Happened in Five Years?

Why has the movement toward workplace systems stalled after an explosive spurt of acceptance? Was it merely a phase? Was the problem structural (how it was organized and funded and evaluated) rather than conceptual? Have events superseded its original value?

The following are my perceived reasons for the lack of growth of integrated conflict management systems in the workplace. Some factors were identified in our text, while other reasons are new.

1. Institutional memory about the original reason (precipitating justification) for creating the workplace system has been lost.

Some workplace systems were originally created as a response to some major event, such as settlement of a class action lawsuit, a difficult merger of two organizations, a labor dispute, or a scandal involving employee relations. Memories fade quickly in corporate America, and an attitude arises of "That is old history."

2. Resistance from internal corporate stakeholders was stronger than anticipated, particularly the law department and HR department.

This barrier was clearly anticipated in the original research. Although law schools have slowly embraced ADR, most practicing attorneys have a "rights-based orientation" to their jobs. They understand but do not intuitively value a preventative focus in the law. The same could be said for human resource executives, who today see their primary role as instruments of business strategy and less employee engagement and morale. Both professions may view workplace systems as a loss of control for them. Of course, there are exceptions to any characterization.

3. Turnover or departure of original champions and program leadership has left gaps in ongoing institutional support.

There are several examples of workplace systems that floundered due to the turnover of their original champions or original leaders. When the original champion or original program director retires or relocates, the workplace system may be moved lower in the organization, or defunded, or staffed with a lower-level executive with less influence.

4. Two problems have arisen concerning mandatory employment arbitration as the last step of the system: companies with mandatory arbitration clauses have received public criticism due to perceived unfairness, and management (with legal advice) reverted back to a legalistic attitude favoring disposition of employment disputes by legal maneuvering.

As noted previously, the majority of workplace systems established in the 2000–2003 time period included mandatory arbitration. One of the uneasy questions about employer motivation about workplace systems is whether "it was all about arbitration," even though 98 percent of all workplace disputes are resolved during the negotiation or mediation steps. Clearly, mandatory employment arbitration is under attack due to concerns about fairness and public policy. In addition, employers seem to be regressing to a more power-based attitude toward employee conflict, seeking legal means to quash conflict rather than take the time to embrace and resolve it. Bottom line, those employers who embraced workplace systems due to arbitration are now thinking twice about the decision.

5. The range of motivations toward systems narrowed: at one time the motivations included productivity, employee retention, quality improvement, culture building, and even branding as an employer of choice. Those reasons are not mentioned anymore.

This observation reinforces our original view that ADR has generally been viewed by employers more as a reactive response rather than a strategic choice. However, coauthor David Lipsky has a contradictory theory. His view: In the beginning, corporations had a sharp focus on saving the time and money associated with litigation. Those two goals justified the program. Later, an expanded range of motivations may have raised unreasonable expectations and diluted the sharp focus of earlier approaches, and led to contradictory prescriptions on how best to serve all of those ends.

6. Hard research data from universities or corporations to justify cost savings is not available. Most corporate ADR systems do not invest in evaluation of their outcomes.

Workplace systems have knowable costs but uncertain benefits. Corporate leaders demand data to support business decisions. With few exceptions, most workplace systems did not invest in such data, or instead gave it lip service. When budget reductions occurred, there was not the hard data needed for the systems to survive the cuts.

7. Support from outside employment law firms regressed, as they never valued conflict management systems and disparaged the idea.

Five years ago, it was common to hear defense employment attorneys complain about the waste of time and money in the litigation process and praise clients who had a preventative focus. Today, that theme has disappeared. At legal conventions, defense employment attorneys now praise the use of motion practice to knock out most employment cases. Within the defense bar, there is a general disdain toward the motivation of plaintiffs. Today, the defense firms discourage arbitration, because in theory some arbitrators disfavor motions to dismiss. The irony of this observation is that the top twenty-five employment law firms today all represent themselves as offering expertise in ADR.

So What Is the Future of Workplace Systems?

In the short term, we do not expect to see a reemergence of workplace systems. The barriers outlined in our book, together with the barriers described, are overwhelming the perceived opportunities. However, I remain optimistic. In that much of life is cyclical, I can foresee a new era of workplace systems, perhaps different than the prior era. Described next are five possible scenarios that could encourage employers to embrace the benefits of workplace systems.

One scenario involves a backlash by employees against financial corporations tainted by the recent U.S. financial meltdown and associated images of greed. In an effort to reduce or address employee discontent, these financial corporations may draw attention to protections they offer that address both internal process justice and distributive justice through workplace systems.

Another scenario involves employers using workplace systems to collaborate with labor unions. Contrary to common perception, unions can embrace workplace systems that do not infringe on rights within the collective bargaining agreement.

A third scenario involves potential passage of the federal Arbitration Fairness Act, which would eliminate the enforceability of arbitration for employment disputes. As of September 2009, the Arbitration Fairness

Act is being vetted through various committees in Congress. A recent lawsuit between the State of Minnesota and the National Arbitration Forum over ties to consumer groups has increased the likelihood of some form of passage. The ACR Board of Directors has commissioned a national taskforce to explore options concerning the AFA. A recommendation will be made to the board in early 2010. This issue is being greatly overshadowed by health care legislation.

Without the option of mandatory arbitration, some employers may place more emphasis on mediation and other preventative measures to avoid court litigation.

A fourth scenario involves the expected growth in union organizing which may accompany the federal Employee Free Choice Act (EFCA). Some version of EFCA is expected to become law, and some employers may embrace workplace systems to convey a culture of internal justice and due process. As of September 2009, the proposed Employee Free Choice Act is stalled in Congress. Resistance to the card check provision has been more intense than was anticipated by the sponsors. Some labor law reform is still expected to pass Congress is 2010. The issue is being greatly overshadowed by health care legislation.

A final scenario involves the eventual rebound of our economy. In a down economy, most employees keep their heads down and hesitate to sue their employers. In a growing economy, employees have more confidence to push their rights. As our economy recovers, employers may preempt this litigation-prone environment by embracing workplace systems.

Note: Dick acknowledges the insightful contributions of Professor David Lipsky and Professor Ronald Seeber of Cornell University. The author also thanks Warren Cunningham (formerly of Raytheon Corporation) for his insights as well.

CULTURE AUDITS

In order to know what changes need to be made to an organization's conflict culture, it is first necessary to understand the current culture. Every organization has one, although they are implicit in most. If you ask people, they can tell you how they think conflict is handled in their organization, even if the vision and mission say something quite different. However, different people may provide you with different pictures depending on their position and location in the organization. Sometimes it is necessary to first conduct a *culture audit* to get a better sense of where things stand. Mike Bice, Senior Health Care Fellow at the Center for Conflict Dynamics, shares his experience with a cultural audit of a health care organization.

REGIONAL MEDICAL CENTER CULTURAL AUDIT

I was hired by the new CEO of the Regional Medical Center (RMC), to conduct a cultural audit. He had been hired to reverse the fortunes of an ailing medical center and had been on the job for eighteen months. Try as he might, he could not change the culture to realize his vision of a market-leading, high-quality provider as rapidly as he'd like. There was a gap between his vision and the operating reality, and he was eager to fully understand the nature of the gap and to develop interventions to alter the historical culture.

A department head meeting was held prior to the audit to allow me to present my model of the culture change process. The CEO then announced that I had been retained to conduct a cultural audit and that the findings of the audit would be presented to the group upon completion of the study.

The culture audit began with a document review. The review included the current HR policy manual, the process used to hire new employees, employee newsletters, and CEO memos to employees for the previous eighteen months. RMC annual reports for the previous three years were studied, as well as minutes from the management executive committee for the past twelve months. Two employee attitude surveys were examined, and the most recent Joint Commission survey was studied.

After this paper review, a series of structured interviews was held with thirty individuals: ten from top management, ten from middle management, and ten direct caregivers or care support staff. Since each person was asked the same set of questions, there was an opportunity to compare and contrast the answers for each group. Not surprisingly, there were material differences between top management and the other two groupings.

The top management group "got" the CEO's message, for the most part, and were trying to move the organization forward. The other two groups hadn't internalized the CEO's vision, and based on past experience, were hunkering down until it was evident the new CEO meant business and was going to stay long enough to make significant changes. All three groups were unified in one respect: they all described the historic culture in nearly the same terms. A comparison of the historical culture and the desired culture was then prepared. Figure 6.4 shows the results of this comparison.

The next step in the process was to identify two high-leverage interventions, which had the potential to change the organization's culture. One intervention fell in the human resources category (Human Relations Philosophy) and the other fell into the organizational development category (Enhance Innovation). In the first instance, it became evident that the HR department was firmly embedded in the old culture. Policies were based on controlling behavior, and rigid rules and procedures were enforced. The HR director was not a member of top management and probably could not have passed muster as a contemporary CHRO. As the organization moved forward, she was falling further and further behind. An early retirement package was developed, and she accepted, after some counseling and due process.

The other intervention, Enhancing Innovation, began with a thorough reordering of the organization's system for handling employee suggestions. Suggestion boxes were placed on all patient floors, in the cafeteria, and inside the two main entrances to the facility. (Before this, there had been

Figure 6.4
Regional Medical Center Culture Audit Findings

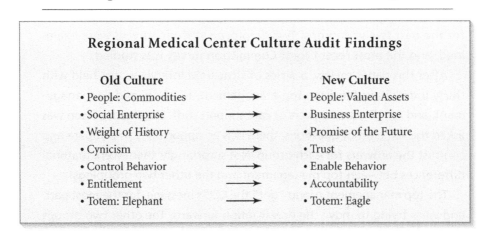

Source: Mike Bice.

one suggestion box, located outside the HR office.) Every quarter, an employee was recognized for suggesting an improvement, and a monetary reward was given by the CEO at a department head meeting. Continuous quality improvement (CQI) programming began, and achievement reports were published widely. Team-building efforts were redoubled, with CQI and daily, incremental improvements becoming part of the routine.

The final step was to present the findings of the cultural audit to the department heads, after the program was underway and taking hold. We were not interested in a one-off improvement but rather in sustained changes. Today, the same CEO is in place, and the RMC has been recognized as a market leader by JD Power & Associates.

THE LEADER'S ROLE IN ORGANIZATIONAL CONFLICT COMPETENCE

Cultural change is a key component of developing organizational conflict competence. Leaders can play a big role in supporting this change. They can model the constructive behaviors that make a difference in conflict settings. They can serve as coaches and mentors to help others improve their conflict skills. Finally, they can champion the organizational and cultural change processes needed to achieve the comprehensive benefits of conflict competence. Jean Wright is a coach and organizational development practitioner who works with leaders to improve their abilities to manage conflict. She graciously shared her insights.

COACHING AND PRACTICING CONSTRUCTIVE BEHAVIORS: PATH TO UNEXPECTED DISCOVERIES

Machu Picchu, the Inca Lost City, was discovered by Hiram Bingham as he searched for something else. Hiram Bingham and my coaching clients share the experience of exploring and discovering something unexpected that proved more powerful than their initial intention. The Conflict Dynamics Profile (CDP) opens an opportunity for clients to dig deeper into some key beliefs that contribute to not just one specific conflict but to many of their workplace conflicts. By opening themselves to reflection and challenging existing stories, coaching clients gain a greater awareness of themselves and how they contribute to conflict. The CDP's constructive behavior responses are potential areas for client practice during all phases of the coaching process.

Phase I: Exploration

Using open-ended questions, explore the client's context of presenting conflict, internal conflict, values, goals, and meaning making. Client explores the presenting issue and sets a coaching goal, which could be directly tied to one of the CDP behaviors or to a current conflict. Through this exploration, the client gains insight into self. The coach may assist the client's practice of several of the CDP constructive responses: perspective taking, expressing emotions, and reflective thinking.

Application. This client's position required listening to diverse groups and considering their concerns—a hotbed of conflict. During exploration, this client revealed that he could listen for short durations and stopped listening when he thought that he heard all he needed to hear or started hearing impertinent information. The client also revealed that he drove the conversation, focused mainly on facts, discouraged hearing about "personalities" as they were "insignificant," and easily became impatient with listening. The client made physical body shifts when he talked about the "fluff" in conversations. The distinction between "fluff" and "facts" led the client to question if he was missing valuable information. Client felt he was operating in a "fallacy" that he listens but does not give it his full attention. As the client told stories about work situations and how he listened, I noticed and shared my observation about the types of questions he asks and the imbedded suggestions of the "right" way of doing something. We explored using open-ended questions and the origin of his questions. We created an observation exercise to notice what he says to himself when he is listening to others.

Phase II: New Awareness

Through reflection and observations on current conflicts, the client becomes increasingly aware of their making meaning and the thinking and feeling behind the action; becomes aware of new sensations and makes connections among three domains (mind, body, and language); begins challenging his own assessments; realizes that the presenting conflict is rooted in something much deeper than was first thought.

During this phase, the coach continues to build on perspective taking, expressing emotions, and reflective thinking, and the client begins to notice behaviors connected with the CDP constructive and destructive responses.

Application. The client practiced active, authentic listening and quickly realized that he was missing information. He was hearing what he wanted to hear and imposing his suggestions on others. Some of the mental distractions included formulating responses prior to the other person finishing his or her sentence, not pausing to reflect on what was said, assuming he already knew the solution and situation, and holding assessments of the person and situation. The client also recognized physical distractions to his listening, such as people waiting in the hall, e-mail alerts, papers on the desk, and so on. The client became more curious about missing information and practiced listening with curiosity and asking questions. The client created a list of strategies to focus and refocus his listening and identified conversations in which to practice the strategies.

Phase III: Unexpected Discovery

My clients usually find something unexpected and become more self-directed in their learning. With anticipation and hope, one of my clients said, "This is going unexpected places." The client's unexpected discovery impacts the presenting conflict and other areas of his or her life. Client reflections and self-observations are strong and intentional; somatic work becomes a practice; between sessions observations lead to new behavior; takes risks; adapts in the moment or shortly after; and welcomes accountability.

I find this part of coaching gratifying, as clients begin asking themselves coaching questions and making their own observations. I enjoy witnessing the clients' hope in their progress and eagerness to learn. I simply hold an open space and hold them accountable.

I can see the constructive behaviors practiced as part of the coaching process carrying over into the work setting and conflicts.

Application. The client immediately started noticing and hearing other perspectives and identifying emotions during conversations. He effectively dealt with many of his mental distractions to listening, which opened an opportunity to reexamine his leadership style. He found that his listening and communication was more directive than he intended. This discovery surprised him. As a result, he began reaching out to others, collaborating, and asking more questions. He noticed increased participation in creating solutions, learned more about people and the situation, and experienced less conflict.

Phase IV: New Direction
With new awareness, the client refocuses on the presenting conflict. This time, the presenting issue looks different to the client. New options unfold out of new distinctions and choices.

Application. The client's discovery prompted him to reshape his coaching goal to listen and reach out to people at all levels. He started observing others' behavior and created meeting processes that involved others. By involving others, the client learned more about situations, noticed improvement in his relationships, and engaged in conflict in a new constructive way.

This client noticed that he used to say, "I think you are wrong." Now, he listens, observes body language, pauses, and responds. He receives positive feedback from others. He uses questions instead of telling and notices that others enjoy responding to curious questions. When listening to others, the client finds opportunities to praise them. The client also worked on slowing his rapid pace for the sake of better listening, discussion, involvement, and openness.

Closing Phase
I end each coaching agreement by asking about the client's key takeaways, the impact of coaching, and their commitments to themselves. I inquire about strategies to overcome potential obstacles and

enlist support from others. This phase is an opportunity to return to the CDP results and celebrate improvements.

Application: The client used a breathing practice to slow his pace, listened better by focusing on what he doesn't know, accomplished more based on "new" information received from listening, involved others, passed leadership onto others, talked more to others, and put his BlackBerry away to reduce reaction and slow the pace. An unexpected benefit is that he feels less tense and has created boundaries that help him decide if he really needs to be involved or if others can handle the problem. Previously, he escalated conflict by inserting himself in situations that could have been resolved without his intervention. The client also has a better idea of what coaching really means.

Championing Organizational Conflict Competence

When we reviewed TSA's experience developing an integrated conflict management system, we saw that TSA leaders gave early buy-in to the process. Cultural change does not come easily. Leadership support is critical in helping sustain momentum. Leaders need to model the kind of behaviors that they want others to use. It provides credibility to leaders' calls for new norms that support constructive engagement of conflict. We strongly recommend that leaders show the way by participating in training to improve their own skills. We suggest they work with coaches to refine those skills. Finally, we encourage them to be personally involved in efforts to develop conflict competence in others so that their organization can achieve the benefits that stem from it. After all, they and their organizations face conflicts on a regular basis—why not get the best results from them?

RESOURCES

We work at Eckerd College in St. Petersburg, Florida. Tim is the director of custom programs at the Leadership Development Institute at the college. His group conducts programs for leaders and managers in leadership development, team building, and conflict management. You can reach Tim at:

Leadership Development Institute

Eckerd College

4200 54th Avenue South

St. Petersburg, FL 33711

800–753–0444

flanagta@eckerd.edu

www.eckerd.edu/ldi

Craig is director of the Center for Conflict Dynamics at the college. His group oversees the Conflict Dynamics Profile® assessment instrument and other products that can be used to help in assessment and training in conflict management. You can reach Craig at:

Center for Conflict Dynamics

Eckerd College

4200 54th Avenue South

St. Petersburg, FL 33711

888–359–9906

rundece@eckerd.edu

www.conflictdynamics.org

Contact Information for Contributors and Other Resources

Bob Acton
Gilbert Acton
347 Sierra Morena Place SW
Calgary, Alberta T3H 2X3
403–862–7246
bobacton@gilbertacton.com
www.gilbertacton.com

Don Albert
Don Albert & Associates
415 Newport Drive
Indialantic, FL 32903
321–953–2223
DONALBERTLEAD@cs.com

Edmond Bazerghi
Center for Executive Assessment
2002 Plumbrook Drive
Austin, TX 78746–6230
512–656–0007
edmondbazerghi@centerexec.com
www.centerexec.com

Michael Bice
Senior Health Care Fellow
Center for Conflict Dynamics
Eckerd College
4200 54th Avenue South
St. Petersburg, FL 33711
888–359–9906
mobice@eckerd.edu
www.conflictdynamics.org

Dr. Heather Brown
Professional Solutions, Inc.
462 Herndon Parkway, Suite 108
Herndon, VA 20171
703–593–2901
hbrown@professionalsolutions
.com
www.professionalsolutions.com

Rita Callahan
Working It Out
175 West 90th Street
New York, NY 10024
646–438–9899
www.mediate.com/RCallahan

Curtis Curry
Quality Learning International
1050 Hollow Brook Lane
Malabar, FL 32950
321–724–1917
curtis@leadershipqli.com
leadershipqli.com

Dan Dana
Mediation Training Institute
International
5700 West 79th Street
Prairie Village, KS 66208–4604
Phone 877–338–1113
Fax 913–273–1919
http://www.mediationworks.com/
index.html

Debra Dupree
Relationships That Matter
4075 Alder Drive, F1
San Diego, CA 92116
619–417–9690
debradupree@relationshipsthat
matter.com
www.relationshipsthatmatter.com

Richard Fincher
Workplace Resolutions
3420 Shea Boulevard Suite 200
Phoenix, AZ 85028
602–953–5322
RDF@workplacesolutions.com
www.workplacesolutions.com

Beverly Fletcher
Federal Executive Institute
1301 Emmet Street
Charlottesville, VA 22903
434–980–6360
Beverly.Fletcher@OPM.gov

Susan Gunn
Working Dynamics
P.O. Box 25778
Richmond, VA 23260–5778
804–353–9527
info@workdyn.com
www.workdyn.com

Maya Hu-Chan
Global Leadership Associates
San Diego, CA
858–668–3288
mayahuchan@earthlink.net

Marcia Hughes
Collaborative Growth
P.O. Box 17509
Golden, CO 80402
303–271–0021
mhughes@cgrowth.com
www.cgrowth.com

International Institute for Conflict
Prevention & Resolution
575 Lexington Avenue, 21st Floor
New York, NY 10022
212–949–6490
info@cpradr.org
www.cpradr.org

Debera Libkind, Ph.D., and Dennis
Dennis, Ph.D.
Care Full Conflict, LLC
16541 Redmond Way, #525-C
Redmond, WA 98052
314–330–5558
Debera@carefullconflict.com
Dennis@carefullconflict.com
www.carefullconflict.com

Jan McKenzie
The Weather Channel
300 Interstate North Parkway SE
Atlanta, GA 30339
770–226–2154
JMckenzie@weather.com
Janmckenzie@comcast.net

Sherod Miller
Interpersonal Communications
Programs
30772 Southview Drive Suite 200
Evergreen, CO 80439
800–328–5099
icp@comskills.com
www.i-skillszone.com

Mark Nevins
Nevins Consulting
90 Bedford Street Suite 1-D
New York, NY 10014
212–675–6137
info@nevinsconsulting.com
www.nevinsconsulting.com

Cinnie Noble
Cinergy® Coaching
Toronto, Ontario
416–686–4247
cinnie@cinergycoaching.com
www.cinergycoaching.com

Denise Pearson
University of Denver
2199 South University Boulevard
Denver, CO 80208
303–871–3964
Denise.Pearson@du.edu
www.du.edu

Michael Rawlings
Federal Executive Institute
1301 Emmet Street
Charlottesville, VA 22903
434–980–6280
rawlingsm@aol.com

Dennis and Michelle Reina
Reina Trust Building Institute
560 Black Bear Run
Stowe, VT 05672
802–253–8808
info@reinatrustbuilding.com
www.reinatrustbuilding.com

Judy Ringer
Power and Presence
76 Park Street
Portsmouth, NH 03801
603–431–8560
judy@judyringer.com
www.judyringer.com

Dr. Daniel Siegel
Mindsight Institute
11980 San Vicente Boulevard F1
Los Angeles, CA 90049
310–447–0848
info@mindsightinstitute.com
www.mindsightinstitute.com

Sue Strong
Strong Consulting
4 Beechwood Drive
Morristown, NJ 07960
973–267–7720
sjstrong@strongconsulting.biz
www.strongconsulting.biz

Tim Ursiny
Advantage Coaching and Training
480 East Roosevelt Road, Suite 105
West Chicago, IL 60185
630–293–0210
info@advantagecoaching.com
www.advantagecoaching.com

Rick Voyles and Carol Rice
Conflict Resolution Academy, LLC
P.O. Box 724506
Atlanta, GA 31139
770–435–5009
Conflictacademy@aol.com
www.conflictresolutionacademy.com

Jean Wright
Leadership Coaching 911
240–299–9744
jean@leadershipcoaching911.com

A good source for synergy exercises:
Consulting Psychologists Press
1055 Joaquin Road
Mountain View, CA 94043
650–969–8901
custserv@cpp.com

REFERENCES

Allred, K. "Anger and Retaliation in Conflict: The Role of Attribution." In M. Deutsch and P. Coleman (eds.), *The Handbook of Conflict Resolution.* San Francisco: Jossey-Bass, 2000.

Amason, A. "Distinguishing the Effects of Functional and Dysfunctional Conflict on Strategic Decision Making: Resolving a Paradox for Top Management Teams." *Academy of Management Journal,* 1996, *39,* 123–148.

Argyris, C. *Overcoming Organizational Defenses: Facilitating Organizational Learning.* Upper Saddle River, N.J.: Prentice Hall, 1990.

Armstrong, D., and Cole, P. "Managing Distances and Differences in Geographically Distributed Work Groups." In P. Hinds and S. Kiesler (eds.), *Distributed Work.* Cambridge, Mass.: MIT Press, 2002.

Begley, S. *Train Your Mind, Change Your Brain: How a New Science Reveals Our Extraordinary Potential to Transform Ourselves.* New York: Ballantine Books, 2007.

Bridges, W. *Managing Transitions: Making the Most of Change.* Cambridge, Mass.: Perseus Books Group, 2003.

Capobianco, S., Davis, M., and Kraus, L. *Managing Conflict Dynamics: A Practical Approach* (5th ed.). St. Petersburg, Fla.: Eckerd College, 2008.

Carmeli, A., and Schaubroeck, J. "Top Management Team Behavioral Integration, Decision Quality, and Organizational Decline." *Leadership Quarterly,* 2006, *17*(5), 441–453.

Center for Creative Leadership. "Conflict Poll Results." *Leading Effectively e-Newsletter,* 2003. http://www.ccl.org/leadership/enewsletter/2003/FEBjanpollresults.aspx?pageId=436.

Center for Creative Leadership. "Conflict in Teams: Maximize Potential, Limit Pitfalls." *Leading Effectively Newsletter,* 2009. http://www.ccl.org/leadership/enewsletter/2009/APRlessonsLanding.aspx.

Cohn, A., and others. "Happiness Unpacked: Positive Emotions Increase Life Satisfaction by Building Resilience." *Emotion,* 2009, *9*(3), 361–369.

Cooperrider, D. *Appreciative Inquiry: Toward a Methodology for Understanding and Enhancing Organizational Innovation.* Doctoral Dissertation: Case Western Reserve University, Cleveland, Ohio, 1986.

Dana Cost of Conflict Survey, 2009. http://www.mediationworks.com.

Dana, D. *Managing Differences.* Prairie Mission, Kan.: Dana Mediation Institute, 2005.

Davidson, R., and others. "Alterations in Brain and Immune Function Produced by Mindfulness Meditation." *Psychomatic Medicine,* 2003, *65,* 564–570.

DeDreu, C., and Weingart, L. "Task Versus Relationship Conflict, Team Performance and Team Member Satisfaction: A Meta-Analysis." *Journal of Applied Psychology,* 2003, *88*(4), 741–749.

Edmondson, A. "Psychological Safety, Trust, and Learning in Organizations: A Group-Level Lens." In R. Kramer and K. Cook (eds.), *Trust and Distrust in Organizations.* New York: Russell Sage Foundation, 2004.

Edmondson, A., and Smith, D. "Too Hot to Handle? How to Manage Relationship Conflict." *California Management Review,* 2006, *49*(1), 6–31.

Ekman, P. *Emotions Revealed.* New York: Henry Holt, 2003.

Elangovan, A., Werner, A., and Szabo, E. "Why Don't I Trust You Now? An Attributional Approach to the Erosion of Trust." *Journal of Managerial Psychology,* 2007, *22*(1), 4–24.

Fisher, R., and Shapiro, D. *Beyond Reason.* New York: Viking Press, 2005.

Frederickson, B. "The Role of Positive Emotions in Positive Psychology: The Broaden-and-Build Theory of Positive Emotions." *American Psychologist,* 2001, *56*(3), 218–226.

Frederickson, B., and others. "Open Hearts Build Lives: Positive Emotions, Induced Through Loving-Kindness Meditation, Build Consequential Personal Resources." *Journal of Personality and Social Psychology,* 2008, *95*(5), 1045–1062.

Garland, E., Gaylord, S., and Park, J. "The Role of Mindfulness in Positive Reappraisal." *EXPLORE,* 2009, *5*(1), 37–44.

Goleman, D. *Destructive Emotions.* New York: Bantam, 2003.

Goleman, D. *Social Intelligence.* New York: Bantam, 2007.

Gosline, A., and others. *Guidelines for the Design of Integrated Conflict Management Systems Within Organizations.* Washington, D.C.: Society of Professionals in Dispute Resolution, 2000.

Gross, J. "Antecedent- and Response-Focused Emotion Regulation: Divergent Consequences for Experience, Expression, and Psychology." *Journal of Personality and Social Psychology,* 1998, *74*(1), 224–237.

Hambrick, D. "Corporate Coherence and the Top Management Team." In D. Hambrick, D. Nadler, and M. Tushman (eds.), *Navigating Change.* Boston: Harvard Business School Press, 1998.

Hammer, M. "The Intercultural Conflict Style Inventory: A Conceptual Framework and Measure of Intercultural Conflict Resolution Approaches." *International Journal of Intercultural Relations,* 2005, *29,* 675–695.

Harris, A. "Effective Teaching: A Review of the Literature." *School Leadership and Management,* 1998, *18*(2), 169–183.

Hiam, A. *A Dealing with Conflict Instrument.* Amherst, Mass.: HRD Press, 1999.

Hotz, R. "How Your Brain Allows You to Walk in Another's Shoes." *Wall Street Journal,* August 17, 2007, p. B1.

Hughes, M., and Terrell, J. *The Emotionally Intelligent Team.* San Francisco: Jossey-Bass, 2007.

International Institute for Conflict Prevention & Resolution. "Why Programs Are No Longer Enough: An Interview on Collaborating at the U.S. TSA." *Alternatives to the High Cost of Litigation,* 2009, *27*(4–5), 81–102.

Johnson, D. *Reaching Out: Interpersonal Effectiveness and Self-Actualization* (10th ed.). Columbus, Ohio: Allyn & Bacon, 2008.

LeBaron, M. *Cultural Issues in Conflict Management.* San Francisco: Jossey-Bass, 2003.

Lipsky, D., Seeber, R., and Fincher, R. *Emerging Systems for Managing Workplace Conflict.* San Francisco: Jossey-Bass, 2003.

Luft, J., and Ingham, H. "The Johari Window: A Graphic Model on Interpersonal Awareness." *Proceedings of the Western Training Laboratory in Group Development,* 1955.

Lynch, J. "Beyond ADR: Integrated Conflict Management Systems." 2005. http://www.pdggroup.com.

McCraty, R., Atkinson, M., and Tomasino, D. "Impact of a Workplace Stress Reduction Program on Blood Pressure and Emotional Health in Hypertensive Employees." *Journal of Alternative and Complementary Medicine,* 2003, *9*(5), 355–369.

McCullough, M. *Beyond Revenge: The Evolution of the Forgiveness Instinct.* San Francisco: Jossey-Bass, 2008.

Miller, S. *I-Skills Zone.* Evergreen, Colo.: Interpersonal Communications Programs, 2009.

Mooney, A., Holahan, P., and Amason, A. "Don't Take It Personally: Exploring Cognitive Conflict as a Mediator of Affective Conflict." *Journal of Management Science,* 2007, *44*(5), 733–758.

Morrison, T., and Conway, W. *Kiss, Bow, or Shake Hands: How to Do Business in Sixty Countries.* Cincinnati, Ohio: Bob Adams Publishers, 2006.

Niebuhr, R. *The Essential Reinhold Niebuhr: Selected Essays and Addresses.* New Haven, Conn.: Yale University Press, 1987.

Ochsner, K., Bunge, S., Gross, J., and Gabrieli, J. "Rethinking Feelings: An fMRI Study of the Cognitive Regulation of Emotion." *Journal of Cognitive Neuroscience,* 2002, *14,* 1215–1229.

Ochsner, K., and Gross, J. "The Cognitive Control of Emotion." *Trends in Cognitive Sciences,* 2005, *9*(5), 242–249.

Prati, L., and others. "Emotional Intelligence, Leadership Effectiveness, and Team Outcomes." *International Journal of Organizational Analysis,* 2003, *11*(1), 21–40.

Rapisarda, B. "The Impact of Emotional Intelligence on Work Team Cohesiveness and Performance." *International Journal of Organizational Analysis,* 2002, *10*(4), 363–379.

Reed, J. *Appreciative Inquiry: Research for Change.* San Francisco: Jossey-Bass, 2007.

Reina, D., and Reina, M. *Trust and Betrayal in the Workplace: Building Effective Relationships in Your Organization.* San Francisco: Berrett-Koehler, 2006.

Ringer, J. *Unlikely Teachers: Finding the Hidden Gifts in Daily Conflict.* Portsmouth, N.H.: OnePoint Press, 2006.

Roberto, M. *Why Great Leaders Don't Take Yes for an Answer.* Philadelphia: Wharton School Publishing, 2005.

Runde, C., and Flanagan, T. *Becoming a Conflict Competent Leader.* San Francisco: Jossey-Bass, 2007.

Runde, C., and Flanagan, T. *Building Conflict Competent Teams.* San Francisco: Jossey-Bass, 2008.

Schön, D. *Educating the Reflective Practitioner: Toward a New Design for Teaching and Learning in the Professions.* San Francisco: Jossey-Bass, 1996.

Siegel, D. *The Mindful Brain: Reflection and Attunement in the Cultivation of Well-Being.* New York: Norton, 2007.

Siegel, D. *Mindsight: The New Science of Personal Transformation.* New York: Bantam, 2010.

Stone, D., Patton, B., and Heen, S. *Difficult Conversations: How to Discuss What Matters Most.* New York: Penguin, 2000.

Thich, N. H. *Touching Peace: Practicing the Art of Mindful Living,* Berkeley, Calif.: Parallax Press, 1992.

Thich, N. H. *Anger: Wisdom for Cooling the Flames.* New York: Riverhead Trade, 2002.

Thomas, K., and Kilmann, R. *Thomas-Kilmann Conflict Mode Instrument.* Mountain View, Calif.: Xicom, 1974.

Thomas, K., and Schmidt, W. "A Survey of Managerial Interests with Respect to Conflict." *Academy of Management Journal,* 1976, June.

Ting-Toomey, S., and Oetzel, J. G. *Managing Intercultural Conflict Effectively.* Thousand Oaks, Calif.: Sage, 2001.

Tolle, E. *A New Earth.* New York: Dutton, 2005.

Tugade, M., and Frederickson, B. "Resilient Individuals Use Positive Emotions to Bounce Back From Negative Emotional Experiences." *Journal of Personality and Social Psychology,* 2004, *86*(2), 320–333.

Tugade, M., Frederickson, B., and Barrett, L. "Psychological Resilience and Positive Emotional Granularity: Examining the Benefits of Positive Emotions on Coping and Health." *Journal of Personality,* 2004, *72*(6), 1161–1190.

Ursiny, T. *The Coward's Guide to Conflict: Empowering Solutions for Those Who Would Rather Run Than Fight.* Naperville, Ill.: Sourcebooks, 2003.

Ury, W. *The Power of a Positive No: How to Say No and Still Get to Yes.* New York: Bantam, 2007.

Watson, C., and Hoffman, R. "Managers as Negotiators." *Leadership Quarterly,* 1996, *7*(1), 63–85.

Weeks, H. "The Art of the Apology." *Working Knowledge for Leaders.* Cambridge, Mass.: Harvard Business School, 2003. http://hbswk.hbs.edu/archive/3481.html.

Williams, J., Teasdale, J., Segal, Z., and Kabat-Zinn, J. *The Mindful Way Through Depression: Freeing Yourself from Chronic Unhappiness.* New York: Guilford, 2007.

Williamson, B. "Managing at a Distance." *Business Week,* July 27, 2009.

THE AUTHORS

Craig E. Runde, Director of the Center for Conflict Dynamics at Eckerd College, oversees training and development on the Conflict Dynamics Profile® assessment instrument and other products and services of the center. He is a frequent speaker and commentator on workplace conflict issues and is coauthor of *Becoming a Conflict Competent Leader* (Jossey-Bass, 2007) and *Building Conflict Competent Teams* (Jossey-Bass, 2008). Before joining Eckerd he was the director of the International Center for Computer Enhanced Learning at Wake Forest University. Craig has a B.A. from Harvard University, an M.L.L. from the University of Denver, and a J.D. from Duke University. He has practiced law in Colorado and has taught at the University of Minnesota Law School and Wake Forest University.

Tim A. Flanagan, Director of Custom Programs for the Leadership Development Institute at Eckerd College, earned his M.A. at the Ohio State University and worked in higher education for eight years before entering the human resource development field in 1985. Tim's experience includes leading the senior leadership development programs at the Harris Corporation, managing consulting services for Development Dimensions International, building the training program at AAA, Tampa, and guiding the custom development of discovery learning programs at Paradigm Learning. Tim is a frequent presenter at professional conferences and has consulted with scores of leading national and international firms. He is coauthor of *Becoming a Conflict Competent Leader* (Jossey-Bass, 2007) and *Building Conflict Competent Teams* (Jossey-Bass, 2008).

Tim and Craig are available for speaking engagements, webinars, and presentations. Visit their website for more information at www.conflictcompetent.com

INDEX

Page references followed by *e* indicate an exhibit; followed by *fig* indicate a figure.

BPOK (Breathe, Present, I'm okay), 44

Brainstorming, 173–174, 186–187

Bridges, W., 135

Britt, R., 218, 224, 227

Building Conflict Competent Teams (Runde and Flanagan), 13, 46, 140, 142

Bunge, S., 49

"Button pusher," 38

C

California Psychological Inventory (CPI), 94

Callahan, R., 81

Canadian Human Rights Commission, 59

Capability trust, 143

Capobianco, S., 18, 34, 106

Carmeli, A., 152

CCA (Corrections Corporation of America), 217

CDP (Conflict Dynamics Profile) 360: appreciative inquiry (AI) used with, 134, 136–137; blind spots identified by, 135–136; description of, 134–135; Johari Window showing four quadrants of, 135–136

CDP (Conflict Dynamics Profile): administering the, 18–20; coaching and practicing constructive behaviors of, 237–241; debriefing the, 20–21; description of, 17–18; destructive behaviors measured by, 20, 23, 105–128; fundamental team functionality improved by, 168–169; "It's All About the Business" discussion using the, 22–24; measuring hot buttons reactions, 18, 19, 36–41, 90; team shared knowledge of, 210. *See also* Conflict management; Constructive behaviors

Center for Creative Leadership: CEO conflict study by, 1, 12; on costs of conflict, 15; mindfulness exercises used at, 56

Centering: *aikido* approach to, 45, 46; description of, 45; emotional regulation using, 45–49

Champion, J., 89

Change Style Indicator (CSI), 94

Changing focus approach, 60–61

Checking for understanding, 185–186

CINERGY Coaching, 63

Clearing the air, 191–192

Climate. *See* Competence climate

Close-ended question, 90

Cognitive reappraisal, 49–52. *See also* Reframing

Cohn, A., 62

Cole, P., 201

Collaborating conflict style, 25

Collaborative outcomes: adapting to facilitate, 20, 94–95, 131–132; constructive communication for, 169–171; creating solutions to facilitate, 19, 102–105, 131–132; reflective thinking to facilitate, 19, 96–102, 131–132

Collaborative problem solving: comparing beginning and ending solutions, 133; participants engaging in, 132–133; planning for, 131–132

Collaborative Skills System, 119–120

Collette, D., 72

ColourBlind exercise, 85, 92

Communication: closed-ended versus open-ended questions, 90; expressing thoughts, interests, and emotions, 91–94, 130–131; intent to address emotional damage, 73; listening for understanding, 80–84, 129, 164–166; offer to take responsibility and apologizing, 73–76; reading between the lines for good, 88–91; structured disclosure, 176–178; team meetings on, 149–152; tips for effective cross-cultural, 208

Communication exercises: Animal, 90; Constructive Communication, 128–133; Getting to Know You in deep listening,

M

McCraty, R., 63

McCullough, M., 34

Machu Picchu, 237

McKenzie, J., 110

Maddon, J., 197–199

Managing Differences (Dana), 88

Mediation: used as conflict resolution, 10, 63; examples of, 64–68; four basic tenets or guidelines for, 198–199; "Peace Makers" (student program), 72; reading between the lines during, 88

Micromanaging behavior, 19, 36

Miller, S., 70

The Mindful Brain (Siegel), 57

The Mindful Way Through Depression (Kabat-Zinn), 54, 55

Mindfulness-Based Stress Reduction (MBSR), 53, 54

Mindfulness (or awareness): description of, 52–53; practicing to build skill in, 56–57; techniques used for, 53–56

Mindsight (Siegel), 57

Misunderstandings level of intensity, 125–126

Mooney, A., 152, 155

Morrison, T., 208

Motivation for conflict competence, 3

Multiple Uses exercise, 95

Myers Briggs Type Indicator (MBTI), 94, 210

N

Nevins, M., 167

New York–Penn Baseball League, 176–177

Noble, C., 63

O

Obama, M., 203

Observation, 53, 189–191

Ochsner, K., 34, 49, 51

Open-ended questions, 90

Organizational conflict competence: addressing conflict systematically for, 217–218; benefits of, 216–217; challenges of managing conflict, 228; championing, 241; components of, 6, 10*fig*; constructive behaviors coaching/practice for, 237–241; culture audits on, 234–237; *Emerging Systems for Managing Workplace Conflict:* on issues of, 228–234; ICMS approach to, 10, 217–227; leadership role in, 237; TSA's case study on, 215–216, 218–228

Organizational support, 10*fig*

Overly analytical behavior: as hot button, 19, 36; "It's All About the Business" on, 23

Overt invitation, 73

P

Pace, A., 170–171

Paraphrasing exercise, 82–84

Park, J., 52

Peace Corps training centers, 206–208

"Peace Makers" (student mediation program), 72

Pearson, D., 134

Pena, C., 198

Performance management conflict, 119–120

Periodic peer feedback, 199–201

Personal hot buttons, 36–38, 40–41

Personality styles, 94

Perspective taking behavior: ColourBlind exercise for, 85, 92; constructive communication using, 164–166; description of, 19, 80; focus on content, 84–85; focus on emotions, 86–88; listening for understanding for, 80–84; planning and engaging in, 129–130; preliminary perspective sharing, 178

Poetic principle, 136

Polarization level of intensity, 127–128

Positive emotions: cultivating, 62–63; description and power of, 61–62

ABOUT THE CENTER FOR CREATIVE LEADERSHIP

The Center for Creative Leadership (CCL) is a top-ranked, global provider of executive education that unlocks individual and organizational potential through its exclusive focus on leadership education and research. Founded in 1970 as a nonprofit educational institution, CCL helps clients worldwide cultivate creative leadership—the capacity to achieve more than imagined by thinking and acting beyond boundaries—through an array of programs, products, and other services.

Ranked in the top ten in the *Financial Times* annual executive education survey, CCL is headquartered in Greensboro, North Carolina, with campuses in Colorado Springs, Colorado; San Diego, California; Brussels, Belgium; and Singapore. Supported by more than four hundred faculty members and staff, it works annually with more than twenty thousand leaders and two thousand organizations. In addition, twelve Network Associates around the world offer selected CCL programs and assessments.

CCL draws strength from its nonprofit status and educational mission, which provide unusual flexibility in a world where quarterly profits often drive thinking and direction. It has the freedom to be objective, wary of short-term trends, and motivated foremost by its mission—hence, our substantial and sustained investment in leadership research. Although CCL's work is always grounded in a strong foundation of research, it focuses on achieving a beneficial impact in the real world. Its efforts are geared to be practical and action oriented, helping leaders and their organizations more effectively achieve their goals and vision. The desire to transform learning and ideas into action provides the impetus for CCL's programs, assessments, publications, and services.

Capabilities

CCL's activities encompass leadership education, knowledge generation and dissemination, and building a community centered on leadership. CCL is broadly recognized for excellence in executive education, leadership development, and innovation by sources such as *BusinessWeek, Financial Times,* the *New York Times,* and the *Wall Street Journal.*

Open-Enrollment Programs

Fourteen open-enrollment courses are designed for leaders at all levels, as well as people responsible for leadership development and training at their organizations. This portfolio offers distinct choices for participants seeking a particular learning environment or type of experience. Some programs are structured specifically around small group activities, discussion, and personal reflection, while others offer hands-on opportunities through business simulations, artistic exploration, team-building exercises, and new-skills practice. Many of these programs offer private one-on-one sessions with a feedback coach.

For a complete listing of programs, visit http://www.ccl.org/programs.

Customized Programs

CCL develops tailored educational solutions for more than one hundred client organizations around the world each year. Through this applied practice, CCL structures and delivers programs focused on specific leadership development needs within the context of defined organizational challenges, including innovation, the merging of cultures, and the development of a broader pool of leaders. The objective is to help organizations develop, within their own cultures, the leadership capacity they need to address challenges as they emerge.

Program details are available online at http://www.ccl.org/custom.

Coaching

CCL's suite of coaching services is designed to help leaders maintain a sustained focus and generate increased momentum toward achieving their goals. These coaching alternatives vary in depth and duration and serve a variety of needs, from helping an executive sort through career and life issues to working with an organization to integrate coaching into its internal development process. Our coaching offerings, which can supplement program attendance or be customized for specific individual or team needs, are based on our model of assessment, challenge, and support (ACS).

Learn more about CCL's coaching services at http://www.ccl.org/coaching.

Assessment and Development Resources

CCL pioneered 360-degree feedback and believes that assessment provides a solid foundation for learning, growth, and transformation and that development truly happens when an individual recognizes the need to change. CCL offers a broad selection of assessment tools, online resources, and simulations that can help individuals, teams, and organizations increase their self-awareness, facilitate their own learning, enable their development, and enhance their effectiveness.

CCL's assessments are profiled at http://www.ccl.org/assessments.

Publications

The theoretical foundation for many of our programs, as well as the results of CCL's extensive and often groundbreaking research, can be found in the scores of publications issued by CCL Press and through the center's alliance with Jossey-Bass, a Wiley imprint. Among these are landmark works, such as *Breaking the Glass Ceiling* and *The Lessons of Experience,* as well as quick-read guidebooks focused on core aspects of leadership. CCL publications provide insights and practical advice to help individuals become more effective leaders, develop leadership training within organizations, address issues of change and diversity, and build the systems and strategies that advance leadership collectively at the institutional level.

A complete listing of CCL publications is available at http://www.ccl .org/publications.

Leadership Community

To ensure that the center's work remains focused, relevant, and important to the individuals and organizations it serves, CCL maintains a host of networks, councils, and learning and virtual communities that bring together alumni, donors, faculty, practicing leaders, and thought leaders from around the globe. CCL also forges relationships and alliances with individuals, organizations, and associations that share its values and mission. The energy, insights, and support from these relationships help shape and sustain CCL's educational and research practices and provide its clients with an added measure of motivation and inspiration as they continue their lifelong commitment to leadership and learning.

To learn more, visit http://www.ccl.org/community.

Research

CCL's portfolio of programs, products, and services is built on a solid foundation of behavioral science research. The role of research at CCL is to advance the understanding of leadership and transform learning into practical tools for participants and clients. CCL's research is the hub of a cycle that transforms knowledge into applications and applications into knowledge, thereby illuminating the way organizations think about and enact leadership and leader development.

Find out more about current research initiatives at http://www.ccl.org/research.

For additional information about CCL, visit http://www.ccl.org or call Client Services at (336)545–2810.

Printed and bound by CPI Group (UK) Ltd, Croydon, CR0 4YY

16/04/2025

14658525-0001